Art, Crime & Lithium

On the Road with Literature and Delirium

O.Z. Lysiak

Concord, New Hampshire

Art, Crime and Lithium
On the Road with Literature and Delirium
by
O.Z. Lysiak

© 2013, Oleh Lysiak. All rights reserved.

All Rights Reserved. No part of this book may be reproduced in any form or by any means, electronic or mechanical, including photocopying, recording or by any information storage and retrieval systems, without the written permission of the copyright owner or the publisher.

I have tried to recreate events, locales and conversations from my memories of them. In order to maintain their anonymity in some instances I have changed the names of individuals and places, I may have changed some identifying characteristics and details such as physical properties, occupations and places of residence.

Paperback ISBN 13: 978-1-61807-097-5
Mobi (Kindle) ISBN 13: 978-1-61807-098-2
ePub (Sony, Nook, iPad) ISBN 13: 978-1-61807-099-9

Library of Congress Control Number (LOC): 2013936928

Cover & Interior Design:
Pamela Marin-Kingsley, Grey Gate Media, LLC

TaoFish Books
an imprint of Grey Gate Media LLC
Concord, New Hampshire
Email: info@greygatemedia.com
Website: www.greygatemedia.com

*This book is dedicated to the people who befriended,
helped, and enlightened me.
They enriched my life. If it weren't for
wild women and men I might have turned
out to be a totally boring "suit"
with an equally boring outlook.*

Displaced

Mariyka Lysiak, my pregnant mother, flees Lviv in the western Ukraine to Krakow, to Warsaw to Vienna, where she survives the terrifying Allied bombing in a lightless underground shelter crammed with people uncertain, second to second, of how long they have to live. Decades later, my father claims the reason I'm not normal is my mother's intense experience in that bomb shelter.

My father, Oleh Lysiak, enlists in the First Ukrainian Division to defend his homeland against Russians. Russian czars imposed brutal, tyrannical rule on Ukraine. Stalin starved multiple millions of Ukrainians to death: brutal, grim, no love lost here.

Displaced, refugees, my parents survive the carnage of WWII. They lose everything except each other, a few friends, memories and what they carry.

Conceived in Lviv, I'm born August 27, 1945, in St. Maria's Hospital in Bad Canstatt, a suburb of Stuttgart. I grow up in the Alps, blissfully unaware I'm displaced, a refugee, stateless and homeless.

The Wermacht's First Mountain Division barracks converted to refugee housing are home for the first years of my life. The refugee camp is in Mittenwald, a Bavarian village on the Austrian border famous for centuries of violin making, in the shadow of the Karwendel, Germany's highest mountain. My family shares cots in large rooms, separated from adjoining families by blankets strung on lines, fortunate to survive on post-war CARE packages from Americans.

A burned-out tank on the edge of the refugee camp is my favorite place to play, but I don't recall if the carcass is Sherman or Tiger; it's over six decades since the blackened hulk's fascinating ex-mechanization was a springboard for my imagination, dank darkness my refuge.

The year is 1948. Ukrainian refugee sports enthusiasts organize a makeshift hockey team, scrounge equipment and schedule to play the Military Police hockey team from the US Army School, Europe, in Oberammergau, in a series at the Olympic Ice Stadium in Garmisch-Partenkirchen.

In one of those games my father is viciously forechecked. His head cracks sharply on the ice. Unconscious, he is taken to the hospital and remains out until the following day. On regaining consciousness he suddenly, clearly and simply, realizes he's a genius.

He writes Ukrainian books about the war and emigration, explaining the nature of Ukrainian struggle, the part he and his comrades-in-arms played. The First Ukrainian Division's role in defending Ukraine in WWII becomes the focus of his life. A lawyer by trade, my father becomes a respected Ukrainian author, writer, editor, journalist and public speaker. His books are now sold in his beloved Lviv.

A cobbler in Garmisch-Partenkicken makes my first pair of leather ski boots. My father finds a child's skis and poles. My mother knits a sweater. At three years old, I figure my father is the best thing since chocolate. He teaches me to ski. I'm convinced he knows everything. It doesn't turn out that way, but I have to give him his due. Years later he lets me have the keys to his 1958 Chevrolet Biscayne, twenty bucks for gas and lift ticket, so I can go skiing at Elk Mountain in upstate Pennsylvania on powder-snow days. He doesn't mind my cutting school to ski. In his balance of priorities, skiing is more important than a mere day in school.

A former magistrate and city councilman of the city of Lviv who speaks Ukrainian, Polish and German, my father learns English quickly and serves as a translator at the refugee camp.

Mariyka, my mother, actress and singer from the Lviv theater, teaches knitting classes and does a radio broadcast at the camp YMCA. She and her students disassemble CARE package sweaters, dye the yarn with natural dyes and knit sweaters in their own styles and patterns. My mother knits toddler outfits, my first ski sweater, and more sweaters in her lifetime than I could possibly wear.

The youngest of four children, she rode Boormylo, her St. Bernard, to school in Monastyryska—a small town in western Ukraine, where my grandfather Mykola managed the local tobacco factory. Yustyna, my grandmother managed their home and raised the children. My uncle Orest is murdered by Polish authorities because he was in the Ukrainian underground.

My mother makes the journey to Ukraine in the '80s to see where her parents are buried, and takes a handful of Ukrainian soil from their graves. Later I give that bag of soil to a Ukrainian priest conducting her funeral. He spreads it over her coffin when we bury Mariyka in the Ukrainian cemetery in Philadelphia.

February 8, 1952, we arrive at Pier 51 in New York harbor aboard the *SS General Hahn*, former American troopship, past the Statue of Liberty when there was no Verrazano Narrows Bridge. I vomit across the Atlantic to get here, and wonder where the trees and grass are. My sister Olya doesn't survive the journey; my mother miscarries. I'm fated to be an only child. My half-brother Bohdan goes to Australia with his father, my mother's first husband, something my parents are loath to talk about. I'm too young and wouldn't understand, I'm told.

We live in immigrant neighborhoods with kindred displaced of all races and creeds, and take our place on the immigrant treadmill. Five years later, my parents take naturalization oaths. At sixteen I take my oath.

American citizenship coupled with displacement by association creates a dichotomy. At home everything is in Ukrainian, about Ukraine. Out the front door are street and school, a world anything but Ukrainian. My father wistfully repeats that America has awesome technology but no culture.

Ukrainian living in America, I'm not fully one or the other—confused, stuck in the middle, balancing guilt, not wanting to disappoint my parents, while struggling to develop my own identity in the only home I know, America. I go to Ukrainian school on Saturdays, join the Ukrainian Plast scouting organization, a Ukrainian student club and a Ukrainian sport club.

My father expects I'll continue in his footsteps. He doesn't care about my ideas and dreams, does his best to saddle me with his loss and expectations, remembering and mourning a Ukraine that no longer exists. The enormity of his loss is overwhelming, hardly possible for either of us to deal with.

The possibility of going home isn't available for Ukrainian immigrants then. Most of them have lived in the US longer than they had in Ukraine, despite their memories and dreams, including my parents. America is their home, economic and political. Hyphenated, they're judgmental and status conscious, exceedingly fond of supermarkets, jobs, bank accounts, homes, Buicks, Chevrolets, and Chryslers. Guilty for having abandoned country, home and family, they're happy to be alive and prospering.

I don't understand why my father left his country, especially his beloved Lviv, since he constantly bemoans the fact. I ask him. His reply is he didn't want somebody kicking down the door in the middle of the night to take my mother and me away. While I understand and appreciate his motivation and reasoning, I wonder about Ukrainians who don't escape, who remain and face grim reality with little or no hope. Decades later a young woman doctor, visiting Philadelphia from Lviv before she decides to return home, tells me: "Life without hunger isn't interesting."

My mother sends packages to family and contemporaries in Ukraine for decades, much to my father's chagrin. He claims hers is an expensive hobby. She won't be denied though, the empress of emotional extortion.

My parents sleep in separate bedrooms, their arguments frequent and operatic. I remember my mother shrieking "You'll drive me to my grave!" her favorite refrain as volume rises, doors slam, glass crashes. He's the life of the party, plays piano, smokes, drinks, cynical enough sober—but with a few drinks he berates and belittles her, finds fault with every small thing she does. His affairs wound her, and keep their relationship distant until anger erupts in yet another dramatic, operatic confrontation. The saving grace of their daily combat for identity is Old World European values. They made a deal and stick to it to the end, in classic European fashion.

Having grown up in makeshift refugee housing and displaced immigrant neighborhoods, I expect little from shelter other than minimal basics which are welcome and, thankfully, enough. We live for a short while on the Lower East Side in Manhattan, move to Buffalo where my father builds tanks in a Ford plant, and later Philadelphia—where he takes over as editor of "America", a Ukrainian language weekly. I encounter television for the first time in New York, when a guy on the screen puts his arm on an ironing board and irons it flat. I'm confused and impressed at the same time.

My parents are active in immigrant Ukrainian theater. We tour Ukrainian communities on the East Coast. One of my fondest memories is standing in the wings as my mother downs a shot of blackberry brandy, strides onto the stage, acknowledges the pianist and, resplendent in her performing gown, turns to the audience. The woman had brass balls. She sang solo in a touring Ukrainian

Art, Crime & Lithium

choir, and in the church choir Sundays. She'd kick it up a notch and power over the choir with ease.

Artist, actress and singer, my mother's most appreciable talent in my estimation was cooking. Her creamed garlic spinach was art, divine. I don't understand why American children don't like spinach. My mother cooked traditional Ukrainian dishes: *holubtsi* (cabbage rolls) with creamed mushroom sauce, *pyrohy* (potato dumplings), *borshcht* (beet soup) with *ooshka* (mushroom dumplings), *pliatsky* (potato pancakes with sour cream). She baked cakes, cobblers and cookies. She made her own cherry and coffee liquors. I spent happy hours in her kitchen helping and tasting. The basis of every good thing I cook I learned from her.

Ukrainian Christmas dinner consists of 12 meatless dishes, a major production, days in the making. As the youngest, it was my duty to say the traditional prayer before dinner after the first star appeared. I disliked pretending to pray because I didn't believe it, but understood it was just more theater in an already theatrical and operatic family.

My friend Nancy Welles had occasion to sit at my mother's table. Nancy claims my mother's tomato soup (*pomidorova zupa*) is the best thing she ever put in her mouth.

Reality in America, for my mother and her Lviv theater friends, is rolling panatelas at the Dutch Masters cigar factory on Second Street. We live a few blocks away in a fourth floor walkup on Franklin Street, a couple blocks off Girard Avenue, in Fishtown.

School

My mother holds my hand in the principal's office of the Immaculate Conception Ukrainian Catholic Elementary School at 8th and Brown Streets, entrusting me to the teaching abilities and benevolence of Ukrainian nuns.

"This one is trouble," says Sister David, Mother Superior and a linebacker of a principal.

My father's office is directly across the street from the Ukrainian cathedral and elementary school, on Franklin Street in Philadelphia. His office window looks across Franklin Street to the schoolyard. He spots me at recess with the bill to my cap turned up in the fashion of the time. For some unknown reason, the turned-up bill offends him. He leaves his office, crosses the street, whacks me upside the head and turns the bill down. As soon as he's back in the office, I turn the bill on my blue leather cap back up.

In true central European tradition, my father is an autocrat in his household. The nature of our relationship is changing. I don't measure up to his idea of what his son should be. Public perception is important to him. His perception of himself apparently suffers because I turn up the bill on my cap. According to him, I have no rights and nothing to say until I'm 21. That may have worked in post-Austro-Hungarian Ukraine, but we're in America now.

Every first Friday the nuns herd us into the cathedral to confess our third grade sins, having made certain to impress on us that the devil will dance on our tongues if we lie or don't tell the whole truth in confession. We're forced to go to communion, drink the blood and eat the body of Jesus Christ, not such a savage proposition as one might think for an eight-year-old child with access to comic books.

I lie my ass off and a receive mega-penance: dozens of Our Fathers and Hail Marys to recite kneeling in sight of a life-sized statue of Christ—bloody, torn, wounds in his chest, feet and hands, and thorns embedded in his head. I feel sorry for him. He looks pained and unhappy. I would too if I had a father like his.

The following morning, in my navy blue suit, white shirt and navy blue tie, I nervously mount the stairs to the altar prepared for the worst. I kneel, place my hands over my heart, sneak a quick peek down the row of kneeling fellow third graders, open my mouth, stick out my tongue and cross my eyes to see if there indeed is a devil dancing on my tongue. Nothing. The priest dips into the chalice, and places wine-soaked bread on my tongue. No dancing Fred Astaire of Darkness here. The nuns are full of shit. My young life changes that morning.

The nuns beat me on a regular basis, on general principle. I plot my escape. In eighth grade I take the test for public school, pass, get accepted and enroll at Central High School.

Riding the trolley and walking to and from school, I learn to check streets and alleys before stepping out onto them. Besides the daily beatings by the nuns, I suffer beatings by black gangs, brown gangs and white gangs: street equality—not racism, just Philadelphia the City of Brotherly Love.

My father carries a gun in order to discourage punks of any number of races, creeds, colors and convictions from threatening to rob him when he goes to the corner to buy a paper. He isn't particular about what color the threat is, but is prepared to deal with it. He took to heart the lesson he learned in Ukraine – a guy without a gun is at a disadvantage. He becomes a lifetime member of the National Rifle Association, God Bless America.

I didn't encounter racial bias in Europe as a child, with the exception of stern warnings to steer clear of gypsies—who, we were told, abduct unwary children and fry them in a pan.

In Bavaria, American GIs are the first people of color I see—more a source of fascination than bias, so when I'm attacked by black ghetto kids in Philadelphia, I don't understand. Jews, Ukrainians, Poles, Puerto Ricans and blacks all share the Philly ghetto we live in. Time after time I arrive home with a split lip, a bloody nose, and the colorful evidence of an emerging shiner. My sprint for the #15 Girard Avenue trolley is often successful. I find a seat and breathe easy, having momentarily escaped America's racial reality at one end of the trolley line. Then, to complicate things, the neighborhood Irish gang at the other end stalks me. I often wonder why my parents chose America over Bavaria, where nobody wanted to beat me up. I determine to leave Philadelphia as soon as I can manage.

To their enduring credit, the nuns of Immaculate Conception teach me to read, write and do basic arithmetic. The nuns do an admirable, workmanlike job with a recalcitrant customer like me. They also cure me of religion, for which I'm eternally grateful.

Smart kids in Philly go to Central High School. I get in and get by on mediocre grades, and develop playing hooky into an art form. On my way to school, I decide I'd rather spend the day meandering home rather than sit in a classroom. Enthusiasm for freedom is my undoing. The principal calls my parents in for a conference, once the days I cut outnumber the days I attend school. He gives me a choice; stop playing hooky or go to Dobbins Vocational, where Philadelphia's finest patrol the hallways and white boys don't last. I see his proposal as realistic and benevolent, get straight As in English, and suffer through the rest well enough to be accepted to Penn State University and Temple University with acceptable SAT scores. Central has a great reputation with colleges and universities. My graduating class boasts 47 Merit Scholarship winners. Obviously, I'm not among those.

When I get a driver's license in 1961, my father takes advantage and has me drive my mother to church Sundays. She puts on her Sunday best. I drop her off at the Ukrainian church and head for the Philadelphia Museum of Art. She worships in the traditions of her tribe. I develop an appreciation for world-class art.

I visit Picasso, Van Gogh, Delacroix, Klee, Brancusi, Calder, Matisse, Magritte, Chagall, Reubens and Giacometti, amid galleries of influential artists from a variety of eras—individuals who took leave of their senses to make their own, express their personal vision, insist on their perception of truth.

The museum becomes my refuge from the streets—filled with light, creativity, diversity, expression, freedom—where I get an education by deciding for myself what's worthwhile, what isn't, what works, what doesn't, without having some supposedly authoritative entity lecture me on what is right, what to do or how to do it.

Alexander Calder remains my favorite, his work beyond dimensional, always changing, always the same. My fascination with Calder develops into a 40-year obsession exploring esthetics, kinetics, fractals and balance.

The main branch of the Philadelphia Public Library is another refuge—where I discover Robert Louis Stevenson, Jules Verne, Joseph Conrad, Ernest Hemingway, John Steinbeck, Nikos Kazantzakis, Henry Miller, Jack Kerouac—a building filled with authors nobody mentions at school. I don't like school, but attend because I haven't figured out I can do something else.

Myron Polochaylo gives me a summer job, at his Esso station at 6th and Callowhill Streets in the industrial meatpacking district, so I can repay my father for the

Vespa 125 motor scooter I bought. I wash windshields, check under hoods and pump gasoline.

I proudly ride the Vespa to work and school until the weather is too nasty, when I revert to the trolley and subway, anxiously waiting for spring to ride my scooter, free again. Riding public transportation in Philly is an invitation to confrontation, both neighborhood and race related.

My worried mother expresses reservations about buying the Vespa.

"It's all written in the Big Book," says my father. "The wall may fall on him when he's sleeping."

I get the scooter.

I work for Polochaylo summers. He's a good guy, patient, understanding, easygoing, drives a big green Chrysler and has a hefty stash of nudist magazines tucked away under the clean-rag pile in the toilet. I study un-airbrushed female anatomy in Myron's magazines, in the sanctity of the station's john. A few years later, a black punk robbing the station murders Myron.

Although I had been mad for masturbation for quite a while, later that year I surrender my virginity to a Ukrainian girl, who lives a couple blocks away from our brick row house on Myrtlewood Street in Brewerytown. She looks to be in her twenties, brunette, with wide-set dark eyes: beautiful. She is twelve. I'm sixteen. She needs neither prodding nor convincing. Neither of us knows precisely what to do, but we figure it out.

After phys-ed class in the fall of my junior year at Central, I'm in the locker room getting out of my sweats but can't get up off the bench. The school nurse is summoned. My mother arrives in a taxi. The pain is excruciating. The taxi speeds us to a hospital on Second Street where my mother knows a Ukrainian doctor. Second Street is paved with cobblestones. Each time the taxi is jarred on the cobblestones, I scream. Surgeons determine I tore the mesentery membrane that holds intestines to the intestinal wall: hemorrhage. I'll either bleed to death or die from blood poisoning without surgery. A black nurse preps me.

"Not much hair there. Good," she says.

I wake up taped across my abdomen, navel to crotch. Final visit to the doctor, weeks later, he grabs hold of the tape and rips it off in one mighty yank taking skin, hair and scar tissue with it. If I survive this, not much else can hurt me. I play right fullback on the Central soccer team my senior year.

My father proposes I choose between a trip to Europe or a junker car of my choice for a graduation present.

I board an Air France jet at La Guardia for Paris. Orange tile roofs appear through clouds on our descent into Orly. A train to Munich, and I renew a friendship with Ihor Kordiuk, who I knew in the refugee camps as a child. Five years later he's a painter with a studio in Dachau outside Munich, when I'm the public affairs officer of the US Army School, Europe, in Oberammergau, Bavaria. I visit Kordiuk in Munich. He expands my art outlook at the Neue Pinakotek and other Munich art museums, where he introduces me to the work and history of Wassiliy Kandinsky. Kordiuk goes on to a distinguished art career in Toronto, bohemian after his inimitable fashion, until his death in 2004.

Summer in Venice provides an olfactory cornucopia, based on garbage Venetians throw out their windows into the canals. Trains for Rimini and Brindisi, and I board a ship for Patras, to Piraeus and Athens. First impression of Greece is disgust on encountering a public toilet, which consists of a stinking soiled hole in concrete to which you need to bring your own newspaper to wipe yourself.

The full moon over the Bay of Marathon dwarfs the night, the biggest, most orange moon I've ever seen. Marathon watermelon is the sweetest. One bout with *retsina* and *metaxa* is sufficient.

A passage through the Straits of Corinth, so narrow it seems the ship can't possibly navigate through: I take trains to Brindisi, Rimini, Munich and Paris to a hotel by the Gare de l' Est. My room is on the third floor, with a balcony and a common toilet at the end of the hall.

She spots me right off, approaches and makes her pitch in French. I speak no French. She speaks no English. She has me by the arm, leading me toward a doorway I'm not so sure I want to go into. I interpret she wants an exorbitant fee for her services, all the while calculating if I can afford to indulge in this Parisian floozy's favors. Afraid to and afraid not to, I don't want to get into an altercation, so I break loose and bolt down the street. Calm in the safety of my hotel room, I determine I have plenty of francs to pay her. New francs are worth a hundred times old francs. She had asked for approximately ten dollars to massage my teenage libido. I can afford her easily but am embarrassed to go out in the street again, which may have saved me from coming home with a dose of the clap.

It rains a torrent that night. The toilet at the end of the hall is occupied. I step out on the Parisian balcony in the rain, and piss off it.

First freshman English writing assignment at Temple, I write an essay about exchange rates in France. The professor gives me an "A" and thanks me because he hadn't been to Paris in a long time.

A one-semester attempt at business administration, and I enroll in Temple's journalism school. My father insists I study business. Accounting lab and economics class are beyond boring.

College for me consists of English and literature classes, riding my motorcycle, playing soccer and pursuing pussy. I delude myself into being in love, whatever that is, in order to convince the girl I'm pursuing to drop her drawers. All she needs to be is a looker. I'm shallow, a happy, needy punk with an endless erection and a lot to learn.

I ride my Vespa to Washington, DC to see a green-eyed Ukrainian brunette, to Montreal for a Ukrainian blonde. As I'm constantly in love and horny, a 1,000-mile ride on a motor-scooter doesn't seem totally unreasonable to at least get a sniff at the possibility.

Classes having nothing to do with English, literature or journalism, I barely acknowledge. I walk out of a Psychology 101 class when the teacher reaches over and pulls the blinds closed to shut out street noise. Comparative Religions of the World is bearable. I attend sufficient classes to get passing grades. A "D" in Symbolic Logic completes my mathematics requirement for graduation, once I repeat Psychology 101.

I played soccer at Central, and try out for Temple's team. We win the Middle Atlantic Conference championship for years, never losing more than a game or two a season. Senior year we go to the NCAA tournament, and lose to Michigan State 2-1 in the semifinals. A partial soccer scholarship allows me the luxury of choosing my major without parental pressure or interference.

Secure in the knowledge my BMW R50 motorcycle is parked on Broad Street, seconds away, ready to go, I'm loath to put up with any class even mildly uninteresting. Freedom of the road for me, in college, is much like freedom of the streets in high school.

After school I ride down Broad Street to the *Philadelphia Inquirer,* where I'm a copyboy from 6 p.m. to 3 a.m. I get off work when the streets are empty and all mine. My ride home begins west on Spring Garden Street, past the Philadelphia Museum of Art—lit like a classic spaceship of reason and beauty—past the gilded statue of Joan of Arc, into Fairmont Park and along East River Drive, where I know every curve, crevice, bump and straightaway. The R50's valve covers often scrape on deep turns. On occasion I'm issued citations for excessive speed, but my alderman fixes the tickets in true Philly neighborhood political fashion.

I go to college because it's expected, not quite sure what to do otherwise. Had I apprenticed with a competent cabinetmaker, welder or sculptor, I'd be in the world working, creating, and not dealing with requirements towards a degree. I want to be a writer, and the closest program to that at Temple is journalism, where I learn the basics of news-writing with a realistic expectation of a job.

The Vietnam War is on. I sign up for ROTC so I won't be drafted before I complete my degree, figuring the war will be over by the time I graduate. I figure wrong. As an officer, I'll get paid better and won't have to take as much shit as enlisted men—who apparently shoot Second Lieutenants in Vietnam when it suits them. Bad enough the enemy is going to try to kill me. Now I have to worry about turning my back on our own guys.

Most guys go because they're drafted. Some go because neighborhood buddies go. Others go because they want to be tough guys, Marines; this the only opportunity for them to experience war, Semper Fi. Then there are the gullible, who believe the government's flag-waving is about defending our country, making the world safe for democracy. Unfortunately it's merely grim government bullshit, sold to the unsuspecting as patriotism. This war is a mistake.

Motorcycle Transcontinental

June, 1965, I start the R50, secure my helmet, slip the BMW into gear and make for the Schuylkill Expressway, the Pennsylvania Turnpike and points west. Finals done, saddlebags packed with food and a carton of Camels, camping gear, tent and rucksack secured, I kiss my mother goodbye.

With no destination, thousands of motorcycle miles to look forward to, fifty bucks in my pocket, endless enthusiasm, America before me, momentarily unencumbered by guilt or expectation, I'm free in the wind.

I'm butt-sore from hundreds of miles of switching cheek to cheek, and my first camp is just across the Ohio line. Tent up, sleeping bag laid out, I heat slices of smoked ham in a skillet on a small wood fire, open a can of beans, and light up a Camel.

The following morning I crash the R50 on top of a fairly steep incline when the dirt road to camp crests sharply to the left, too fast for the turn. The R50 is okay, with minor scratches. I suffer a pretty good gash in my right elbow and road-rash. A fellow camper gives me a ride to a local clinic to have the wound cleaned and stitched.

The keystone piece to the Gateway to the West, the enormous stainless arch in St. Louis, isn't in place when I park the bike underneath to snap a photo after crossing the Mississippi. Crossing the Missouri the bike, the stitches and I are one, rolling in rhythm. I master what needs to be done with my left arm since my right arm bends only so far, right hand fine on the throttle.

The spectacular erosions of Badlands National Park in South Dakota are an eye-opening teaser to the

West. In Rapid City I splurge on a motel room, a shower, and take out the stitches.

Mt. Rushmore is impressive, but the fresh hot chocolate doughnuts I enjoy at the cafeteria below the monument early that morning impress me a lot more.

First distant glimpse of snow-capped Rockies takes my breath away on the way to Yellowstone National Park. I spend days camping, see Old Faithful blow, smell the reality of bubbling sulfur amid the grandeur, and meet a girl from Arkansas. I can't get enough of the molasses in her drawl, never having heard anyone speak that way before. She likes my big black motorcycle, and is game to spend the night in my tent despite rumors of bears in the neighborhood.

Snow is stacked several feet high on both sides of the highway over the Continental Divide. It's July and the mountains, snow in summer; the expanse of the West amazes me. A guy in a pickup truck tries to run me off the road outside Reno. I weave through traffic, apply throttle, lose him and continue on my way to Los Angeles—where I get a part-time job, rent a room on Fountain Avenue off Sunset Strip, and go to the beach.

Watts is in riots, National Guard convoys on the freeways. I leave LA. A couple days before school starts, I arrive home.

The following spring I ride to Cape Cod, up the east coast to Montreal. I rent a room close to McGill University. The green-eyed, black-haired, beautiful, buxom Ukrainian girl I met at skiing at Val David in the Laurentians the previous winter, the one I rode my scooter to see in D.C., insists I buy prophylactics before we engage in sex. Her parents don't approve of me. She's a good girl who tries her best to mind them, but has ideas and needs of her own. Forty years later she writes me, via the Ukrainian grapevine, after her symphony conductor husband dumps her for an 18-year-old he knocked up.

Art, Crime & Lithium

Gone in the morning after tearful goodbyes, I ride along the south shore of the St. Lawrence Seaway up the Gaspe Peninsula past Trois-Riveres, Quebec, Montmagny, Riviere-Ouelle, to Riviere du Loup. Madame Villancourt, who lives up the road, invites me for breakfast of sautéed herring sperm on toast. She sets fish traps in the river. I ride through Trois Pistole to Rimouski where I turn right for Mont-Joli, New Brunswick and Halifax, Nova Scotia. From Halifax I ride to St. John on the Bay of Fundy, which boasts the world's biggest tides. Sixteen hours after departing St. John, I'm back home in Philadelphia: my longest single ride ever.

I ride my R50 almost until graduation from college, when I trade it in on a brand new Karmann Ghia. Serious people don't ride motorcycles, I presume. Twenty years later I come to my senses, serious but not any by accepted standard.

In June 1967, I graduate from Temple University with a Bachelor of Science in Journalism. Attending my graduation are my parents and the 19-year-old blonde Ukrainian bombshell who told me I'm the one the previous spring in Central Park. I believe her. We're engaged. Her father owns several apartment buildings in New York, and plays the stock market.

Journalist

I'm editor of *The Ukrainian Weekly* in Jersey City, New Jersey. The Weekly is the English-language publication of *Svoboda*, then the largest Ukrainian daily in the free world.

My life is set. I'll follow in my father's footsteps as a Ukrainian journalist, editor and writer, bone my Ukrainian bombshell and produce Ukrainian children, all for the greater glory of Ukraine. It seems like a good idea—only not my idea.

Leonid Poltava is a Ukrainian language editor at *Svoboda*. I'm editor of the English-language *Ukrainian Weekly*. Antony Dragan is editor-in-chief. Poltava and I walk down to the Hudson River at lunch daily, and speculate about ports of call of the ships steaming through the Verrazzano Narrows, past Red Hook to the Atlantic Ocean. I often wish I were on one of those ships, heading someplace else, instead of grinding away in Jersey City at a dead-end second-rate job, looking forward to marriage to a girl who increasingly reminds me of my mother. A mortgage, children, responsibility and social standing in Ukrainian immigrant society are not high on my list of things to do.

Dragan refuses to publish an editorial I write accusing the *Washington Post* of being anti-Ukrainian. I tell him to stick it, and pack my Castilian yellow 1967 Karmann Ghia and drive to Wildwood, New Jersey, to inform my parents. My father isn't pleased. It's okay with me. My mother packs shopping bags of goodies when I tell her I'm leaving for Oregon. I don't say goodbye to my spectacular Ukrainian blonde.

My father never calls me by my name again. Now he addresses me as *Pane Redaktor*—Mr. Editor. Old-school Ukrainians are afflicted with a disease for titles. He was never one for displays of affection. The title keeps us at a comfortable distance for him. I love my father because it's my duty. He's an alcoholic, egomaniac, cynical, judgmental bully obsessed with appearances, a brilliant writer and public speaker, disappointed in his wife and son because they don't measure up to his standards. We exist in an uneasy truce. He is frightened I'll fuck up and how that will reflect on him. I make it easy for him and leave.

Jonathan Block and I meet at Temple, become friends. Jonathan is from Seattle, now in Portland enrolled at Reed College. We agree to share a house. I pack my mother's lunch, a Smith-Corona, a Pentax, a change of clothes, and strap a ski rack with my Head Downhills over the engine, and drive west.

Jonathan rents a small two-bedroom cottage on SE Insley, close to Reed, has a BMW R60 and a redheaded Irish girlfriend when I arrive. I move in and set out to find a job. Two opportunities open: one a job at the Portland Zoo and one at *The Oregon Journal*, Portland's afternoon daily. The zoo won't have me. I interview with Ed O'Meara, managing editor. He hires me. On the city desk on obits and rewrites at first, I convince the editorial staff that I do a fair—albeit inexperienced—impersonation of a reporter covering meetings, bank robberies, fires, ships sinking, celebrities, bigwigs, and political heavies: something new to write about every day, fresh meat on the street. Daily, I check the front page for my byline.

The city editor asks if I speak Russian, since several Russian-speaking people from South America are at Portland International Airport and we need someone to find out what they're about. I speak fluent Ukrainian and studied Russian: the obvious man for the job.

The Russians at the airport are émigrés from Punta Grossa, Brazil: members of the "Staroviery" (Old Believers) sect, with sect sponsors in Woodburn, Oregon.

I write a story for the late edition. The next step is interviews with the Old Believers in Woodburn. The city editor agrees, and I'm given time off from my regular reporting duties to pursue the story. Ron Bennett, who later takes photographs of the Bobby Kennedy assassination at the Ambassador Hotel in LA, accompanies me as photographer. With his photographs and my story, we create a three-part series advertised on the *Journal*'s front pages.

Religious intolerance is why the Staroviery leave Russia, settle in Harbin and Sinkiang in China, but are forced to leave when Mao comes to power. They immigrate to Brazil where everything other than poverty is fine, send envoys to the U.S. who settle in Woodburn, and sponsor other members of the sect. Affluence is the problem here. Their children want cars, televisions, education, jobs: no longer willing to follow the old ways. The elders send envoys to the Kenai Peninsula to establish another base.

A few years later, *National Geographic* does a feature on the Staroviery. My *Journal* piece remains one of my best journalistic efforts. I beat *National Geographic* to the story by years.

I have a job on a major daily, a new Karmann Ghia, strange streets to explore and pick of available, attractive young women at the *Journal,* and Reed.

James Brown is playing Portland's Oriental Theater. I have tickets. The Oregonian's 19-year-old, quasi-innocent, apple-cheeked assistant librarian agrees to accompany me, hasn't seen James Brown in action. After the show, as I close the front door, she asks, "Are you going to fuck me now?"

Art, Crime & Lithium

Jonathan goes to Reed, bangs his redheaded girlfriend's head against the wall pumping away nightly, marries her, has four children by her, divorces her after forty years, and is now a crazy geezer on the road, having fun.

He gets a photographer job at the *Journal*. Weekends at his family home on Capitol Hill in Seattle, the cook makes delicious German pancakes with powdered sugar for breakfast. Jonathan has a key to his father's wine cellar. We appropriate select bottles of expensive wines, which we drink out of the bottle on the drive home to Portland. Or we drive to the beach, camp and make driftwood fires.

The *Journal*'s trio returns from the legislative session in Salem. Managing editor Ed O'Meara advises me to look for another job. I apply at *The Oregonian*, whose offices are downstairs in the same building. They hire me with the understanding that no job will be waiting for me when I return from the service. I work at the cop shop until I leave for induction in February, on a fourth journey across United States, this time in mid-winter. The ride is uneventful until I turn north for Montreal. Snow is mild at Syracuse, but by Watertown it's a blizzard. I push on, anxious to see Fran before the roads close.

The Ghia is dead the next morning, frozen, covered in snow with below zero temperatures, outside Fran's parents' home in Montreal. Fran is blonde, 20 years old, and a virgin when I arrive. We remedy her virginity and enjoy enthusiastic days in the sack. Fran knows I'm on my way to officers' basic in the US Army, and wants me to stay with her in Canada, adamantly opposed to the war in Vietnam. I explain that I'm an American citizen, an officer in the US Army with responsibilities, and have to deal with it my own way. She doesn't like what I have to say. That's OK with me.

O.Z. Lysiak

My mother cries when I arrive in Philly on my way to officers' basic at the Army Transportation School in Ft. Eustis, Virginia. My father beams, his son a college graduate, a professional newsman and an officer.

The Army

Six weeks of officers' basic and I'm assigned to honcho a truck company of recruits, not thrilled with the Army's choice of assignments for me. The portfolio of features and stories I accumulated at *The Oregon Journal* and *The Oregonian* is on the desk of the colonel in charge of *The Wheel*, the Ft. Eustis base newspaper. He calls my commander, whom he outranks, to inform him I'm immediately reassigned.

My job is to research and write a weekly feature, which presents the Army, the school, the paper and especially the colonel in a positive light. No sweat. I write features about wharf-building and pile-driving, operating room technicians, base security and MPs, any and everything as long as it makes the colonel look good.

Not at all enthused about running a truck company up and down Highway 1 in Vietnam, where convoys are ambushed with alarming and deadly regularity, where a second lieutenant's life expectancy is minimal, I intend to do any number of things with my young life other than participate in a war I consider an unfortunate mistake. I reserve the right to make my own decisions, government be damned. Killing Vietnamese isn't part of my agenda. Being killed by Vietnamese or disgruntled GIs isn't either. I sign on "voluntary indefinite" to get my choice of assignment.

Three important things I quickly learn in the Army: you're on your own, do not trust authority, and learn the rules so you can abide by, bend or avoid them.

Much is publicly made of the "ultimate sacrifice" by self-serving "citizens", usually politicians not likely to make that sacrifice. We cannot continue to have our children die around the world for the sake of oil, convenience, economics, religious dogma, or political advantage, obviously. Making a case for war based on casualties caused by political and ideological mistakes defies logic.

I'm outraged about the wasted youth of my contemporaries, whose names are inscribed on two long black marble triangles set in the ground in Washington, DC, and the veterans who endured unendurable treatment in VA hospitals.

How our parents handed over responsibility for our lives so easily to inept politicians and egomaniacal military brass, I'll never understand—although I rationalize they were doing what they considered their duty as good, albeit ineffective, citizens manipulated by government they elected.

The top-sergeant at *The Wheel*, recently returned from a tour in Germany, knows the colonel in charge of information in Heidelberg, and puts me in touch. My orders for running a trucking company up and down Route 1 in Vietnam are changed. I'm on my way to Oberammergau, Bavaria, to take over for outgoing info-officer Maj. Robin Luketina, as Public Information Officer of the US Army School, Europe. The DP camp of my youth in Mittenwald is 40 kilometers away.

My primary job as PAO is to keep commandant Col. Jack Lane's name out of the press unless the story is to his advantage. I like Lane and do my best to keep his career blemish free, an easy job since he's a good man.

Maj. Robin Luketina is a battle-hardened, seriously decorated, professional soldier with three tours in Vietnam. I am a liberal, an ROTC officer and graduate of an eastern university. It never gets in the way of our becoming friends. We share a difference of opinion, and 40 years later continue to understand that differences of opinion serve as intellectual and emotional fuel in working out ideas.

Art, Crime & Lithium

"The white man's burden" is Luketina's explanation for our war in Vietnam. I can't believe he actually spouts this horseshit, and tell him he is full of it, although I am sorry to see him leave since he is scheduled for another tour in Vietnam.

Freddie Schwela is my liason to Oberammergau's Bavarian community. Teutonic swish spectacular, blatantly gay, cunning, resourceful, loyal, Freddie is indispensable. He hires my receptionist out of the secretarial pool: Genvieve, a homely French girl with spectacular breasts and minimal command of English, a blessing. She manipulates callers with her thick French accent and apparent lack of understanding until they give up trying to locate me. She understands full well what they are trying to do. We share the joke. I take advantage of her skills, often being elsewhere when I'm supposed to be at the office. We keep our relationship strictly professional.

Anyone of higher rank outside the office staff is the enemy. Lt. Col Lassiter, a bald, Texas good 'ol boy and executive officer of the school, has it in for me. We endure each other at weekly staff meetings. Lassiter jacks me up at every opportunity, assures me he'll make me walk, talk, and act soldier. He knows I don't care about the Army, but there is very little he can do. I'm a member of his fraternity by act of Congress. Col. Lane protects me because I do my job well protecting him. I don't have to tell Lassiter he can stuff it up his ass; he knows. He flusters in retreat at Genvieve's accent, wile, and magnificent tits.

My staff and I practice small-unit guerilla tactics with tight security, on the highest level, directly under the nose of high-ranking enemy. We pool our monthly gasoline and liquor ration-coupons. I have an arrangement with a Bavarian who takes the liquor coupons, buys Class VI booze at discounted prices, and resells it to bar owners in Munich. I disburse the profit among my staff in exchange for gasoline coupons. I make certain everyone on my staff is promoted on time. I take care of them. I cover for them. They cover for me.

Every lieutenant in Europe is hot to buy a Porsche. I buy a BMW 2000 Tilux—a screamer, snarky-nosed, white sedan with four side-draft Weber carburetors—with cash from the sale of my Karmann Ghia. I'm proud of the boxy white BMW rocket-ship with navy blue velour interior, mahogany trim and steering wheel. A silver-haired gentleman in a white lab coat carefully, and with great showmanship, makes final adjustments to the sedan's high-output 2000cc engine when I arrive to take possession, at the BMW dealership in Garmisch.

As public-affairs officer I publish the post newspaper, conduct community relations, cover the post commander in the press, drive a hot BMW, smoke hashish, drink excellent Bavarian beer, ski whenever possible, drop acid weekends so the tripping hopefully won't conflict with military duties, screw every available female who'll let me —including one hot, curly blonde, blue-eyed Bavarian barely-teenage cutie delightfully and abundantly developed, enthusiastic and intent on slut greatness.

Hashish is readily available from a variety of sources at Army recreation facilities in Garmisch. The MPs at the school are a reliable source in case availability is in short supply elsewhere. Europeans don't smoke pot but prefer hashish or kif imported from Afghanistan, Nepal, Lebanon, Israel or Morocco. They mix kif or hash with tobacco and smoke it in hand-rolled cigarettes, or in traditional chillums. It takes getting used to, but works well once the coughing abates.

July 1968, I'm glacier-skiing on the Zugspitze above the Eibsee outside of Garmisch, 40 kilometers from where I first learned to ski. The Alps are spectacular, exotic, historical, traditional, with powder and style. Crossing European borders with a U.S. Army officer's ID card is a breeze. The Tilux will do 130 mph plus on the autobahns, allowing me to ski Verbier, Champery, St.

Anton, Kitzbuehl, Cortina d'Ampezzo for long weekends. When lights flashing behind me indicate I should vacate the passing lane, I move aside for Mercedes sedans, Lamborghinis, Porsches or Ferraris that blow by at 150 mph or better.

Ray L'Hommedieu and I both live in the Oberammergau BOQ. Ray is from Rochester, New York. We're immediate friends. An OCS graduate, he is headquarters company commander. Ray continually tinkers with a Fiat 650 sedan, which winds up in a lake after he dons a helmet and drives it off a cliff. There's more to Ray than meets the eye.

Invited to Formula 1 races at Nurburgring, Ray and I meet Cpt. Bill Welles—a pleasant guy married to Nancy, an equally pleasant young redhead. Our group sets up camp. We watch Ferraris, Lolas and Porsches take practice laps, and distinguish who is who on the straights by the distinct timber of engine tone at maximum RPMs.

Bill Welles is officer of the day at his unit, starting at midnight, and leaves early to make his duty assignment with time to spare. Nancy and I shred her vows in my sleeping bag. Bill asks her to choose. She chooses me.

Col. Lane calls me to his office and indicates I close the door. Living with a captain's wife in the Bachelor Officers Quarters is not acceptable behavior, and he suggests I get Nancy out of there.

I rent a second-story apartment by the Isar River in Garmish, from Herr Johanssen. He is relieved that a white officer is willing to take the apartment, since he had been approached by a black non-com.

Nancy's comment is, "That stupid Bavarian son of a bitch will be sorry. He has no idea."

We set up house. I never felt about a woman the way I do about Nancy, a skinny redheaded triple–Scorpio, born on Halloween, with brains and moxie that make standard expectations and accoutrements superfluous. In my arrogant enthusiasm, I don't take into account that what she did to Bill Welles she'll do to me. I have a lot to learn. A perpetual hard-on and the best of intentions aren't enough.

Garmisch-Partenkirchen is on the Brenner Pass route through the Alps. Smugglers use the Brenner Pass as a primary artery. American expatriates, hashish smugglers, ex-GIs with European discharges, fresh friends and diverse influences frequent our Garmisch apartment.

Art Rowell is one of our new friends. Art takes a European discharge, and runs off with gypsies in Spain to learn flamenco guitar. He has beautiful large hands, made for music. He knocks up Trudy, a local Bavarian girl. Art comes back, marries Trudy, and they're raising a daughter. He works as a hotel night clerk when we meet. Trudy has a dim view of Art hanging out with us, correctly assuming we we're up to no good.

We discover lysergic acid diethylamide, little blue dots of LSD. Art is at our apartment one evening when we're coming down after dropping acid. Trudy calls, looking for him. I hand him the phone. He listens, shrugs, smiles and leaves. I've known Art 40 years, and never have seen him flustered.

On a two-week walkabout I catch a train to Frankfurt, a taxi to Rhein-Main airbase, and a ride to Oslo on an Army transport. In Oslo I take off my uniform, give it to the pilot with instructions to mail it to my office, hoist my pack and hitch-hike to Stockholm and the *Af Chapman*, a square-rigger floating hostel.

Easy Rider blows my mind in a Stockholm movie theater. Bobby Kennedy had been shot, the Democratic Convention in Chicago was riotous, Kissinger was bombing Cambodia, American kids were killing and being killed in Vietnam for reasons none of us understood, we were defoliating Vietnam with Agent Orange, and images of a burning chopper on a Louisiana back road flash in my brain.

Art, Crime & Lithium

I catch a ferry for Helsinki, where I find a bookstore that carries all of Henry Miller's work. At the time Miller's books aren't available in the States, but are in Finland.

In a coffee house adjacent to the bookstore a young woman dressed in purple and orange, my favorite colors, sits at my table. She speaks no English. I speak no Finn. We finish our coffees, then shop for bread, wine, cheese and a room. She is noticeably pregnant once she takes her clothes off, but that doesn't diminish her enthusiasm. By morning we enjoy an understanding, although in no spoken language.

On the ferry to Copenhagen a young black man engages me in conversation. I'm reading Miller. The black guy is pleasant, interested in my book. I hand him *Sexus*. He reads for a bit, eyes wide. He looks at me directly.

"Henry Miller," I say. "Keep it."

The young man is from Cameroon, a medical student in Moscow. It's my turn to be surprised.

"If you live in the house of the devil, it doesn't mean he can tell you what to think," he says.

Copenhagen hippies offer me a place to sleep in a government-sponsored building they maintain and use. I visit Tuborg and Carlsberg breweries daily. The hippies give me directions to the Club 27, a "free zone" drug-disbursing establishment, located in an old multi-storied brick factory building. Copenhagen cops leave local druggies alone, as long as they do their business in the "free zone." Authorities keep drug business centralized, local and under control.

A hole in the brick wall on the third floor is the entrance to Club 27. Purveyors of whatever interests you are set up for business. A quick tour, and I stop at the hashish sellers. The one I choose has stacks of black Nepali, a scale, a large burning candle and a knife. He heats the knife blade on the candle, slices the hash, weighs it and announces the price. I buy black Nepali to take home, and fit it into the lining of my coat. German Customs don't check me traveling on my U.S. officer's ID. I hitchhike the length of Germany to get home to Nancy.

John Beaver is one of our smuggling pals who frequents our apartment to regroup, repackage, and relax before making his appointed rounds. John is arrested at the French border and is put in prison in Colmar. I put on my best Republican undercover outfit and drive to Colmar to see what can be done to get John out of the French joint. The French are obstinate pricks, no surprise. I speak with John's lawyer. I can leave money and cigarettes, and he'll make sure Jack gets them.

Months later, after Beaver is released, I ask him how it was. He says the Moroccans love French prison, because they get three squares a day and fuck each other in the ass waiting for the next meal.

Our time in Bavaria is winding down, my two years almost up. I take 30 days leave, due for orders for Vietnam. Nancy and I meet in Philly. I mail 25 grams of primo Nepalese black hash to myself in a Valentine's candy box. We see a drive-away ad to deliver a red '67 Corvette Stingray to LA. The Corvette belongs to the owner of White Whale Records. He hands us the keys at his offices on City Line Avenue, and tells us to have a good time. The Vette has room enough for a couple toothbrushes, a change of clothes and the hash.

Seventeen hours later we're in Omaha, visiting Luketina enrolled in ambulance-chaser school. In Denver I call the owner and tell him the tires on the car need replacing, two go flat when we stop to refuel. He wants red raised-letter tires. His distributor has red raised-letter racing tires put on the car. Nancy drops me off in San Francisco. We put 6,000 miles on the Corvette on our cross-country binge. I catch a flight to Philadelphia with serious things to arrange.

The war hasn't ended in two years, as I figured. My objection to the war isn't moral or ethical; it's practical. I object to stupidity. Vietnam is a sovereign nation. What they choose to do is none of our business. We invade their country, which has nothing to do with protecting America or its people. They defend their country against invaders, just as we'd defend ours. Conviction and reason are on their side. The result is predictable. We're wrong. The French found out. Arrogant Americans aren't smart enough to recognize the lesson. Communism isn't the issue; stupidity is.

After researching my options, I apply for a hardship discharge based on the fact I'm the only surviving son in a family that was decimated in WWII. Desertion isn't an option; nor is psychodrama staged to promote psychiatric evaluation and a stint in the loony bin, a shaky proposition. I did my duty, two years, and want out.

While making arrangements for necessary documentation I suffer a series of debilitating migraine headaches. I assume the headaches are temporary since I never experienced them before. I'm wrong.

Steve Kaczak, a childhood friend who played goalie for Temple, who I protected at right fullback, gives me a ride to the Pentagon. We park a few blocks away. I change from my civvies into my uniform in his Mustang. Armed with notarized paperwork asserting my case, I stride into the Pentagon.

March 27, 1970, I'm relieved from active duty with an honorable discharge. Processing out, I go to the Naval Hospital in South Philadelphia, walk through corridor after corridor of America's youth in sickbeds and wheelchairs, missing limbs, eyes or brain function. It doesn't make me want to go to Vietnam and kill Vietnamese. At that moment I'm a prime candidate to kill the idiot sons of bitches in Washington who conceived of, approved, and conducted this insanity.

On The Road

Nancy and I are on the road the following day, in a white '63 Ford Econoline van I buy In Philadelphia for $700 and sell in Alaska months later for $1,200. Ray gets out a couple months earlier. In an old milk van, "MOTHER'S MILK" painted in bold letters on the side, Ray drives to Ketchum, Idaho, wearing a gas mask to keep from being asphyxiated by leaking exhaust. We meet and set up camp in an abandoned log cabin with a creek nearby.

Late afternoon, nearly dusk, shadows lengthen as I approach pink-tinged riffles on the Wood River in the alpenglow of rounded brown mountains south of Ketchum. A flight of mallards rises, startled from a bend downstream, quacks at my intrusion, circles and heads south in search of another spot to bed down for the night. Sweet pinewood smoke hangs, incense-like, on the pale blue September breeze.

I walk amid aspen and spruce, fishing pole in hand, hook baited with salmon eggs, a virgin about to embark on a journey I'll travel the rest of my days in search of the wild and wily trout.

Nancy the Bear, my girlfriend and traveling companion, has talked me into fishing for the first time in my life. Recently discharged from the service, I'm on a quest to see if the exotic names of places in the world have equally exotic stories.

With my limbs and faculties intact, instincts dictate I get as far away from my parents, government and schooling as I can.

The Bear rigs my pole and line, and baits the hook with scarlet, salty eggs. I'm a fishing virgin, and the Bear is the only human I dare trust.

Ketchum is where Ernest Hemingway blew his brains into the orange juice when he figured he didn't have what it takes.

The ducks disappear downstream. I toss the bait into riffles, unaware what is about to happen will transform my life.

By Ketchum I'm prepared to lose my fishing cherry. A woman turns my attitude around, points it in the right direction. The Bear grew up fishing the High Sierras, knows what fishing is about.

The salmon eggs make their journey through the riffles, along glistening gravel on the Wood's bed. I watch the mallards flap and quack when the monofilament straightens, feel the first indelible electric jolt, adrenaline rushing, when the trout strikes—as powerful today as it was then. The power of other feelings in life pales with time. The feeling of a fish on the line improves, the moment when you know—and the fish knows, although neither see the other—the power of realized possibility, the primeval sense of the hunt, connection to a wild overpowering instinct, return to the pagan despite the lure of technology. Gear may have changed over hundreds of thousands of years. The jolt remains the same.

Knee-deep in the river, I don't know what to do. I horse the fish in, grab hold of the pole in one hand and the line with squirming fish in the other, and run full bore, crackling leaves and branches with every step, stumbling, tripping, screaming: "Hey, Bear, hey Bear - I got one! I caught a fish! Hey!"

I'm breathless at the door. Bear's laughing, framed in the hot buttered-muffin glow of the cabin's log interior. I'm soaking wet, still yelling, and totally amazed: no longer a virgin, hooked.

We tell Ray about our plan to see if the exotic names and realities of the world match. Alaska begins with "A", and is our first destination. Ray is aboard. Gary Marbut is in Missoula, Montana. Gary, a Montana native—The Stripe From Missoula"— rode a Honda 450 in striped ski–pants, in the winter in Garmisch. He invites us to Montana if we're in the neighborhood.

Gary lives on the Grant Creek Ranch, up Grant Creek, on the outskirts of Missoula. His parents raise world-class polled black Angus; a serious cattle raising operation with a show barn, sperm sales, and mega-reputation in the world-wide cattle community. We help work a true-to-life cattle drive, play cowboy, ride horses and make our goodbyes, off on our quest to match exotic places and realities.

Canadian border guards are concerned that we want into their country to take advantage of Canuck largesse. We explain we're on our way to Alaska and their country is in the way. They want to know what skills we have. We tell them we're entertainers. Show us, they insist. Nancy, Ray and I sing "Egg Sucking Dog", which we sing for our own amusement on the road. A couple choruses and they wave us through, glad to be rid of us.

An expedition up the Alaskan Highway, a really long dirt road, looms. We develop a system for choosing campsites by taking turns. If the site is good, the person is showered with praise. If not, they take abuse in silence. Places with snake names are immediately disregarded.

It's June, and we drive further north daily. Fish morph from bass and trout to Arctic grayling. We cross from British Columbia into the Yukon Territories, into Alaska. At Tok Junction a solitary figure sits on a rucksack with what looks to be a guitar: Gary Marbut. He strums his 12-string all the way into Anchorage, where we take up residence in Goose Lake Campground.

A few days of Anchorage, Gary and Ray try their luck in Fairbanks. Fire crews won't hire us. Neither will canneries. I sell my shotgun, a Parker 12-gauge Damascus twist with hammers, for gas money and go job hunting. Conn Murray—owner of Murray, Kraft and Rockey, an Anchorage advertising firm—hires me as a copywriter. Nancy gets a secretarial job with the state. We rent a basement apartment on 4th Street, overlooking Cook Inlet. I chuckle about working for an ad agency with an owner named Conn.

A few months in Anchorage, and we find Mr. Natural LSD. Coming down on the kitchen floor, Nancy or I move an arm and watch multicolored flashing translucent images long after the arm stops moving. We burn our mail and traces in the fireplace and make reservations on the trans-polar flight from Osaka to Paris, which stops in Anchorage. At the airport the Air France rep informs us the flight is totally booked except for two seats in first class, which we're assigned. Nancy and I are dressed in our Alaskan best – plaid shirts, jeans, boots and jackets. The upper crust French are decked out in furs, jewels, double-breasted suits. The stewardess, not your ordinary run-of-the-mill economy class Molly but a tall, shapely, divine babe with a throaty French accent, inquires if we want red or white wine. Yes. Cheese plate? Yes. Fish? Beef? We say yes to everything. The French upper crust stew in well-bred silence.

In Paris we get a flight for Munich, and then the train to Garmisch-Partenkirchen. In Garmisch we see Art and John Beaver released from the French joint. Nancy, John and I hitchhike to Stockholm to visit Mike Boren and Gunnela. Mike and Art were MPs in the Army.

Mike is taking Swedish lessons, paid for by the Swedish government. He and Gunnela live in a small apartment. We smoke hash mixed with tobacco in chillums, and play Frisbee daily. Twenty years later, Mike tells me Nancy and Beaver do the dirty deed on the floor of his apartment while I sleep. A piece of ass is no reason to disrupt a friendship. John Beaver is a slut, but Nancy has a talent for bringing that out in a guy.

Mountain Ranch

We need to build something or dissipate. Nancy suggests we go to Mountain Ranch in Calaveras County, where she and her brother Mike Kizer have a gold-mining claim in the foothills of the Sierra Nevadas. We get hold of Ray and meet in Mountain Ranch. The mining claim is off Whiskey Slide Road, a few miles past Mountain Ranch, left down a dirt road, right down a barely discernible track, to a clearing surrounded by huge sugar pines with a makeshift platform. Mountain Ranch is a general store, a tiny post office, a community center building, sugar pines, oak trees and ponderosa.

Ray knows what to do, having learned the basics of how things work from his father and grandfather. I help, watch and learn. What I learned from my father, as far as practical things go, is that a smart guy makes enough money to pay other people to do carpentry, plumbing or mechanics. He refers to people who work with their hands as "two by fours." I have a degree in journalism, but don't have a clue how anything other than a short, simple sentence actually works.

Ray and I build a platform, frame walls, and sheathe them in intricate plywood mosaics—from pieces laboriously cut to fit from scrap. We straighten used nails. Ray teaches me how to use a tape, lay out a wall. We find windows, doors, and a wood cook stove. We haul water in 5-gallon containers from a spring a quarter mile down the gully, dig and build an outhouse, and hang a tire swing over the gully.

Art, Crime & Lithium

This isn't father-knows-best by any stretch, but is warm, dry, human-friendly and real. We know what needs doing and figure out how to do it.

Ray and I shore up and level the platform, frame and install walls and go on material-gathering forays in the county or to the dump, to liberate or requisition whatever isn't nailed down and looks like it might work. We find enough stuff to build a competent one-room with loft, kitchen, and living room shelter—with enthusiasm. We don't have whole sheets of plywood, so we sheath walls by cutting and fitting a mural out of pieces of varying patinas from plywood remnants we scrounge, and straighten bent used nails to hold our creation together.

We don't have jobs, rent, phone or electricity. Jobs aren't necessary. We get by and have fun. Decades later, what we do is called living "off the grid."

Ronn and Charlie Alexander give Nancy a ride home from Mountain Ranch in their yellow VW one fateful afternoon. We hit it off, become and remain friends forty-plus years later.

Our first Thanksgiving is held under the sugar pines, on a makeshift table. Friends join us to celebrate. Nancy's friend Chappel and my childhood chum Steve Kaczak show up. We have a traditional Thanksgiving with all the trimmings.

Alex Nikorovich, another childhood pal, shows up later from San Francisco. He leaves me a Sunbeam Alpine convertible. Ray and I rebuild the Sunbeam's engine on our kitchen table. A year later Nikorovich, alcohol impaired, is killed in car wreck in Augusta, Georgia. Alex has a history of crashing automobiles. I'm saddened but not surprised.

Kaczak is committed to the looney bin in Manteca. Although I feel a responsibility for his welfare in the bin, I also have concerns about entering the facility myself. Steve is locked in a rubber-room in straightjacket. I request the orderly remove his jacket.

We have a short conversation in Ukrainian, which distances Steve from his rubber-room situation. Later he plays a role in a production of *Marat/Sade* at the community college in Jackson, California. I hear through the grapevine that Steve is married and now lives in the Northwest.

In the hammock on the hill above our shack, I listen to squirrel-chatter in the tree above me. Evening slips into dusk—still, sweet, peaceful. Nancy comes up the hill, puts a hand on the hammock and announces she's pregnant, later has an abortion. Forty years afterward I ask about the abortion.

"We were never pregnant," she replies.

Like all good things, it comes to an end. After three years together Nancy and I split up, the reality of relationship more than we can handle. In a Sausalito gas station after hitchhiking to Big Sur, Nancy announces she's had enough. With twenty bucks in my pocket I get change, give her ten and continue up the coast. Devastated, I won't admit it to myself or anyone else. As far as I'm concerned, there is nobody I can't get along without. For years I have put my faith, trust and everything I have in Nancy. She's gone. Whatever she needs I don't have.

If, back then, you had asked me how I felt I would have told you to shut the fuck up, stick it up your ass and mind your own goddamned business. Decades later I realize how fragile everything is, and how lucky we were to have survived.

Nancy gets herself knocked up in Stockton and has son Matthew Jasper, her dose of stability. She later has second son, Nick, by a different guy on Whidbey Island, Washington. For me, it's pathetic but over. I'm home on the road, on my own. Getting over Nancy takes awhile, but I have nothing else to do but ease and lubricate the process.

Ray goes his own way. I've been best man at two of his three weddings, and wonder how a guy can "till death do us part" a third time with a straight face. It's theater. Maybe third time's the charm.

I hitchhike to Ketchum, Idaho, and hook up with Mike Randles whom I know from the Army. He owns property on the Wood River south of Ketchum, with an antique wood silo. I convert the silo to shelter with a layered leaf and visqueen roof, carpet and accoutrements from the local dump. I dig a shitter, put up snow-fencing sides and a Cinzano umbrella to keep me dry. Ducks and trout are plentiful on the Wood, so there's no lack of stuff to do or good things to eat. Everything is swell until his girlfriend shows up and takes me to a local hot springs. We repeatedly do the dirty deed in the steam, even though we know repercussions are imminent. I'm a slut without moral or ethical dilemma. Apparently so is she, propriety or political correctness no issue.

The situation at the silo becomes untenable. She tells Randles, for whatever reason. Maybe she wants to get his attention. He's wounded in one of those "how could you" moments, backed with the injured might of the righteous when it's just a piece of ass between friends.

Bumpers That Bump

Lucky for me, and I've always been lucky, Ray shows up in a voluminous 1948 four-door DeSoto he bought in Stockton for fifty bucks, with bumpers that bump and fenders that fend.

"Let's go," he says.

Nepalese black hash in my pocket, I throw my pack in the trunk and we drive east on the original Mom Tour. The two French kids we pick up sit in back, silent, until we drop them off in upstate New York.

We spend Christmas with the L'Hommedieu clan, at their compound on the shores of Lake Erie, at Blackpoint outside of Albion, New York. Ray's parents, John and Georgia, are glad to see us, potential still on our side.

My mother cries when we arrive. My father holds cynicism in check because he likes Ray. I discover Nacky Smith, a good woman and my girlfriend for a short while in college, is in town. She invites us to a New Year's Eve party on the Main Line. Hits of Mr. Natural are available. In the spirit of togetherness and adventure, Ray and I both drop some and save a few hits for the ride home to the West Coast.

At my parent's home on 10th Street in Olney-Nicetown at 3 a.m., us stoned, there's no deterring my mother from feeding whoever is left standing at that time of the morning. Ray is exceedingly polite, eats some chicken and potatoes, and ducks out to the basement where he has a bed waiting.

I tell my mother about the Rolling Stones and "Sympathy For the Devil" and try to explain, in Ukrainian, the gist of the lyrics. My mother nods and loads my plate with more food.

In her glory the following day, when Ray and I watch four consecutive football games, she keeps the goodies and cold beer coming as we groan through football into the night.

At that time, the soul and jazz stations in Philadelphia incessantly advertise "Maximus Super" malt liquor for an audience specifically non-Main Line. We load a couple cases in the DeSoto's space between the grille and radiator, there's that much room, and after goodbyes head home to the coast. The weather is nasty, snowing, cold, but the DeSoto's heater works fine and its rounded mass gives the tires excellent traction.

Our decision to put off dropping the acid until the Midwest road doldrums proves fortuitous. The lunch my mother packed for us holds out nicely. The Maximus Super is cold and keeps the radiator hot. Iowa is on the verge of being boring. No matter what station we tune the DeSoto's cream, raspberry and pistachio radio to, Don MacLean sings "American Pie". Anticipating the stark flat boredom of Nebraska, we drop Mr. Natural.

The change requires a little while to take effect. What normally is an interminably boring flat drive takes on otherworldly aspects with curves and hills. Time is moot as the sky and clouds breathe cosmic, multi-colored, incredible largesse around our 1948 time-capsule hurtling along at what we hope is 60 mph, hanging on for dear life. Apparently we hold it together, since the Nebraska State Police don't pull us over for going 15 mph on the interstate.

The DeSoto's radio's multicolored lights throb as MacLean sings:

> And the three men I admire most:
> The father, son, and the holy ghost,
> They caught the last train for the coast

The day the music died.

And they were singing,
"Bye-bye, miss american pie."
Drove my chevy to the levee,
But the levee was dry.
And them good old boys
were drinkin' whiskey and rye
Singin', "This'll be the day that I die.
"This'll be the day that I die."

On what I assume is the following night, on a subzero Idaho two–lane, a semi decapitates a nice four-pointer in mutual headlights. The buck steps out onto the roadway. The semi takes his head off. Orange and red lights recede into the night. We stop, wrap the dispatched venison in a tarp and lash it to the roof. I roll a daybreak doobie. The acid, Maximus Super, and the lunch my mother packed for us, are gone. We split the final Snickers. Later that day we present frozen road kill to our pal in Ketchum, and drive on to Stockton, as close to home as we have at the moment.

Ray and the DeSoto stay in Stockton. I hitchhike north. Jonathan Block is in Stanwood, Washington, blowing glass at Pilchuck, a former tree farm turned glass-blowing facility in a development founded in 1971 by Dale Chihouly, Anne Gould Hauberg and John H. Hauberg.

Jonathan gets me in at Pilchuck to learn to blow glass. Annie Hauberg graciously provides me with a modular living unit: a trailer furnished with white Italian furniture, rugs, and accoutrements.

I find a job tending bar at the Red Lion on the outskirts of Anacortes, with Bill, a guy I picked up hitchhiking years before on my way to Alaska with Nancy and Ray. The clientele at the Red Lion are on the lower end of the social scale in that part of Washington, which suits me just fine. I trade beers for whole salmon with Indian

Art, Crime & Lithium

fishermen, and console the ladies pool team with free beers when the other ladies pool teams in the league refuse to play at the Red Lion for status reasons.

First paycheck, I buy a 1959 Oldsmobile stationwagon for $50 from a guy at the end of the bar. Now I have my own transportation, a place to live and glass to blow. I blow glass mornings and days, work evenings and nights. For added inspiration Jonathan, Mike Nurout and I retire to the barn where Chihouly keeps his '50s Hudson Hornet. We smoke hash until we can't see out the windows.

I blow glass until my palms resemble blackened sandpaper. The closer you hold the pipe to the hot glass, the more control you have over the slumping mass in a carefully orchestrated neverending dance with gathers, blow pipes, glory holes, marvering tables, rolling benches, annealing ovens and a dizzying variety of hand tools to manipulate the glass to shape.

One night after work I drive to LaConner to the 1890s, a locally infamous bar where Tom Robbins reportedly hangs out. I read *Another Roadside Attraction* and want to meet Robbins. He isn't there that night, but a half dozen literary-minded local heifers out for a good time decide I'm the right guy to discuss literature with. We hit a snag discussing Norman Mailer. I say *The Naked and the Dead* is the best war novel I ever read. They counter with Mailer is a misogynist. I say I don't give a fuck what his religion, he is a great writer. They offer to kick my ass because of my literary taste. I think about taking them up on it, certain I could take most of them down, but politely decline since there are six of them and they look pretty mean. They act more like Norman Mailer than I ever did. At that moment misogyny makes perfect sense. I ease out and never go back. Robbins writes more books. I work on perfecting the day to day on the road. It seemed like a good idea at the time; one thing leads to another philosophy of being.

O.Z. Lysiak

Nancy entertains a long-standing dream about living in the Northwest. I have a place to live in the Northwest close to the Pacific, a job and an artful reason: learning to blow glass. I call her. She takes a bus. Our first night together, Nancy vomits attempting to make love. We order shrimp for dinner. I have an allergic reaction to the shellfish; my face swells to grotesque proportions. Nancy takes the bus home, frisky times now history.

Wandering through the Cascades at night, coming on to acid, I feel pulsating red lights on the crest of the mountains as Cat Stevens sings "Longer boats are coming to win us, they're coming to win us, they're coming to win us. Hold on to the shore; they'll be taking the key from the door." I interpret it as a sign, load the Olds and drive south until I run out of gas, park it by the side of the road and hitchhike to Mountain Ranch.

My sign is a stop sign I ran in another life in North Philadelphia. Time and space tumble out of synch. A fat one and a pot of coffee is my morning ritual. For years, I'm stoned first thing in the morning. Nobody sees my eyes clear, because I'm stoned to deal with remnants of reality I refuse to or am unable to recognize. When brandy or rum is available I lace my coffee, put a different perspective on the day. LSD is a regular occurrence. Somewhere in this jumble of drugs, Ray and I go to see *2001: A Space Odyssey* in Stockton ripped on pink mescaline, a baggie-full we snort through a straw. We emerge from the theater after dark. Ray makes a right turn in his blue VW van, the door opens and I find myself sitting in the street with the rear wheels whizzing by. The streetlights are miraculous, exuding multifarious dancing colors. I'm a happy, albeit too stoned to move, camper when I hear the van back up, the door open and Ray say, "Hey, O, get in. Let's go."

Alternative Lifestyle

If you remember the '70s, you obviously weren't there.

In Bear Valley, California, uphill from Stockton, I meet Andre Potochnik: Society of Friends member, ski patrolman, and Grand Canyon boatman. He and I hit it off, hike cross-country from Bear Valley to Yosemite—often naked save for socks, boots and packs—the beginning of many Sierras hiking adventures. Our hiking naked is cause for consternation for at least one family on a Sierras horse pack-trip; parents look away angrily while daughters, smiling, check us out and demurely wave.

I hike solo down the Grand Canyon of the Mokelumne River, from Ebbetts Pass to Bear Valley, a stretch of the Sierras infamous for rattlesnakes. Civilization drives them to seek shelter in the canyon. The canyon's snaky reputation leaves it pretty much tourist-free. I find a stout stick, cut and shape it to length, and tap the granite in front of me on my descent, careful not to step on sleeping rattlers as I progress. I encounter fewer rattlesnakes than the reputation warrants, although I'm chilled on occasion when we share sudden encounters. The snakes probably are as frightened of me as I am of them. Mutual respect is the key. I leave them alone and they reciprocate.

At what I approximate to be directly below Bear Valley I make camp, find an old but useable can, clean and cook the peyote buttons I brought just for this occasion. By morning the buttons have rendered down into awful-tasting viscous brown paste, which I painstakingly ingest. I emerge on the rim of the canyon not far from Susie Lemoo's house, after a 4000-foot vertical climb with no direct recollection of the climb, although I remember speaking Ukrainian to what I assume are imaginary people along the way. Susie sees the state I'm in, and cares for me until I recover.

Andre hears of an alternative-lifestyle family on Sun Mountain, outside of Sheep Ranch, not far from Bear Valley. The last part of the ride to Sun Mountain requires an adventurous spirit and a vehicle capable of driving through a running stream, over oil-pan punishing rocks, and around boulders. We arrive when the family is gathered in the cook shack involved in a deep OM.

Unsure what the chanting means, I stand outside the shack, reluctant to join in. Lawrence, a tall, wiry family member approaches me, assures me it's cool and invites me to share their meal. In short order I'm "OM"ing along, checking out braless and panty-less women.

At Kikubudwini, a Miwok Indian name for the waterfall downstream from the road crossing to Sun Mountain, a group of naked bathers gather the next morning. Invited, I go along. Whatever misgivings I might have about the hippies and their quasi-religious malarkey dissipates at the sight of youthful female bodies with cold-water hardened nipples cavorting in the waterfall and pool below. Not even lush expanses of pubic and underarm hair, as well as hair down thighs and legs, dissuades me. These girls are juicy with a blush of innocence. Not all are nubile maidens.

I live in my Jansport dome-tent, well away from the "spirituality" of Swami Satchadenanda and Guru Gi followers, who are magnetized to the cook-shack. The devotion of lost American children to sleazy purveyors of questionable dogma amazes me. Family meetings are nothing more than opportunity for strong personalities to henpeck the weak. Oh, we "OM" and do yoga and pretend we participate in "higher consciousness", but we simply can't deal with the reality of an America gone mad, and are hiding out in the woods seeking enlightenment from eastern philosophies none of us have the depth or cultural heritage to understand. Smoking dope, ingesting peyote, mescaline or LSD is nothing more than fueling confusion, no matter how many times you call it "sacrament". Timothy Leary, the Harvard professor who tuned in, turned on and dropped out, simply buys into the confusion and has the means to mass-distribute his bullshit.

Needing to get further away from the cook-shack and the swami slingers, I find a spot on a sloping hillside between two huge sugar pines, hand saw 20' long 2x12 shop planks in half, haul them on my back, and build a platform and a rock firepit for warmth and esthetics. This is going to be my home for however long it takes, away from the cook-shack and family politics. Sawing and using the shop planks haunts me for decades. Apparently the mechanically-minded contingent intended to use the planks for a shop floor. For 30 years John Aadland incessantly reminds me I hauled his planks away and sawed them in half. I offer to replace them with 3x13x 22' planks but he declines, opting to remind me instead.

Women visitors to the family bring their own ideas as to what alternative lifestyle is about. They come loose, ready and willing. A comely blonde student, with a group from the medical school at UC Davis, strips down to panties on arrival. I introduce myself and escort her to the platform, where we engage in anatomical research and the finer points of liberated engagement. She and I remain friends all through her medical studies, into her professional career.

My role in the family evolves into devil's advocate. Lawrence, the Leo and leader of the "spiritual" faction, and I never come to blows but it crosses my mind. I call bullshit on the questionable philosophy of swami slingers, the "sacrament" nomenclature mistake, the need to throw our shoes and any leather products away to save the world. I make up my own lyrics to Amazing Grace: "Amazing Grace sat on my face and 'oh my God' said she…"

Having survived the nuns at Immaculate Conception Elementary, who were armed with corporal punishment and the threat of eternal damnation, I'm not about to buy into mediocre wishful thinking.

Word of the first Love Family gathering, at Strawberry Lake at Granby in the Colorado Rockies, spreads throughout alternative communities. The Sun Mountain family decides to attend. Everybody kicks in what they can to finance the journey, buy a school bus and get it ready. Once prepared, we move to Barn Meadow, high in the Sierras to tighten up for the journey, where I meet Dr. Bob Jacobs, former psychiatrist and Miami Playboy Club physician. Jacobs is one of the founding forces of the Sun Mountain group. He is connected to the UC Davis Medical School, where he shows the freshman class a film of faith healers tossing live venomous snakes around, and claims it's bona fide medicine. Jacobs loses his license to practice medicine after getting busted for selling LSD. After that he's known as "de-frocked, de-doc-ed Bob." Bob works emergency rooms weekends to help support the family.

Bob Jacobs sports a never-ending smile, like he knows something special. What he knows is transparent bullshit, which he induces desperate people to believe.

Besides Jacobs we bring along a couple UC Davis doctors, a couple vets, students, medical ability, supplies, sacks of rice, beans and a variety of staples.

The day we leave for Colorado, we're a VW van and the schoolbus. By the time we arrive, more than 30 vehicles are in our caravan.

Our first order of business is to relieve the medical staff at the emergency tent. They're happy to get a break, working non-stop day and night, tending to stoned out-of-control hippies.

A stoned hipster jumps headfirst into the lake, and nearly tears his scalp off. We clean him up, and Jacobs stitches him without benefit of painkillers as we "OM"

Art, Crime & Lithium

in a circle around him. When Bob is done, the guy sits up and chats with him. A chopper is summoned. I'm on one end of the stretcher as we haul this chump to the meadow where the Huey prepares to land. A Vietnam vet, one of ours, guides the chopper in with hand signals as we crouch in the grass, loaded on LSD. We load him on the chopper. Who knows? We might have saved that guy's life, provided he doesn't die of infection.

Approximately 300 people "OM" holding hands, eyes shut, in a giant circle. I recognize maybe 20, drop the hands of chanters on either side, hook them up, hoist my pack, hike to the nearest highway and hitchhike to Breckenridge, Colorado, done with swami baloney scammers and America's deluded youth. It's July, 1972.

South

On the outskirts of Breckenridge, up a dirt road, I find the remnants of a 3-story mining mill built of heavy timbers. Above the mill in the aspens, in a small clearing, I build a platform out of timbers and planks, fashion a frame from dry, curved aspens and cover it with visqueen. I dig a hole for a shitter on the back side of a fallen log. I'm home.

First order of business is to traverse the ridge above town, which begins with Peak 13 at the top of the ski area and ends with Peak One directly above Interstate 80. With a sleeping bag for shelter and Snickers for fuel, Peak 13 is a walkup. The traverse is no big deal. I find a relatively soft and flat spot to sleep in the rocks and lichens midway. The difficult part is descending from Peak 1 to the valley floor; once committed, there's no turning back. I hang and drop from shelf to shelf—dicey. At timberline I hike again.

Peak One Survey in Dillon, CO, advertises for a surveyor grunt. I apply. The crew boss hands me a measuring pole, a radio, instructions, and directions to the peak I'm to climb. At my destination I radio in, hold the pole vertically until readings are made, and meander back to the staging area. Colorado is bidding for the Winter Olympics. We survey a potential downhill course near Beaver Creek. Cowboy surveyors ride to the summit. I decline horseback, climb straight uphill instead, and meet the cowboys at the top. They zigzag; I don't.

Peak One assigns me to survey the tailings ponds at the Climax molybdenum mine. I learn to operate a

Art, Crime & Lithium

theodolite, climbing the surveyors' success ladder. My enthusiasm for surveying wanes, working above growing acres of toxic tailings.

Eve, a curvy brunette mountain-momma looker in hiking boots, wool socks, hairy legs and armpits, picks me up at the Gold Pan Saloon one night, takes me home to Monte Cristo on the pass above Breckenridge and fucks me until I'm too sore to move, a woman with amazing capacity and drive. I might have stayed longer, but her 3-year-old daughter climbs in bed with us while we're screwing, and bucks her little hips in rhythm with our grinding. I'm not that liberated. Following my world-class Rocky Mountain fucking I drag ass back home, momentarily consider going back but refuse my ravaged, battered, but nonetheless hopeful libido.

A foray to neighboring Lincoln Gulch yields a shopping-bag full of *amanita muscaria* mushrooms. I very nearly poison myself, squirt out of every orifice with the exception of my ears, for an entire night and the better part of the next day. This is not an experience I'd try again, nor would I recommend it. In a painful way, it was an exercise in enlightenment.

I have no intention of spending winter in the Rockies. A letter from my mother says my friend Alex Nikorovich finally succeeded in killing himself by driving an automobile into a bridge abutment. Alex is buried in the Ukrainian Cemetery in Bound Brook, New Jersey. Intending to work until I have $10,000, I have a grand stashed, and the molybdenum tailings help make my decision. I hit the road for LA.

In Los Angeles, an ad for a drive-away offers a Cadillac repo that requires delivery to New Orleans. I call Ray and wait for him to show. We pick the car up in a downtown LA parking garage.

The attendant kid's stringy tattooed arms drag a battered and rusted battery-charger to a baby-blue white rag top Caddy layered in months of greasy downtown dust, his destiny linked to limp, pallor, slouch, and a cheap underground LA outlook on life.

The beast contained in the convertible's expansive power cradle receives the required jolt, fires, belches, blows black smoke out dual exhausts, and settles into a retracted claw purr. My estimation of the clammy-skinned kid grows. His scowl turns to the unfamiliar territory of a grin.

Ray roots through the trunk for spare and tools, finds a tiny black suit and a pair of patent leather shoes that'll maybe fit a dwarf. Script on the tarnished glovebox plaque proclaims that this Caddy was built expressly for WILDCAT FRENCHIE. The ragtop plays dead in the low light of the parking dungeon. Ray hands the kid a $10. The kid grunts, back in the head-bowed cowl of his sleaze.

Hazily layered smog parfait, rubber, concrete and metal rhythms of endless reasons for somewhere to go, fill the tightly-packed Southern California bowels of The Great American Highway. We escape against gridlock grain, intent on finding a car-wash to cleanse the free-at-last Caddy of transgressions past. Crankshaft and pistons weave us into morning's viscous fabric. Four barrels open wide, hungry as a Great White Shark on a feeding frenzy, senseless. She rides like an ice cream float with the edge of a tequila shooter, waiting at the end of a slurp that never comes. Endless juice. Pedal to the metal and the Caddy leaps, a baby-blue linebacker in a top down tutu, dancing through traffic on 35 psi.

Toked, stroked, Snickers for breakfast, white leather, door locks, cruise control, stereo: Ray points to the Cucamonga exit observing silence in the haze, as if a word'll break the spell of our escape. It's time for a sixer, car wash, reality check, quarters-free dials and nozzles. Stoned and flying on an Indica and Snickers high, THC and sugar, we're crazed for a high shine boogie. The ragtop receives her high-pressure baptism soaped, brushed, rinsed, waxed, buffed, whitewalls scrubbed, resurrected, freed from the darkness, reborn to be wild.

From Los Angeles to New Orleans, through Arizona, New Mexico, Texas and Louisiana, we smoke California weed and feast on Snickers, shine the convertible, power the top up, power the top down, set the cruise control, steer the beast with a finger, pick hitchhikers up, drop hitchhikers off, dawn to sunset, night after night, gloriously loose in America, on the road in a Cadillac.

In a New Orleans carwash on a Saturday morning, crazed, we're in need of another high-shine boogie to chill out. The carwash is a latter-day Sportin' Life in N'Awlins, doing the shuck and jive, putting the buff and shine on prize Caddys.

At the yacht basin we shop for boats, with the Caddy as a front visible in the parking lot. A few mildly adventurous yachties who entertain in the basin on weekends invite us for boat drinks and tales. Monday we're in Chalmette, delivering the car on time as promised. The repo agent gives us a ride to the French Quarter.

Ray and I work out a plan, over the course of the journey from LA to New Orleans, to find a berth on a freighter going to South America. The reality of our scheme is nothing like the reverie. No freighters with berths leave for over a month, and they're booked well in advance. There is a flight leaving for Merida, Yucatan, in the morning. We spend the night at a flophouse in the Quarter, catch a bus for the airport in the morning, Cadillac days long gone.

Hammocks hung in a cheap room rented in downtown Merida, we sort through all our stuff, pack three-quarters of it in a box and ship it home. Without the Caddy, we'll travel light. Yucatan is hot, humid, foreign and different. Since neither of us speaks Spanish, we order by pointing and figure out what it translates to what once it arrives. *Pulpo en tino,* octopus marinated in octopus ink, is one of our more adventurous meals, washed down with a chilled *Modelo Negro* in a beachside café on the Gulf of Mexico in Progresso, a few kilometers north of Merida. We catch the local bus for the ruins at Chitzen Itza.

The sun is going down when we arrive at the ruins, and rather than get a room we opt to camp in a covered dugout on a baseball field outside town. Everything goes well until it starts raining. Fire ants invade our sleeping bags. Ray and I do vigorous dances ripping off our sleeping bags, slapping at the ants to stop the stinging, in the dark, in a totally foreign place famous for the fer-de-lance, the bushmaster, arguably the deadliest snake in the world.

Composed, we walk back to town, pound on the door of the local motel, rent a room intending to get in the shower to get the sting out of the ant bites. The water, the proprietor informs us, doesn't get turned on until 10 a.m. It's getting light.

The ruins at Chitzen Itza stand in mute tribute to the Mayan ball players who played a game putting a ball through stone hoops on the walls of the court, where winners took all and losers lost their heads. Ray and I play Frisbee up and down the court, skipping and skimming the Whamo disk off ancient walls, and catch the next bus for Puerto Juarez for a ferry to Isla Mujeres where Mundaca the pirate kept women.

Isla Mujeres lies on the northeast coast of Yucatan, where the Caribbean and the Gulf of Mexico blend. The thatched-roof, beach sand floor of La Hamacas, where backpack travelers from around the globe hang their hammocks and share road tales, is where we land. French divers in obligatory minimal bikinis come in daily with lobster and fish, which they prepare with extravagance and share. Several New Zealand girls, who leave home for years to go on walkabout, share road stories and

Art, Crime & Lithium

lubricious generosity under cover of darkness, in warm tide-pools under Caribbean stars.

Ray's decision to go home to upstate New York, become an alderman and a member of a bowling league, catches me by surprise. I'm sorry to see him go.

One spectacular French Canadian blonde—Lyse, the queen of the beach—is involved with Perry, an American with a place on the island.

Lyse announces she is leaving the island, and requests I join her on the train to Palenque, a famous Mayan ruin. We take the bus for Merida and the overnight train through Yucatan, Campeche, and Chiapas to Palenque.

"Whatever you want," Lyse says in the sleeper.

She knows what I want and does it before my request. Lyse has a husband in Chibougamou, Quebec. She is on a journey of self-discovery. Maybe she wants to know exactly what she'll be missing being married. She certainly spreads the joy around, an exceptionally beautiful, brave young woman, not someone who would allow herself to be owned. By Palenque I assume she gets what she wants, and certainly gives me what I want. I give her my dog-eared copy of Henry Miller's *Big Sur and the Oranges of Hieronymus Bosch* before we split up at the railroad station.

I hoist my rucksack and get directions to the ruins off a road leading to a forested jungle hillside. Just before the last turn, an innocuous road leads into the jungle with a small abandoned house at the end. A trail leads from the house to a stream and a waterfall further into the jungle.

A group of disparate travelers occupy the house, some with hammocks slung, other with bedrolls laid out on the concrete floor. Communal meals are cooked over a primitive outside fire pit. A traveling American family, Phil and Linda Hall and their infant son Poco, feed the fire when I arrive. Phil is short, with braids, steel-rimmed glasses, in basic native Mexican campesino garb. Linda is tall and gaunt.

Psychedelic mushrooms are plentiful in fields on the opposite side of Palenque, where cattle graze. It's December 21, 1972, winter solstice, full moon, four days until Christmas, at a major Maya ruin in the Chiapas jungle. We're about to get ripped on shrooms in a pagan celebration of our own.

The *hongos* we find are plentiful and potent. At the jungle house we gather large banana leaves, spread them on the floor and lay our psychedelic stash out, plenty for everybody several times over.

The *hongos* kick in, vibrating moonlight in undulating, pale, primary colored waves. Phil and I launch my Frisbee, lock into the sound of the plastic disc spinning, slicing through vibrating colored-light waves, at first on the road and eventually through the ruins. Music from a Mexican's Chevy parked on the hill above us serenades our moonlit ballet. Although we can't see each other, we remain connected by the sound of the spinning disc.

A bath in the waterfall, and I'm on my way to South America again. Phil invites me to go tree planting with him out of Crested Butte, Colorado, in case I'm back in the States by spring. I thank him, but it's unlikely.

Locals in black outfits with red sashes promenade to midnight mass on Christmas Eve, along the candle-lit cathedral square in San Cristobal de las Casas. The smell of hot pancakes and syrups hawked by vendors permeates the square. I cross into Guatemala the next day.

Huehuetenango and Quezaltenango are the first Guatemalan towns I encounter on the Pan American Highway, on the way to Lago Atitlan. I'm in road flow mode, garnering information about where to go and what to avoid in conversations in bars, around campfires, in hostels and cheap hotels, from fellow travelers who also pick tips up from a usually reliable on-the-road underground information system. A road master or mistress applies their own instinctive bullshit meter to information obtained in suspect places from shaky sources.

Art, Crime & Lithium

I learn about the hammock place in Panahachel on Lago Atitlan from somebody up the road, just as I learn about the *hongo* fields outside Palenque, exotic names a language magnet.

The hammock establishment in Panahachel is an international road master destination on Lago Atitlan. I hook up my hammock. A curly-haired young man in a lounge chair is immersed in a book, intent. I'm intrigued, and walk over. He is reading my dog-eared copy of *Big Sur and the Oranges of Hieronymus Bosch*.

What strikes me about Atitlan is the contrast of the villages to the ostentatious intrusions of concrete, steel and glass villas perched on hillsides about the lake. Inequity is shockingly apparent. The names are exotic, but the economic and political bullshit remains the same. The farmers who till terraced fields and gather coffee honey are secure in their place and apparent poverty. Patrons in the mansions higher up on the hillsides, and in bellicose motor launches raising hell on the lakes, are shakier with a long way to fall.

Richard McNeese, president of the Great American Sales Institute, Seattle, Washington, leans on the shiny long hood of his pale green Oldsmobile Toronado in the street outside the national palace in Guatemala City. He hands me a business card to establish veracity. I have a room on the rooftop of an apartment building in the center of town, and am on the street looking for a ride south. Richard is my ticket, with the Olds for bait, trolling for riders to help with fuel and driving. Fate, instinct or good timing, we come to an understanding. A young French couple, and a looker blonde with a cop daddy from Detroit, fill out our road crew.

By El Salvador the blonde and I are a number. She dumps me for a boat captain in Panama when things get tough.

We arrive in Managua, Nicaragua, a couple days after the city is hit with a devastating earthquake on

O.Z. Lysiak

December 23, 1972. Bodies stacked in the streets are doused with gasoline and set aflame. Confusion, soldiers and police are everywhere. Richard decides this is an opportune time to sell the Olds to government officials or diplomats whose vehicles are destroyed, on the phone to some embassy. I look at him in disbelief. We're in a third world city devastated by an earthquake, under martial law, with corpses burning in the streets, and he's selling our ride out. I hang up the receiver and calmly advise Richard to get in the car or be left behind to be stacked with the corpses.

Inept Costa Rican beach-thieves, in an attempt to gain access to the Toronado, manage to spider-web the rear window with a blow but don't gain entrance or get away with anything. We take it as a sign and drive south. Surprised to see MacDonalds' golden arches on the main street of San Jose, having covered nearly the entire length of Central America, I'm not ready to deal with Ronald MacDonald hustling Big Macs on the main drag of the capital city of Costa Rica. Central American cuisine – rice, plantains, beans, and occasional fish, chicken or pork, although bland and unspectacular, is an improvement over corporately processed white bread and mystery meat.

A man with a stick chases what looks to be a dog along the gutter, as we cross the bridge over the Panama Canal into Panama City early enough in the morning for it to still be dark. What the man with the stick is chasing is a large rat, once we get a good look under a streetlight.

Richard continues to sell his car. The French kids take off. My blonde finds a frizzy-haired boat captain to latch onto. I'm on my own.

Camping in Panama City happens at the National Racetrack downtown. I find a soft grassy spot under a palm tree in the parking lot. Theft isn't an issue. The Panamanian army patrols the racetrack, heavily armed. Early morning I climb into the grandstand with coffee I buy from a vendor and, with the soldiers, watch jockeys exercise their mounts.

Camped next to me is a rotund gent with a gray flattop, dressed in Sears polyester, with white shoes and belt. He is in a gargantuan Winnebago he intends to airfreight to Columbia.

I'm road lean, with blonde hair down my back, dressed in a T-shirt and white bellbottomed Navy-surplus trousers and huaraches. I live out of my red internal frame rucksack.

One day the gent takes it on himself to impart advice.

"The key to life," he says, "Is being the right man at the right place at the right time." Only thing he ever says to me. The next day the Winnebago is gone.

I speak with a Scotsman who crossed the infamous Darien Gap between Panama and Columbia on foot. Attempts at building highways and railroads have failed. The Scot pulls a three-foot long worm out of his leg, and is getting medical attention in Panama City. I weigh my options and take the train to Balboa.

A dismasted trimaran is home for a few months. The owner of the tri needs somebody to care take his rig while he arranges to have it repaired or sold. I need a place to live. We make a deal which gives me access to the harbor, the yacht club, jobs fixing boats, jobs taking boats through the Canal, and opportunity on the streets of Balboa.

Sanding and painting pay a dollar an hour, sufficient since I don't pay rent. Local food is inexpensive, as is the justifiably infamous Panama Red. I score the Panama Red through Captain Pluto, a diminutive Panamanian who befriends me at the Café Florida in the center of Balboa. The Florida is open to the street on two sides, with tables on the sidewalk, a good place to see and be seen in Balboa. A lot of business, legal and otherwise, is conducted here. The café is an excellent place to sip and watch the sluts, cruisers, scammers, and how those in the know operate. Pluto arranges my first Panama Red score. A black woman in her 30s approaches our table, indicates I should follow her to the john where she lifts her skirt, pulls down her panties, and presents me with a paper bag with primo red. I pay her. She asks if there is anything else I'd like. Not at the moment, I reply.

    Days, I work on boat projects. I sand and varnish a 60-foot mast, in a bosun's chair high above the harbor. From my lofty perch, I watch baseball games on the diamond blocks away. I sand and paint hulls and waterlines, with as much work as I can handle.

    Nights find me on the grassy knolls above the Panama Canal smoking potent red weed, watching ships glide through the slice, an unusual and eerie sight. Big Brother garbles through muscular loudspeakers attached to concrete buildings with bright orange tile roofs.

    I keep an eye on boats coming in which will have to pass through the canal to get to the Pacific, offering to crew. The going rate is lunch, drinks and a train ticket back to Balboa. We motor to the locks first thing in the morning, wait for canal workers to launch tether lines, catch the lines, secure them, and wait for the lock to fill. The top of the lock is a long way up. Sometimes we're in behind a freighter, bouncing around as the lock fills, intimidating. Up the locks on the Caribbean side, we motor across Gatun Lake and down the Pacific side.

    The *Moala* sails into the harbor with Aussie Graeme Tait at the helm, a no-frills wood 34' sloop. While his mates are at the pub weekends, drinking, Tait decides to sail around the world in a boat he designs and builds. He works on his dream in his backyard for six years, saves his money and, while his mates are still drinking at the pub, launches. Two years later Graeme needs $60 to pay canal fees so he can start on his last leg home. I

Art, Crime & Lithium

give him the $60, figuring to never see the money again. Flush, with a place to live, work, all the Panama Red I can smoke, tropical weather and a sunny disposition, I give Graeme a hand through the canal and buy my own ticket back to Balboa.

The Galapagos

The *Maid of Malham*, a former racing cutter from the Channel Islands, sails in and docks. Crew is off her instantly, and gone. Malcolm Robson, her skipper, is looking for crew to sail the Pacific on a round-the-world cruise with his wrinkled paramour, getting their last laughs while the getting is good. He offers me a berth as first mate. Maybe things are too good for me at the Balboa Yacht Club. I agree, score a pound of red and pack my gear, still on my way to South America.

On the Pacific side of the canal, Robson beaches the *Maid* with wood supports to hold her upright between tides, and inspects the shaft and propeller. The shaft bearing is worn, and we can fire up the Perkins marine 2-banger only in case of dire emergency.

The sail to the Perlas Islands is days of constant vomiting for me. I wake up with my sea legs one morning, hungry. The sky is filled with clouds of sea birds feeding on mackerel, explosions of pelicans, cormorants and varieties of birds I'd never seen before diving and impacting the boiling ocean. I have a hand line rigged with orange, red and white feathers on hooks I scored in Balboa, in the water quickly. Soon I have mackerel for dinner.

British cuisine, at least the sort Robson and his sweetie practice, is bland, mostly boiled without imagination. I take every opportunity to get at the meager spices aboard. The mackerel is an opportunity to eat something with flavor. Adrift in the doldrums, common in the Bay of Panama, at the mercy of currents and tides since Robson won't fire up the Perkins, I take every opportunity to fish and cook. We acquire a stalk of bananas in Panama, which all go ripe at the same time. We eat banana bread, bananas mushed, bananas raw and any way possible. The rotting stalk leaves a sticky mess on deck, which I, as last in the succession, clean up. The wind picks up after interminable days, finally off for the Galapagos Islands, a thousand miles away.

Malcolm Robson is a diesel engineer, former police chief of Sark, an English Channel pilot, a captain, navigator and sailor. He brought electricity via diesel generators to Sark, a grim, humorless son of a bitch who expects me to be at his beck and call 24 hours a day. Malcolm is a rigid taskmaster who imparts basics of sailing, navigation and dead reckoning. I read and saw *Mutiny On the Bounty*, Capt. Bligh and Mr. Christian parallels appropriate. I don't sign on for the rigors of British square-rigger naval discipline. Robson assigns me the midnight to 8 a.m. watch. I'm thrilled, eight hours without Malcolm and his prune-skinned sweetie—heaven. They're "dahling" this and "dahling" that, in a smarmy facsimile of '30s British black-and-white chick flicks, ridiculous and embarrassing, tea on the foredeck every afternoon.

I hear the flutter of the mainsail's luff, and look up from the star charts. A halyard slaps against the metal mast. The wind picks up. A hemisphere of constellations defines the horizon in every direction, clear as a sorcerer's dream. The bow slices phosphorescence with a steady, comforting whoosh, through opal-froth swells. This is the third night I'm privy to both the Big Dipper and the Southern Cross. In a few days I'll be in the Galapagos Islands.

I check the compass, adjust self-steering a few degrees into the wind, and the banging halyard stops. I stand to take a turn around the deck to check halyards, hatches, stays, turnbuckles, knots, sails and rigs. She's shipshape, seaworthy, heeled over, smooth running with the trades. In a saltwater sailor's squat stance, I survey my midnight-to-daylight realm on the bow in amazement of proportions of ocean to sky, of below to beyond.

Once I determine the *Maid* is shipshape and we're steady on course, I make my way to the bow, shimmy out on the bowsprit as far as I dare and hang on. I ride the *Maid*, a gypsy on a stolen mare though the night. When she dips deep I'm showered with salt spray, a madman grinning, laughing, hung out over the Pacific, wild in starlit darkness.

Riding the bowsprit one particularly phosphorescent night, I see a tailed, brilliant starburst move directly up at us from deep in the ocean. I'm frozen, welded to the bowsprit at the possibility of being rammed. No need to wake the others; we'll be dead in flash, sunk into darkness, devoured by predators. I'm mesmerized. The prospect of death doesn't fill me with fear. Amazed at this huge sparkling torpedo gaining speed, I can't clutch the bowsprit any tighter as a dolphin leaps from the waves shedding phosphorescence over the bowsprit and into the night on the opposite side, a starburst scooting through the sea.

Able to breathe moments later, I pry cramped fingers out of the wood, shimmy off the bowsprit ever so carefully, and slowly make my way to the stern. The wake trails curly trickles in a dazzling, moon-tipped sea.

Days from the Galapagos the sky is clouded over, negating use of the sextant to get our position. We dead-reckon landfall on Isla Espanola, the southernmost island in the archipelago and drop anchor a quarter-mile offshore.

Come morning, Robson and his ancient hoochie babe row ashore in the dingy to explore the island and enjoy precious privacy. I remain on board. After a time I look to the beach. His concubine waves, I wave back, realizing the dingy is gone. Robson is swimming for the *Maid*. In his ardor, he does a half-assed job tying off the painter. The dingy bobs away in the distance. I help him aboard, worn out, useless, panicked. If we fire up the Perkins, the bearing might not last and we won't have a half hope in a real emergency, with no dingy and no motor. I dive in, swim, board the dingy and row it back to the boat. Sharks frequent these waters, but not today. Robson retrieves his parchment-skinned girlfriend and says nothing as I take the dingy ashore, armed with a net bag containing a bottle of water and a sandwich.

Brilliant red-orange Sally Lightfoot crabs leap rock to rock in front of me in the shallow surf. I find a stick and poke around tide pools, stir up miniscule octopi and alarm small darting fish. The beach stretches for miles. I push on. Suddenly, a shadow sliding fast over my right shoulder startles me to leap for the sand. I look up. A large Galapagos hawk glides close over me, pulls up with wings spread full, perches on a rock and studies me in a side to side motion, totally unafraid and apparently curious as to who I am cruising his beach. Lifting myself, I walk down the beach. The hawk rises, flaps his great wings and flies over me again, landing a few yards above me down the beach.

I approach the hawk arm's length away. He continues to check me out side to side, unconcerned. I whistle. He cocks his head, looks around me to the bag with the water and sandwich I have in hand. I hold on to the bag in case the bird tries to attack me, figuring I need some sort of defense against this wild raptor. Apparently the hawk means me no harm. I drop the bag on the sand. He sees it. I lift first one arm, then the other. He watches me. One at a time I lift my legs, then do my best Motown routine. He continues to watch me. I sing the St. James Infirmary Blues. He listens. After a while I run out of creative stuff, pick up my sandwich and water and walk down the beach. The hawk flies over my shoulder again and lands up the beach, anticipating my arrival. I drop bag and pants and jump in the bay, swim a long way, not thinking about what just happened, steadily stroke. Rolling over, floating in the bay, I look at the sky. Two hawks circle above me.

Swimming back to the beach I feel something brush against me, an uncomfortable feeling. No fins slice the surface, so I dive to investigate. A dark, sleek form brushes against me, not aggressive but suggestive. Sea lions try to induce me to play. I dive, do a loop, come up for air and dive again deeper. Sea lions dart around me until I gain footing in the surf, stride out and lie down in the sun, exhausted. Two hawks continue circling high above. This is a curious place, indeed. I never experienced a place where wild animals aren't afraid of humans.

Back on board Robson thanks me for retrieving the dingy but our relationship, which erodes to minimal courtesy over weeks aboard, suffers over the incident, exposes him as being capable of making serious mistakes. His bout with being human is fine with me, but Robson can't stand the idea. A few days sailing and exploring islands and we drop our hook at the harbor at Puerto Ayora on Isla Santa Cruz, and check in with the local authorities who stamp our passports with a stamp unique to the Galapagos: a penguin with a parasol walking on a beach.

The *Moala* is in port. Graeme Tait repays the $60 I fronted him in Panama. He receives funds from home, and prepares to leave on the last leg of his circumnavigation.

If it weren't for Robson I probably wouldn't have seen or experienced the uniqueness of the Galapagos, learned the basics of sailing or understood that a person needs sound judgment rather than desperation or hope to sign on for a voyage on a buoyant sliver of wood where a walk consists of 20 paces back and forth and privacy is nonexistent. At times I consider dumping him overboard, but we share a relationship based on survival. Despite all that, by Puerto Ayora I had enough. So had he. According to maritime law, Robson is liable for providing me with an airline ticket to the port where he picked me up. I relieve him of that responsibility, quite happy to be away and on my own.

Art, Crime & Lithium

A few weeks later a skipper of one of the larger yachts moored in the harbor returns from business in England, where he visited Lloyd's of London. He brings news that the *Maid of Malham* sinks en route to the Marquesas; keel drops off. Robson and his ancient paramour survive. He has a claim with Lloyd's.

Franklin Angermeyer looks like an unusually tall version of one of the Fabulous Furry Freak Brothers, a definite stoner. His favorite song is the Grateful Dead's *Casey Jones*. Franklin has a dream. He wants to set up a wooden toy train business and export the toy trains—packed with cocaine—to the U.S. I sail over a thousand miles with tight-assed Robson to meet a loose kindred spirit. I hoist my rucksack. Franklin and I hike miles out of town, over lava beds, past towering cactus plants to a beach where other hardy souls camp. A South African surfer shows me the basics of body surfing, which I do daily until I spot two sharks in the waves behind me. We have one pair of diving fins, one pair of gloves and a couple of diving masks between us. Franklin and I dive on reef rocks for *langostino*, Pacific crayfish. He wears one fin and one glove, I wear the other, working holes in the reef together. We boil the *langostinos* in ocean water. A Canadian kid has a telescoping fishing pole. We bait hooks with *langistino* bits and fish for small shark. Knife lashed to a pole, we hunt skate in the surf. The cactus sports fruit, purple and edible. Oatmeal is the only staple we buy. Life is good until a current catches me and pulls me out to sea. I swim for my life. Beyond exhausted, I manage to break the pull of the current. Time to explore other possibilities. I say goodbye to my pals, the beach, and hike back to town.

I meet Jack Nelson, of the Hotel Galapagos in Puerto Ayora, on one of my excursions. His father Don established and runs the operation. Jack runs boat tours. They offer me a handyman job at the hotel. In exchange for handyman skills from 6 a.m. till noon daily, I get my own cottage on a hillside overlooking the harbor, three squares a day, and access to their library and bar. Jack and I build a new launch out of *roble*, South American oak, in the hotel workshop.

Mornings I work with Jack on the boat, or fix plumbing, or rake the grounds, or whatever Don wants. Afternoons I'm free to explore the island, swim, read, or work on my own projects.

Avocados as big as footballs grow here. Local farmers feed them to their chickens, as well as numerous varieties of bananas and plantains. King fruit—a purplish, edible variety of pear—grows in extremely tall trees, difficult to harvest. The Ecuadorian Navy, in American surplus ships with barely enough freeboard to remain afloat, show up monthly with supplies. For a few weeks chocolate and beer are abundant. I steer clear of opportunities for dalliance with local dusky doves. Then I discover sores all over my body, staph infection.

The local pharmacy is ill-stocked to deal with staph. I try washing the sores in boiling water, with citrus juice, seawater, urine. Nothing works until a Canadian kid offers his jar of tetracycline. The tetracycline works. The Canadian kid and I decide to leave the islands together, catch a boat for Baltra and a flight for Guayaquil, where it takes hours of cajoling to convince the Lufthansa rep to accept the kid's Canadian visa for tickets to Miami. Otherwise we're in for an arduous and dangerous journey home.

I kiss the tarmac in Miami. Customs officials put me through a rigorous shakedown, pull me out of line and make me go to the ominous little room where they tear my pack and everything in it apart. I ask the uniformed official why would a person who looks like me do anything obviously illegal? I get a hint of a smile as the guy keeps tearing my rig apart and eventually waves me through.

Points West

Thumb out, smile on, Frisbee in hand, I hitch-hike north out of Miami across country to Crested Butte, Colorado, invited to plant trees. A black Cadillac slows down. A black driver smoking a black cigar checks me out, stops, gets in the back seat, amused to have a white boy be his driver through the South. He sits in back enjoying his cigar. We share non-stop driving until he drops me off south of Chicago on I80 west on his way to Winnetka.

A Jesus-freak on his way home from work picks me up in Davenport, Iowa, in rush-hour traffic, and harangues me with how his life got better when he found Jesus, how he got a new TV and new furniture. I tell him to stop the car and let me out. Jesus needs people like him, I'm sure. A line from Leonard Cohen's "Suzanne" – "and when he was certain only drowning men could see him, he said all men will be sailors then until the sea shall free them," runs through my head as I hoist my worn red rucksack and head on down the road.

No rides. I hunker down under an interstate underpass and sleep with an eye open. Days later I'm in Crested Butte, high in the Colorado Rockies. Phil Hall, his wife Linda and their son Poco, in town as advertised. Phil recruits and organizes a tree-planting crew for a job at 11,000 feet, that he negotiates with the United States Forest Service. It's on Virginia Creek above Crawford, over the mountains and through the West Elk Wilderness, yet another strange place so uniformly unfamiliar, home on the road high in the Rockies.

A meadow on Virginia Creek serves as base camp. Remnants of winter snow-pack cling to shadows in the aspen and fir forest, perfect for planting seedlings that begin their journey as cones collected in local forests, germinated as seeds and sprouted in a nursery in Nebraska. The USFS delivers a reefer with the precious infants.

A hoedad isn't a hooker's daddy but is a steel blade about a ¼" thick, 6" wide, 18" long, beveled on both ends with a rounded front and square rear attached to a recurved wood handle. A planter cleans off a spot with the beveled square end of the hoedad, swings the hoedad over his or her head, plants it in the ground, opens a slice in the earth, extracts a infant tree out of a planting bag slung off a hip, places the seedling in the slice—taproot first, pointing down—tamps the slice firmly with the squared end and moves on, keeping in mind the required spacing between planters on either side.

Hitting a rock on a full-bore downswing numbs hands and sends shivers up to the shoulders. Extended planting in a rock-field makes people consider getting a job as a shoe salesman or a McDonald's flunkie. There's a reason why they plant trees. Planters can't hack regular jobs. Planting trees isn't rocket science but does require strength, stamina, rhythm, dedication—ability to live in the woods, deal with less than optimum circumstances, and a requisite sense of humor. This is hard work. The entire crew gets the squirts a few days into the job, plants on anyway with a roll of toilet paper handy in the planting bag. The altitude, extreme planting angle and an occasional squat are nothing we can't handle.

Stanley Richardson eats beans and rice out of a hubcap, plays sketches of planters around the fire on a varnish-absent road guitar. Soupy Campbell passes the Henry McKenna Kentucky table whiskey. Soupy, from Mississippi, occasionally drops a syllable pronouncing the name of his home state. His given name is Bobby. Soupy sports a full beard but will tell anyone who'll listen that

Art, Crime & Lithium

he has whiskers, like Gabby Hayes had whiskers. Bruce Blackwell is a Mississippian from Jackson who retains the dropped syllable. Leonard Casey, from N'Awlins, sells the last under ten-dollar ounces of pot in America.

The crew is made up of young, tough, willing, able Americans from every part of the country. Planters from the South are memorable with a laid-back manner and engaging drawls. Several are veterans home from Vietnam, uninterested in dealing with American mainstream society. For whatever reasons, we find ourselves camped at 11,000 feet, living and working in a southwestern Colorado forest. Phil and Linda have a tipi set up in the meadow. The rest live in tents, pickup campers or panel-trucks.

We eat beans and rice, peanut butter and jam sandwiches, and poach occasional venison to add flavor and substance to potato, onion and carrot stews once we've consumed roasted back-strap and hams.

Inspectors check planting quality, spacing and women in camp. On subsequent jobs we find inspectors unusually friendly and likely to skip inspections altogether when girls plant topless. Not only are women who plant tough, they have a sense of humor.

A planter is paid a nickel a tree for his efforts. On the Virginia Creek job I plant a thousand trees one day, not something I could or would care to do every day. I make fifty bucks, a tough way to make a living, but it suites me fine. We're tough, happy and free in the mountains and woods, doing something green although it isn't called that then, as close to the earth as we can be and get paid for it. We don't get paid much, but we don't need much.

Job done, with a few bucks in my pocket, I hoist my pack and set out on foot across the Gunnison National Forest and the West Elk Wilderness for Crested Butte, and later Aspen.

O.Z. Lysiak

I have topographical maps, compass, a nose for the trail and everything I need on my back. Afternoon of my first day on the trail, I hear rumbling and duck behind a tree in time to see several hundred elk thunder by. Another day I follow bear prints for miles on the trail, anxious but relieved when the bear saunters off the trail and heads cross-country.

In Crested Butte I sip Henry McKenna with Soupy Campbell and Bruce Blackwell before hiking to the town of Gothic, a right up the trail past Copper Lake, over snow-covered Conundrum Pass. I sit on my trusty red pack, legs out for stability, holding the straps like reins, and ride the snowfield down almost to the hot springs below Electric Pass. Steam from the hot springs pool reveals blue eyes, blonde braids and an inviting smile. I smile back and ease into the heat.

The trail from Conundrum Hot Springs is downhill to Aspen. Art Rowell shares a house with Roy Palm, over the bridge on the Roaring Fork on the east side, across the street from the Kingdom Hall of Jehovah's Witnesses. I check in, drop a hit of Orange Sunshine and go downtown to check out the bright lights, eagle feathers tied in my hair. What I gauge to be a short while later, I'm under the bridge listening to the gurgle of the Roaring Fork, Aspen's bright lights and Gucci profiling too much to deal with. The next morning Art's German Jehovah's Witness landlord complains about me doing yoga on the lawn, claims the pagan rites I'm performing half-naked on his lawn threaten the moral fiber of the neighborhood.

My parents intended for me to become an educated, successful, upscale gentleman, schooled in Euro-Ukrainian traditions and values. Stoned in the '60s, I stay stoned on marijuana, hashish, LSD, peyote, mescaline, speed, cocaine and tequila, snort heroin once, stay up all night puking and scratching, don't like it and don't understand the attraction. My aversion to needles keeps me from becoming a classic junkie. After serious, dedicated research, I accept tequila as my personal savior. At age 27, on my own, loose in the world, I'm a drug-addled, sex-mad pagan vagabond despite my parents' best intentions.

Two weeks solo hiking through the West Elk Wilderness, I run into Joanne Sloane in Aspen. Joanne and I break a gasthaus bed in Garmisch- Partenkirchen one frisky afternoon three years before. We meet later in Bear Valley, CA, and again in the alternative family, leave well enough alone and no longer get frisky on strange beds, friends at last. She is the girlfriend of Robert Scott. Scott and Jim Collins, American Indian antique rug traders, antiquities dealers and scammers, organize the Faire Ecclesia.

Robert recognizes a kindred drug-addled, sex-mad pagan vagabond, and offers me a job working with John Woodjack. John is barefoot with silver rings on his toes and fingers, shirtless with an Indian-style breastplate, with steel-rimmed granny glasses with a venerably soft cowboy hat topped with a beaded hatband. He's a set builder and crew boss with California's Renaissance Faires, who provides the next step in my education. John learned classic set building from his father and other old-timers on LA's movie lots.

A secluded spot away from the main faire grounds in Snowmass serves as my campsite. Woodjack indicates the pile of timber—jacket slab wood—that should manifest itself into ticket booths and an imaginative entrance to the faire, and leaves me on my own. I get Art a job helping me build the entrance. We combine ideas and efforts into a makeshift wood building with two eyes for ticket windows, a long wood nose in between, and a smile underlining the philosophy of our concept. We bury four stout fir poles for structural integrity, and incorporate a deck on top with banners flying off the poles.

The morning the Faire Ecclesia opens, in the zone on a dose of legendary Orange Sunshine I drop the night before, I paint my face to resemble wild jungle. John smiles at me and says, "What's new?"

Woodjack offers me a job with his crew, building and taking down the Renaissance Faires. I accept, happy to have discovered a sub-nation of kindred spirits.

"You're snake bit," says John. "See you in California."

California

I check in with Ronn and Charlie Alexander in Mountain Ranch. They let me stay in Shaw, their bus, until I find a trailer perched on a hillside in California oaks, over an intermittent creek that runs in winter when rains reappear. The cabin Ray and I built on Nancy's gold mine claim on Whiskey Slide Road is torched, so there is no shelter there. The small '50s trailer I move into is charming, paneled in wood, remote, and accessible in trade for watching the property. I set up housekeeping and enclose the space under the deck for chickens. When I first return from working the Northern Faire in Blackpoint, a predator kills every one. The bright side is that the raucous rooster chorus doesn't wake me at first light anymore.

Ronn refurbishes furniture in a white barn on the outskirts of San Andreas, and upholsters a wooden barber-chair in hot red velvet that came out of a gold-mining era Calaveras whorehouse. We get together and share what drugs are available. Charlie is a serious gardener, often gardens in the nude. It's hot in Mountain Ranch in July and August. She also cooks, bakes, puts up delicious preserves, marmalades and jams, runs an orderly house and keeps a well-stocked freezer. We play cards, drink coffee and talk about whatever is worth discussing. Seth, their son, is born in Mountain Ranch.

John Aadland and Larry Allen reclaim control of Sun Mountain when the barefoot longhairs refuse to contribute by making soapstone pipes, sales of which make monthly payments on the property. Lawrence and his band move to the Rainbow Ranch, where the owners have more money than sense and can afford social experiments promising free lunches in the wonderfulness of it all.

John and Larry finish the shop, build homes and move their families onto the property. They're can-do guys, mechanical magicians, scammers extraordinaire, with an ever-present vial of crank or drink of whiskey. John is from a Greek-Norwegian family in Oakland, a graduate of California College of Arts and Crafts. Larry is from Michigan, came to Calaveras for "the warmest breeze and the tallest trees." He is also a Hell's Angel. "Hell hath no fury like the Hell's Angels in the fast lane" is painted prominently on the kitchen wall in his home.

Larry and John are both good guys, but you have to be careful with Larry because he'll talk you into something you have no intention of doing. He isn't evil, or malevolent or malicious. He really is a lot of fun. You just have to be careful and keep your hand on your wallet.

Back in Calaveras I'm with friends, a place to live, a job and Susie —a hot brunette looker with spectacular gravity-defying breasts. My enduring vision of Susie is camping at night by a glacial tarn above Ebbetts Pass, warmed by a campfire beneath a brilliant crystal star-speckled sky. Susie straddles me, rocking sweetly, head thrown back. The fire reflects off her nakedness in orange and pale yellow licks.

Susie takes me home to Palo Alto to meet her folks, lovely suburbanites with apparently no objections to our coupling. Her father is a graduate of Virginia Military Institute, where he wore a navy blue full-length wool cape with red lining. He gives that cape to me, just the thing for Sierras winters. I cherish and wear it when I visit my parents the following spring.

The cape makes my father uneasy. On the bus from the terminal to the parking lot he demands I not wear the cape in his neighborhood for fear the neighbors, who he holds in complete and utter disregard, might have reason to call me Batman. He's still worried about his public image.

Art, Crime & Lithium

At home he announces I should come upstairs to his office for a talk. I climb the stairs. My father insists only he will speak. I'm to say nothing. I turn around and walk down the stairs to check on my mother—who had eaten hashish-laced brownies I brought, giggling while knitting with her favorite soap opera on.

In his best command voice my father summons my mother to come upstairs. She giggles and tells him, in Ukrainian, to go get stuffed.

Meanwhile, back in Mountain Ranch, Ronn and I organize the Howdy Boogie: a dinner, dance and get together at the Mountain Ranch Community Hall, on December 20, 1973.

Hand drawn, machine-copied invitations read: "Howdy. You're invited to show up at the town hall in Mountain Ranch, California, where we're getting together to BOOGIE! Come as your best fancy. Bring folks you want to boogie with. Bring your highest boogie juice & a lotta friendly & your appetite because there's an Italian spaghetti dinner happening at 7 p.m. Be on time. Bring your friends. SUTRO SYMPATHY ORCHESTRA will play after dinner. Have your dancing shoes on! Proceeds go to Mountain Ranch Scholarship Fund. That's it."

We send extra invitations out to everyone we know, and have them send invitations out to everyone they know. The reason we can pull this boogie off is that Ronn and Charlie enjoy a great reputation in the county. When the sheriff and county cops show up to investigate the gathering of longhaired subversives, Ronn calms them down.

The hall is packed. The SUTRO SYMPATHY ORECHESTRA, from Silver City Nevada, kicks ass and we dance the night away. I wear a set of tails that Ray bought in a secondhand shop in Montana and dry-cleaned to rid it of crabs. I slip a few hits of acid into a jug of generic California red we all share. Flying in tails, I catch Ronn's eye.

"You son of a bitch," he says eyes pinwheeling.

The Howdy Boogie draws pirates, scammers and alternative-lifestyle practitioners out of Northern California's hills, valleys, flatlands, nooks, crevices and crannies. "Doctor Bob" Jacobs arrives with a hot LA redhead on his arm. He leaves with Susie Creamcheese. I leave with the hot redhead. She leaves in the morning with a mobile: smoky quartz suspended beneath a compass, with a faceted crystal sphere a millimeter above the face of the luminous dial. Gilah is an art teacher at Cal State Mission Hills, married, living in LA until her husband picks Bob Jacobs up hitchhiking. She's an artist, teacher, painter, philosopher, communicator, public speaker, adventurer and world traveler. And we're still friends decades later.

While other faire crews work with generators and power tools, Monday through Friday with two day weekends off, Woodjack's crew works without power, four tens with three days off. John works barefoot, insists on precision, teaches me to work with hand tools, explains modular building: the importance of gussets, organization, planning, avoiding injury, paying strict attention, giving everything to what you're doing. We're the number one crew at the faires. I'm privileged to be part of it.

We work the southern faire in Agoura outside LA in the spring, the northern faire in Black Point across the bay from San Francisco in the fall, and the Dickens Faire in South San Francisco from Thanksgiving through Christmas. I work security, garbage, parking, and manage ale stands - whatever needs doing. Each faire lasts six weekends with approximately 25,000 people attending daily.

Fresh juicy young girls, looking for work and a hot beef injection from a true-to-life gypsy road king, appear every faire. Between faires we live on the road or in the forests of the southwest, and do what we damn-well please.

Art, Crime & Lithium

Jay Libby invites me to step out into his '53 Chevy hardtop to smoke Nepalese hash, the night Betty Boobs hangs her pantyhose in one of the upstairs dining rooms at Juanita's roadhouse in Geyserville, California, at a crew party celebrating another successful Renaissance Faire.

Juanita weighs over 350 pounds and takes shit from nobody, with a reputation as a fun-loving woman who might deck you if she thinks you're out of line, obnoxious or otherwise displease her peculiar sense of propriety. Pretty much anything goes at Juanita's, as long as you don't piss her off.

Jay and I meet during my first faire, and both work the setup crew with Woodjack. During the faire I work the parking lot, a dusty field spiked with goats-heads, nasty California vegetation capable of penetrating tires and shoe soles. I wear Galibier climbing boots with steel shanks in the soles to protect myself, not only against goats-heads but hard headed drivers who fail to pay attention to directions and either attempt to brush me aside, run me over or park somewhere other than where I direct. A well-placed kick in their door usually gets attention and compliance.

In a couple weeks I'm promoted to working security, pleased to be out of the dust and mayhem of the parking lot. We work in teams, with a radio, on a 24-hour basis with the California Highway Patrol on the faire outskirts, who let us deal with our own problems our own way.

The only time I recall needing the CHP's help is when a fairgoer freaks out on acid, threatening to bite whoever approaches him. I walk up to him, tell him he is my brother, give him a big hug, lock on and carry him to the ambulance, which my partner requests.

We have a garbage detail that continually patrols the faire and keeps it, if not spotless, then clean enough for 25,000 participants to interact in a natural, pleasant theatrical setting with jugglers, jousters, jesters, musicians, craftsmen, belly dancers, flamenco dancers, actors, artists, stages, maids, matrons, plays, games and multifarious food booths to please any palate. We provide the stage, situation and parameters. The people are the show.

Cocaine is our drug of choice, keeps us going without getting too far out of hand. We're responsible for keeping some semblance of order inside the faire grounds, the authorities parked just outside and happy to let us deal with it. Faire brethren who dispense drugs of choice are well known. Paydays, they stand outside the payroll office and collect, business as usual, no chance of getting busted since it is all in the family. The cops are on the other side of an invisible, but effective, agreed-upon line.

The crew camps in the woods at the back of the lot: tents, trucks or station wagons. We have showers and porta-potties. You cook your own grub or work out a deal with food-booth operators. Nobody goes hungry, a latter-day Great American Highway alternative gypsy family.

Hungarian-Sicilian from Brooklyn, muscular with a long brunette braid, a pillar of the garbage crew, John Katroczo sports a pork-pie hat backwards, and falls in love with a fresh-hire teenage twinkie. He offers her a sandwich as a token of his affection. When she opens the wrapper she discovers a dead bird sandwiched between two slices of bun.

Beautiful blond Wendy, faire regular and Jay Libby's girlfriend, expresses concern nobody tried to rape her recently.

Lisa Hagberg is a 17-year-old Lafayette, California, girl working the smoked turkey-leg booth at the Northern Faire in Black Point. Lithe, fresh, young, with a smile to die for: I notice her every time I go by the booth. We connect at the Dickens Faire in South San Francisco later that fall, and spend three years together. She speaks French, plays piano, an enthusiastic lover easily aroused.

Art, Crime & Lithium

After that Dickens Faire Lisa, Jay Libby, John Katroczo and I score a late-model Volvo drive-away sedan and make the cross-country ride from San Francisco to the East Coast on the now established "Mom Tour." We drop Kotroczo off at the 30th Street Station in Philadelphia, where he gets the train for Brooklyn and his mother's house. Jay gets the next train for Rockville, Maryland. Lisa and I pick him up in Rockville in a fresh drive-away for the cross-country cruise back to San Francisco.

Phil Hall scores a big planting contract, at Jacobs Lake on the north rim of the Grand Canyon. Larry Allen, John Aadland and the Sun Mountain crew help us organize, and set our vehicular and mechanical priorities in order. Veteran planters, wannabe's, spouses, kids and dogs arrive to build the West Coast contingent. The contract calls for planting a half million trees in three weeks, because moisture in the ground in the Arizona spring doesn't last long, and the trees need all the help they can get to survive. We need strong bodies with attitude, planters who can deal with living in the wild without whining.

I enlist co-workers from the faires: Lisa Hagberg, Jay Libby, John Katroczo. Ronn and Charlie Alexander from Mountain Ranch join the crew. Ronn drives Shaw, his schoolbus filled with planters, to the Grand Canyon.

Andre Potochnik arrives from Bear Valley, CA, Bob Leeper from Santa Cruz, CA, Tom White from Oakland, CA, John Greefkens from Twain Harte, CA, Soupy Campbell and Bruce Blackwell from Mississippi, Ray L'Hommedieu and JP his poodle from Stockton by way of Rochester, NY. Ray brings a trumpet.

Greefkens drives Babe the Blue OX, his '52 Chevy flatbed loaded with 55- gallon drums of fuel, Leeper his co-pilot.

Our caravan leaves Sheep Ranch, CA, crosses the Sierras north of Yosemite and drives south down the eastern foothills on California Highway 395 to Olancha, where we turn east on 190 for Stovepipe Wells at the base of Death Valley.

The incline to Death Valley is severe and lengthy, requiring driving skill, steady nerves, a solid gearbox and good brakes. I drive Evro the Chevrolet with Lisa Hagberg and Ray L'Hommedieu in the cab, PJ Ray's dog in the bed on top of a tarp, and a trailer with gear pushing us. I gear down at the top of the incline, and we arrive at the Stovepipe Wells gas station none the worse for wear.

Greefkens and Leeper follow us in Babe the Blue Ox. They roll to a stop, not stirring for several minutes. Then the driver's door bursts open, followed by a flood of beer cans. When Leeper's door opens the same thing happens. It might have been embarrassing if it weren't so funny, pilot and co-pilot seriously lubricated.

Shaw the bus appears up the incline in the distance going dangerously fast, brakes smoking. Shaw blows by the gas station with no indication of stopping, Ronn deadly serious at the wheel and Andre beside him looking, for all intents, like the ultimate white boy drained of any hint of color, the rest of the passengers wide-eyed and scared shitless.

We congratulate Ronn on holding it together. Once Shaw's gearbox slips there's no turning back, no saying oops I'm sorry. All Ronn can do is hang on and bring it in whole. He manages.

We drive up and over the lip of Death Valley, through Pahrump, and make camp north of Las Vegas at Mount Charleston Wilderness Area, where we watch the Thunderbirds—the Air Force flying team—practice out of Indian Springs Air Force Auxiliary Field.

Runners are sent to town for automotive parts and groceries. They return with automotive parts, bottles of Henry McKenna Kentucky table whiskey, and cases of Snickers. We're going to be well lubricated and sugared in any case.

Art, Crime & Lithium

The North Rim of the Grand Canyon in Arizona is a short distance from Las Vegas via Kaibab, Fredonia and Jacob Lake. Base camp is set up when we arrive. We unload.

Ray L'Hommedieu plays reveille in camp. Every morning Ray hits precisely the same sour note playing *Cherry Pink and Apple Blossom White* to roust us. Ray plays tuba in his high school band. During one noteworthy public performance Ray plays an unscheduled and unrehearsed tuba solo, causing the band's musical director to request Ray never play with the band again. We look forward to Ray's daily rendition of *Cherry Pink and Apple Blossom White*.

Peanut butter and jelly sandwiches keep us going at lunch. We're happy to have them. Dinner usually is some mix of rice, beans or potatoes with poached venison, which we politely invite to dinner with a crisp, small caliber retort. Phil Sasso, a former member of the Air Force pistol team, is our primary venison provider. On the way home from the day's planting, we keep an eye out for venison. Once it's spotted, Sasso slips off the truck, low-crawls until he has a shot, and pop, meat for dinner.

The sauna committee comes up with a plan to cut down several limber aspens, stake them in a circle, arc and tie them together, then lash smaller diameter limbs in a large wickiup, to be covered with tarps begged, stolen and borrowed. Rocks are collected and a guy in charge of the fire is appointed. He stokes the fire so the sauna rocks are hot enough for steam once water is poured on them. The sauna holds upwards of 20 naked bodies. Often sauna participants provide pennyroyal, marijuana or hashish, giving an altogether different spirituality to the sweat-bath.

The work is hard, intense, and over in a few weeks. We get paid and scatter. Lisa, Ray, JP and I drive west for San Francisco. I remember JP taking a huge shit squatting on the tarp in Evro's bed as we cross the Golden Gate

Bridge. We spent the night at a friend's apartment in the city, and nobody had bothered to take JP out to do his business.

    I pull over, brush the deposit off and tell JP he's a good dog, which he is. Lisa gets off at her folk's house in Lafayette to have wisdom teeth pulled. Ray gets off in Stockton.

    The following winter, Jay is killed in a car crash visiting his family in Silver Springs, Maryland. On the way home from a New Year's party, the Volvo Jay is driving slides and slams into a telephone pole. Jay's brother and other occupants walk away. Jay is DOA. I'm guilty about not having gone with him. We drove cross-country over several winters to visit family on the East Coast, on the "mom tour." That winter I decide to stay in LA, camped out in a school bus parked at Gilah's house in Venice. When Jay's girlfriend Wendy calls to let me know Jay is dead, I buy a bottle of Jack Daniels, drain it on Venice Beach, howl all night and leave, intending to never return to LA again.

Last Plant

Nancy lives at Useless Bay on Whidbey Island. Free to enjoy our relationship as friends without the stress of sex or expectation, we let well enough alone and treat each other with respect, generosity and affection.

A working-class type I meet at a bar in Seattle has an industrial truck with a boom, winch and toolboxes full, interested in art. We talk about mobiles and make a date to meet on Useless Bay by Nancy's house to build one. I buy a 12 pack and a bottle of Jack Daniels. He shows up. We go to work.

A 12-inch piling left over from some long ago construction in Useless Bay is the base. A 30-foot-long telephone pole is dragged to the piling with the aid of the truck, A-frame and winch, hoisted onto to piling at approximately a 30 degree angle and pinned to the piling, after making a notch as a cradle, and spiked with a single jack hammer. Next we roll a 5-foot diameter round onto the base of the telephone pole to counterbalance whatever might hang off the end of the pole, which extends 10 feet over the low tide extreme of Useless Bay.

Basic structure complete, we scour the beach and come up with a natural edged piece of incense cedar 14 feet long. It takes both of us to budge it. The balance point of the cedar piece is determined by lifting it and shifting it back and forth until an approximately close enough point is determined. A steel plate with a welded loop is bolted as close to the balance-point of the cedar piece as we can get it. I shinny to the end of the pole with a spike and hammer. Keep in mind we'd been drinking beer and Jack Daniels since daybreak.

The spike is fashioned into a loop thanks to the incredible array of tools and the ability of my artsy, gutsy, industrial new pal. Once the spike-with-loop is in place, a cable with a universal joint is attached to the plate on the cedar piece. I measure the distance between the end of the pole and the water. A universal joint is attached to the other end of the cable. My pal hoists the cedar piece, with the aid of the winch and A-frame, with a second cable. I bolt the upper universal joint to the end of the pole, and shinny down. The cedar piece revolves dead level but clips the piling a couple inches. I make a notch in the piling with a hatchet. Now the cedar swings free, unencumbered. We're done, drunk, laughing. It is the biggest mobile I made. Nancy later tells me a hellacious winter storm washes it away. I don't build the mobile as a monument, but as something to do with a guy I met in a bar who is possibly as crazy as I am.

Nancy and I walk the beach, hunt geoducks on low tides, cook good stuff to eat and generally have a fine time. Stanley Richardson calls, wants me to meet him in Portland, then drive to Colorado in a Rambler that Stanley claims is ready to go to one last tree planting.

I catch the train for Portland in Seattle. Stanley meets me at the station in a borrowed car. Stanley's '60s Rambler station wagon is anything but ready; it needs brakes, lights, an exhaust. It starts and runs. A couple days work and we have critical parts together. The exhaust is wired with coat-hanger.

Stanley drives to Pendelton. We stop for dinner at a steakhouse with screaming red walls. After dinner Stanley admonishes me to drive the Rambler no faster than 50 mph on pain of death, and crawls in the back seat to sleep.

I have the Rambler up to 80 mph in no time. If it weren't for the road construction I hit south of Salt Lake City about daybreak, that undoes the coat-hanger fixit on the exhaust pipe, Stanley would be none the wiser. I limp the Rambler into the next truck stop off the interstate to Stanley's curses from the back seat.

"Shut the fuck up; I'll fix it. You want some coffee?" I ask.

Stanley knows I'll have the Rambler going fast as it will go and still hold together. He puts an arm over his eyes and groans.

I crawl under the Rambler, manipulate the exhaust pipe back into shape and tighten the wire, fill the gas tank and get us each a large black coffee. Stanley has his surf guitar out, strumming the opening chords to *Yes, Yes, Yes*. The light intensifies to the east over the Spanish Fork turnoff. Stanley strums and sings, "Momma had a chicken, thought it was a duck, put it on the table with its legs stickin' up. Along come sis with a spoon and a glass, and started shovin' stuffin's up its yes, yes, yes." I break out my A-flat harmonica, play and sing along, through the Wasatch, past the Henrys, toward the Uncompaghres—home on the road, easy come, easy go, shrink or grow. The Rambler purrs to Colorado.

Our road rap consists of how we're going to approach this last planting job, what to do about Phil Hall's bullshit, how the money never works out with him and why. The easy come, easy go, shrink or grow theme develops a life of its own in our meanderings.

We make up a new song to be sung in the pay line to Caribbean rhythms: "I come to collect, I come to collect, I come to collect, collect what you owe me." The refrain goes: "Pay me-O, pay me what you owe me; pay me-O, pay me what you owe me."

I'm here to finish it, bury it, the last one and gone, done with planting and the Renaissance Faires since Jay Libby's death. Change beckons.

O.Z. Lysiak

We make the turn to Hwy. 550 south at Grand Junction, another south again at Ridgway for Dallas Divide, privy to some of the most spectacular mountain scenery anywhere on the planet. Once past Telluride over Lizard Head Pass, the Rambler eases down Hwy 145 to the turnoff for the Priest Gulch campground, destination considerably farther up dirt logging roads.

Old home week greets us with familiar tents, rigs and faces. Dunton Hot Springs is the other side of the ridge. We take advantage of the hot springs inside the aged wood-slat building, where the light filters in and plays in steam rising. This job involves planting in muscular slash piles, rigged by D9 Cats dragging a chain between them. Snowbanks stretch out in shady areas. Conditions are good. This isn't the toughest planting or the easiest. It's okay.

On days we're snowed out, planters with 4x4 trucks willing to brave the extreme mountain dirt road head to Dolores, the closest town with a gas station, market and bar.

Playing pool in the Hollywood Bar one off–day, our mostly longhaired planters encounter loggers who suggest they might cut pansy faggot hair.

Several of our guys are combat veterans, who aren't about to take shit from local yokel loggers, and invite them to try. The loggers get a grip and politely decline.

Heavy spring snow comes down with enough force to fold my JanSport dome tent on top of me, and fills my boots outside the inner tent with snow and ice. I brush off the snow and barefoot it to Willie Workman's tipi. Willie has a nice fire going. Willie is from Kansas, a Navy vet whose succinct philosophy is "It ain't the size of your pecker counts; it's your pile-driving ass."

We finish the job and sing *I Come To Collect* for Phil Hall. With no wiggle room, Phil pays up. We're wise to all his tricks. Money in our pockets, we make for the Senate restaurant for dinner and the Roma bar for fun in Telluride.

Art, Crime & Lithium

The Roma is jumping. Fat Franny asks me dance, takes me home to Sawpit and screams, "Fuck me, fuck me, fuck me!" all night long, a soft answer to a horny tree-planter's prayers.

It's spring 1975, and I'm in Telluride, Colorado, in a spectacular box canyon in the heart of the Uncompaghres, sacred to the Utes. The Uncompaghres remind me of the Alps I grew up in. I feel familiarity and kinship with these mountains.

We round up most of the same players for a thinning contract in late fall, at Jacob's Lake where we did the big planting job. Camping in tents isn't practical in severe weather. We share a dormitory with cooking and toilet facilities—another Phil Hall job, but we need the money.

Thinning means working with a Jonsereds 99 chainsaw equipped with a bow-bar and stinger. A worker is assigned a section of forest to thin trees with the smallest diameter, allowing larger trees to grow faster with less competition. A chipper crew chips felled trees over the forest floor. It is dangerous, nasty work in lousy weather. We wear chaps to protect us from 10,000-RPM chains in unsure situations. This is absolutely my last Phil Hall job. I ride back to California with Ronn Alexander.

Done with planting and thinning trees and with the Renaissance Faires, I sell my 1936 Chevrolet Master Deluxe I bought in Stockton to Willy Brown of the Raiders, at his liquor store in east Oakland, and fly to Philadelphia with a wild idea about doing something with my life by applying to the Philadelphia College of Art to study industrial design. I'm accepted after sending an application and portfolio. Tuition is steep, so I apply for a scholarship. They turn me down for the scholarship since I already have a degree.

A friend of my father's with industrial connections gets me a job in Baton Rouge, Louisiana, as a grunt in a bridge-building parts yard on the west bank of the

Mississippi, home to lots of snakes, many poisonous. I last a couple months without getting bit, wondering what the fuck I'm doing here.

Mike Boren's brother John gets my phone number through the grapevine and calls on his way to Key West in a Cadillac. He's captain of the *Capricorno*, a 40-foot sailboat used to run hashish from North Africa to St. Simons Island, Georgia. John offers me the first mate's job. I pick up my last check and go. We stop for the night in a motel outside Mobile, Alabama, in sight of the famous battleship.

In the course of the night I have an uncomfortable, wet, hairy feeling in my left ear. On waking, I find John perched over me with his tongue in my ear, whispering he loves me. I push him off and explain in no uncertain terms that there will be no homosexual hokey pokey. He should cut this shit out and not even think about it if he wants to get to Key West in one piece. We drive straight through. When we get to Stock Island, where the *Capricorno* is berthed, there's a hurricane warning imminent. John wants to take the boat out and face the hurricane on the ocean. I take the Cadillac, find Mike his brother and Mike's girlfriend Terri. We drive to Orlando and go to Disneyland. Mike drops me off at the Orlando airport and takes the Caddy back to Stock Island. I sit in the airport for a couple days and nights wondering where to go. California, here I come.

Pumpkin Festival

I hear through the festival grapevine that Jack Farley, owner of the Pumpkin Festival in Calabasas, California, is looking for a troubleshooter. I interview, get the job and buy a ticket for Telluride—where I arrive with head shaved, a gold earring, and ivory bracelets. I'm wearing flip flops, navy blue shorts, and a purple satin cowboy shirt with white piping I bought at a second hand clothing shop in Venice, styling up.

Roommates, one blonde the other brunette, both lookers, catch my eye in Telluride. Neither will go out with me. Not one to mope, I book a ticket for Rochester, NY. Ray is getting married and I'm his best man.

Ray has a job, is in love, scheduled to marry Donna, a local molly. He is a member of a bowling league and alderman of his district, doing all the stuff that will make his mom and dad proud in the callused-hands tradition of his family.

Nancy flies in. The morning of the wedding, Nancy and I suggest all three of us get out of there to save Ray a world of hurt. Ray won't, convinced he's doing the right thing. He can't see it, but we can. We were road amigos over lively years, through several pharmacological strains of illicit drugs and thousands of kick-ass miles.

I drop Nancy off at the airport. Ray and I go car shopping, adept at finding good inexpensive rolling stock, and this time is no exception. Ray comes up with a green SAAB 99 station, with good tires, for $200. I give him a hug, kiss his momma and shake his father's hand goodbye, stop in to see my folks but don't stay long, with a job troubleshooting the Pumpkin Festival at the end of Topanga Canyon Boulevard in Chatsworth in a few weeks.

My mother packs a usual two-week lunch. I kiss her goodbye and drive west again.

Eve, my libidinous mountain momma, meets me at the Frisco, Colorado, Holiday Inn. This time she leaves her daughter at home with a sitter. We work each other raw again. Come morning I'm on my way to Aspen, where Art has a job managing Frying Pan Anglers for Roy Palm, an Army buddy of Art's with a reputation as a world-class fisherman. Art is married to Carla, an Italian girl from New York who devotes her life to taking care of Art. Carla is a smart woman and a fabulous cook. She is suspicious of me, doesn't like me, and I can't blame her. When I show up, I get Artie loaded and we take off for days. Eventually Carla and I make peace—or rather, Carla decides I'm okay and no threat to her or Art.

On the backside of McClure Pass lies Somerset, a tiny coal-mining town. The road through town is winding, tight and slow, with miners homes crowding the asphalt. Two young women stand hitch-hiking on a gravel lot in the middle of town, one blonde, the other the brunette from Telluride. I pull over. Suddenly we're hugging and laughing. They're on their way to California.

A glance in the rearview mirror reveals wordless surprise and an invitation. The blonde eases her skirt up around her thighs, *sans* panties in the summer heat, and opens her legs. The road through Colorado to Utah passes by in a blur, my attention riveted to the rearview with occasional glances at the road ahead.

The brunette is next to me oblivious, until the SAAB sputters. I stop and open the hood looking for problem. Sandy, the brunette, spots the leak in the fuel line. I do a "Bolivian fix", where I repair what I can the best I can because it's past midnight, I'm on the run and the Bolivian policia are on their way, and I've got just a few minutes' head start. Of course none of these things are true at the moment. I clean and wrap the fuel line with electrical tape, and tighten a hose-clamp as tight as I can get it. We make it to the next town, where I find the correct fuel line. Sandy's ability to deal with on-the-road problems doesn't escape me. Connie, the blonde, gets in the back seat, eases her skirt up and opens her legs. We camp by a river that night. Connie fulfills the blonde promise she made from the back seat while Sandy sleeps.

Sandy is impervious, uninterested, or keeps her mouth shut, while Connie and I carry on at every hopefully discreet opportunity from Utah through Nevada, into the Sierra Nevada to Ronn and Charlie's place outside Mountain Ranch.

The three of us share a bed in Shaw the bus, parked in an ex-chicken coop. Sandy finally gets naked with Connie and me. Done with erogenous lubricious warm-ups on both women I ease into Connie, roll over and ease into Sandy. We ease into and out of each other until daylight. This is a dream: two willing beautiful women in one bed, giving, not jealous.

In the morning Connie says she feels left out while I do Sandy: trouble brewing, possessiveness, jealousy, not quite the dream I envision.

At the laundromat in Stockton, Sandy corners me and declares I have to make a choice. I choose her, rationalizing she can figure out mechanical problems and makes her declaration. Connie's disappointment makes for a grim ride to San Francisco. She sits in the back seat conjuring a black cloud, skirt no longer lifted, legs no longer spread.

Connie is a vastly superior fuck. Sandy protects herself with weapons at her disposal. I get caught in a female trap, pleased as punch fucking two good-looking babes in what I thought was a dream involving friends sharing bodily fluids. I was involved in a Renaissance Faire threesome with Cindy Bush and the Polish Princess, both artistic lookers with a sense of humor and a healthy appetite for sex. We shared ourselves, and went about our business the way friends do when it was over. My fondest memory of Cindy Bush is daybreak; we finish making love in the back of my Mercury station wagon. I'm on my way to work, and look back to see Cindy's legs open in the morning fog, and dew with a faint dribble working its way down her crevice, and she smiling, indicating with a finger that she wants me to come back. Had I known then what I know now, it would have gone differently. My father said sooner or later you pay for everything.

I leave the girls in San Francisco to do what they had set out to do over a thousand miles ago, and tell Sandy I'll meet her in Telluride once my job at the Pumpkin Festival is done. I drive south, relieved to be alone and away from complicated situations brought on by my own stupidity, greed, and lack of understanding of the female political animal.

I check in with Jack Farley at his office in Calabasas. At a Mexican café next door to Farley's office I get picked up, dick in charge of my brain, and set aside the lesson I recently endured to go with this LA babe with good tits and inverted nipples, her clitoris apparently in charge of her brain. We last a week and part friends.

The second level of my hootch, in the eucalyptus by the train tracks, is a garage door balanced on and fastened to a couple of major branches. The lower level is also a garage door, firm on the ground with tent erected on it. A ladder leans against the heftier of the two branches to allow access to the upper level. Trains into LA shake and shiver the eucalyptus on schedule.

The elephant trainer has three pachyderms, in descending sizes, chained to stakes across the road from the eucalyptus. Dumbo, an African elephant, is biggest; Jumba is an Indian elephant and the middle one, and the smallest is named Bomba. I help feed and care for the elephants. Every morning the trainer unchains the elephants, and commands Dumbo to kneel. I climb up onto her neck behind her ears. She heaves up and lumbers off for watering, toilet and training at a circular training ring, with elephant-size stools enclosed by snow fencing. My perspective of the festival grounds changes immediately from twelve feet up, moving along to pachyderm rhythm, Jumba and Bomba the baby behind, trunk to tail.

At the ring, the one-eyed trainer with an atrophied left arm—suffered when a bull elephant shoved him through a wall—commands Dumbo to let me off, then orders all three elephants to rise and shit.

"Shit for me, shit for me, shit for me," he cajoles. Done with morning toilet, the elephants are watered and put through training. This routine goes smoothly until the trainer zaps Bomba with a cattle prod. She isn't having any of this, breaks through the snow-fencing and bolts into suburban Chatsworth. She makes it to Topanga Canyon Boulevard and a shopping center parking lot where we overtake her, calm her down and walk her back to the festival grounds. In the light of morning the hairs on Bomba's back glow purple. Elephant's eyes are extraordinary, large, deep, in multiple colors.

I make arrangements with the fruit smoothie-booth owner to collect his peelings and leftovers a couple times a day, and feed the fruit skins to the elephants. They love their treats, but I have to watch Jamba closely and feed her from a distance. She has a disconcerting habit of shooting her trunk out, snapping it around an unsuspecting watcher's ankles and pulling their legs out from under them, leaving the victim open to her whims. If she has a mind to, she can roll you around or inflict whatever damage she pleases. The clue comes when she peels her eye back and looks at you with a malevolent stare.

Dumbo shoots her trunk out to probe my face, shoulders, arms and hands when she knows I have treats. Bomba often spreads her African ears and trumpets when I approach with fruit yummies.

Another trainer has a more substantial ring set up across the road from the eucalyptus multi-level. He has a bear that rides a bicycle. The bicycle has no seat, so the bear bellows bloody murder when he rides. Included in the act are a German Shepherd and black panther. I stay away from this act because I feel sorry for the bear having to ride a bike with a pipe up his ass.

We build the main stage in the best John Woodjack tradition, booths same genre, bring in straw bales for seating. I set up the drink stands so as little as possible will go wrong. Finally, we're ready and open.

My festival outfit consists of a felt gray top hat, with a gold earring in my left ear, arranged with dexterity by a flame-antiseptic needle from the Polish Princess. She wants to do my ear because it is the absolutely last virgin part of my body after she and Cindy Bush ravage me in Seal Beach. I wear a hand-carved whale on a gold chain, shirtless. The whale is carved by Mel Johnson from Point Arena, California. He annually wins the prize for the best artwork at the Renaissance Faire. The Polish Princess is Mel's wife. We're friends. Red, white and blue sunglasses, to hide stoned eyes, complete my ensemble.

Sally Swan, a Los Angeles streetwise 18-year-old, takes up temporary residence in my eucalyptus home. Into opium, she shows me basics and intricacies, lighting opium balls on a piece of tinfoil covered by a drinking glass, and breathing it in once the opium is smoke filling the glass, suggests we roll opium balls and ease them in each other's assholes for more positive longer lasting results. Sally knows her opium. Unfortunately she fades back into the LA street-scene after a short stay at the festival. I'm sorry to see her go. I like Sally better than opium, never having had been a downer aficionado.

Once the festival is built and in operating condition, my job is to make sure everything, especially the drinks booths, remains operational. The main stage is up, straw bales arranged in a semicircular theatrical arrangement. I look forward every weekend to the bellydancing troupe with the sword dancer, who balances a scimitar on her head while engaged in sinuous gyrations. My favorite is the snake dancer who, accompanied by a hefty python, moves around the stage in unison with the serpent—which invariably slides its tail up the crack between the dancer's butt-cheeks.

Strange, depressive episodes begin, where I can hardly deal with people or problems at the festival, and spend as much time away from everything and everybody as I can. I know something is wrong but don't know what to do about it, so I fake it best I can. Sally seeks me out, since she knows my favorite hiding places. And she knows something isn't right, but I have no way of explaining what is going on since I don't know myself. She eventually leaves me alone to deal with it. I find solace in the friendship I developed with the elephants, kindred spirits.

Eventually the weirdness fades. I complete my troubleshooting agreement with Jack Farley. He asks if I'll return. I'm non-committal since I can't say for certain.

Gilah lets me stay in the bus parked alongside her studio in Venice during the week, in her cooking glory then—French onion soup, ratatouille. She paints large canvases of tomatoes, ice cream sundaes. I wish her well and say goodbye.

O.Z. Lysiak

Telluride

An oil change and a tune-up for my bulletproof green SAAB, and I'm off for Telluride with a stop in Las Vegas for fuel and cheap casino-buffet food. At Grand Junction I turn south on Hwy 50, through Montrose to Ridgway, below the peaks and ridges of the Uncompaghres. Over Dallas Divide downhill to Placerville, a left over Leopard Creek, past Sawpit up Keystone, and a most spectacular valley unfolds with Bear Creek to the right, Bridal Veil Falls cascading in a fine thread of snowmelt below the massive shoulders of Ajax. Fall 1977, shimmering aspen leaves turn yellow and gold, spotting the sacred valley of the Utes with bursts of seasonal color.

In the midst of all this, a small mountain mining town in Victorian dress trails the reputation of a whore with the heart of a banker and the soul of a scammer: Telluride, an extreme place for extreme personalities. I have a good feeling about Telluride as I pull up to the house, next to St. Patrick's Catholic church, where Sandy, Connie and Steve Steed are roomies.

Sandy is glad to see me. I'm glad to see her. Connie makes no appearance. Steve Steed comes out to greet me. Sandy suggests I take my pack upstairs to her room.

Days after I arrive, Sandy asks why I pack my bag every morning and load it in the SAAB. Once I give in to the idea there is nowhere else to go, I leave my pack in Sandy's room until it is time for us to leave together.

Steve was stationed in Europe, a medic. We talk fishing, hunting, skiing and women. He is from eastern Colorado, Lamar, where he was quarterback of the

Art, Crime & Lithium

football team. Steve makes his living as a builder, carpenter, Yoda of all trades. Best of all he's a really good, nice, polite guy. We get along, and spend many a pleasant afternoon around the kitchen table talking about any and everything.

Connie is pleasant enough, but avoids me if at all possible. Apparently Connie and Sandy work it out. I settle in with Sandy, Steve and Connie in John Fahnestock's house, and set out to learn about the town.

Telluride is a small mountain mining town, a leftover from an era when mostly-European immigrants staked their futures in America on hard work in the 350 miles of tunnels they left in the mountains. They also leave behind a huge tailings pond above the town, leaching poisonous heavy metals into the San Miguel River.

The town is infamous for hustlers, hookers, and Bible pounders. Telluride in the '70s isn't changed much. Hustlers sell real estate, and coke whores work The Roma Bar, The Last Dollar Saloon, and the Sheridan Bar. Semi-pro local sluts engage in contests to see who can fuck the most famous musicians at the Telluride summer festivals. Brother Al is on KOTO community radio, preaching the good word on his Sunday morning show.

Alcohol, cocaine and marijuana are drugs of choice. I hear of heroin addicts in town, but don't encounter them. The first ski-lifts are in place, and the future of the town is changing from the grim reality of toxic mining-tailings to a fresh start with skiing in winter, festivals in summer, and full time tourism.

Coming into town along Colorado Avenue, I see Victorian homes line both sides of the street for blocks, until the peaked red-brick San Miguel County Courthouse on the sunny side separates residential from commercial. On either side of Colorado Avenue, homes enjoy a background of arguably the most spectacular mountain scenery in the world.

Small town job possibilities are minimal. The local weekly, *The Telluride Times*, pays $50 a week for a part-time reporter, if the job is available. The Telluride Maintenance Department advertises for an entry-level worker at $5.65 an hour, good money in 1977. Raymond Hughes, as local as a human being can be, since he is born and lives here all his life with the exception of a 2-year stint in the US Navy, interviews me. Being local is important in Telluride, where you wear your years in town like chevrons. Raymond is square-jawed, clean-shaven, wears a wide-brimmed brown Resistol, Levis and a yoked rodeo shirt: the Colorado cowboy look down pat. This is who he really is. I get the job.

Friday mornings I open hydrants on Colorado Avenue, Telluride's main street, and hose the town down. We flush the town's sewer-system a couple times a year. I drive a tanker truck to water severely angled dirt streets on the sunny side of town, learn the routine at the sewer plant outside town.

Raymond hardly ever gets his own hands dirty, and spends most of his time drinking coffee and bullshitting in his office at city hall. He has us do expensive jobs involving serious man-hours, often utilizing heavy equipment, for beer donations from local citizens who certainly could afford to get the work done on their own. Our beer refrigerator at the shop is always full.

KOTO, the local community radio station, sponsors an annual ski-swap and sale in the Quonset hut gymnasium next to the old school in town. I buy second-hand equipment. The surrounding mountains resemble the Alps I knew growing up. No lift lines on the mountain in 1977, and I'm antsy if I have to wait more than 30 seconds to get on a chairlift to the top.

The maintenance department moves a lot of snow that winter, piles it in the middle of Colorado Avenue with a front end loader or backhoe; the snow gets too tall to deal with or cross. Then we bring dump trucks, load the frozen gray mass, and dump it in a field out of town or in the river.

You can walk everywhere necessary in Telluride. The bar tour from the Sheridan to the Last Dollar to the Roma is a three-block turnaround. Each bar has its own ambiance, and caters to a specific crowd. KOTO plays whatever kind of music you're into, with no commercials or interruptions other than airing of the DJ's headspace, a small price to pay and occasionally worthwhile. The town is spectacular and charmingly lit in snow, with 14,000-foot peaks glittering at night to outrageously starlit skies: mega moxie covered in soul sauce, sprinkled with chocolate twinkling jimmies, magic.

In spring Sandy and I drive to The New Orleans Jazz Festival and Heritage Fair and her parents home in Covington, LA. We camp along the way, with a stop at Carlsbad Caverns in New Mexico, where bats leaving the caves at dusk resemble dark clouds shifting and changing against a streaking sky. A ranger in a Smokey Bear hat rousts us at daybreak. Apparently camping isn't allowed in the desert within so many miles of the caverns; some of the bats have rabies. Hot coffee waits at the National Monument entrance. We're on the stalactite/stalagmite magical mystery tour. Attempts to describe the incredible world below fall short of doing it justice. Soon we're in the SAAB winding south to Looziana and N'Awlins.

The circular oyster-shell driveway, white two-story mansion with columns and all-white furniture, throws me for a loss. Not sure if I want to sit down, I wonder what the hell Sandy got me into, but her folks are down-home Cajuns with an uppity streak. Sandy's mother puts me at ease about her furniture. Once I know her father I understand why Sandy figures I'm all right.

Big Steve wants to be a diver, joins the Navy at 15 to fight in WWII; big for his age, he gets away with it. After the war Big Steve stays on, diving. He and his buddies develop hardhat diving techniques used today. He puts in 20 years and goes to work in the oil industry around the world, quits diving and tries his hand at being a building inspector in Washington, DC. This comes to an abrupt end when, stuck in a traffic jam, Big Steve gets out of his car, walks to the car behind his, pulls out the guy who has been honking and beats the shit out of him. Steve's back to diving as soon as the DC cops let him go, a supervisor for McDemott Marine Construction when we meet. We get along fine. Sandy feels at ease with me because I'm a big guy like her daddy, and maybe as crazy. Her mother fades into the white furniture, makes outlandish-good Cajun food, and keeps Big Steve under control.

Connections made, we make for N'Awlins and the Jazz and Heritage Festiva,l held at the fairgrounds in the city, with multiple stages playing jazz, soul, R&B, blues, Zydeco, rock'n'roll, gospel. The parish prison choir sings Sunday morning on the gospel stage. The prison choir singers let loose the most incredibly heartfelt, soulful performance at the festival because it really means something to the prison singers. Southern, Cajun, Creole smells waft from food booths over the festival on invisible spiced fingers and fabrics enticing appetites.

Friends in the city put us up. The Dream Palace and Reality Patio on the edge of the French Quarter are favorite places away from the festival, with good food and music, a great place to meet people. The Café du Monde on Jackson Square, with beignets and coffee, is good for people-watching in a town full of free-thinking and free-styling individuals.

A two-storey Victorian on the sunny side in Telluride is available for fifty bucks a month, an ancient wood structure with 10-foot ceilings and no insulation. We rent it when we get back. I close off a bedroom and bathroom, install a second-hand Ashley stove, insulate the walls with scrounged carpet from the Free Box: a Telluride institution where people put usable discards.

I drive a water-truck to keep the dust down on steep dirt streets on the sunny side, until it loses traction, then slides backwards, determine a hopeful place to turn and get it under control. Colorado Avenue is the only paved street in Telluride. I hose down the main drag weekly. We help build a new water system, and clean up after the campers who use the woods around town for garbage and toilet. The town fathers are thrilled with the revenue the Bluegrass and Jazz festivals generate. The maintenance department gets to clean up leftover shit. Overtime doesn't make up for disgusting big city dickheads who shit where they sleep. Other than that, music and festivals are fine.

As I tow illegally parked festival attendee vehicles, I meet Sheriff Bill Masters. Parked smack in front of the Sheridan Hotel during a festival, a car obviously is in the wrong place, and open. I call the cops to get the okay to haul it off. Masters shows up. Everybody works festival weekends because the town is inundated, overflowing, borderline out of hand. Masters looks inside the car, sees the pot obvious behind the front seat. He can have the guy tracked down and busted. Instead he opens the bag, shakes it out in the street and gives me the OK to tow it: a reasonable cop.

Bill Masters is sheriff of San Miguel County for more than 25 years. I haven't always been on the same side of the law with Bill, but admire him and consider him a friend.

The nights are colder. Fall is here. I get a job as a ski technician at Telluride Sports. W. Lamont Woozley and his brother Tim own it when it's directly across the street from the Sheridan Bar.

I drop off the keys to the maintenance barn early one morning, tell Raymond Hughes thanks and my buddies goodbye and good luck, and walk up the alley behind Colorado Avenue to the ski shop.

Lamont sends me to all the ski, boot and binding tech courses long before first snowfall. The shop is my domain. I make a foray into the retail part of the store early in the season. A matronly woman with a Texas accent shops for a sweater. I politely ask if I can help. She has her eye on one particular item and asks the price. I check the tag and tell her. She puffs herself up, indignant, and says she can buy the same sweater in Dallas for less money. I suggest she get the fuck out of the store, go to Dallas and buy her sweater there. Following that episode I'm on strict orders to remain behind the counter in the shop, which suits me fine; obviously mine is not a retail-type personality.

The back is set up for rentals and repairs. It's still dark outside when I open up the shop and prep rentals, sizing customers, determining ability level, and getting them into comfortable equipment. My enthusiasm for skiing is boundless, and I want everyone who comes through Telluride Sports to share my zeal. Later in the morning, once the rental customers are out the door and on the lift, I pick a pair of skis from reserved sets of the finest skis available for demos. The demos are all my size. A situation where I'd let a pair of my demos out the door is highly unusual. I keep them honed, tuned, and groomed like a stable of thoroughbreds.

The job comes with a season pass. On the mountain, skiing 11 a.m. to 2 p.m., I know what happens, what conditions are, where to go, what to do and how to do it, all part of the public relations aspect of a good shop technician.

Lamont decides we should help local semi-pro ski racers with high tech tuning. We buy an I-beam milled to $10,000^{th}$ of an inch tolerance to determine how flat a ski rides. Edges are honed with stones, tips and tails dulled, depending on when a particular racer wants to initiate turns. We repair edges and bottoms, adjust boots for comfort and performance, and specialize in binding adjustment. Our Victorian rental is more difficult to live in with the temperature drop. I stand in front of the Ashley and sizzle my stomach while my ass freezes, a body-thickness away. A visqueen enclosure over the tub, and we can have a bath or shower without freezing. One night we come home from the movies to a skating rink in the kitchen. The faucet froze, burst, and pressurized water pours out onto a slab of ice. I fashion a wood plug, break the faucet off with a hammer and drive the plug home. The leak stops. We look for someplace else to live.

Old-timer and ex-miner George Cappis maintains miners' shacks out of town, past the cemetery. He lets us know when one's for rent. His wife Gay is the county clerk. The shacks are prized places to live in the valley, with heat and reasonable ceiling heights.

Sandy keeps the little two-bedroom at 90 degrees, happy to be out of the cold. I cross-country ski to and from work through the cemetery.

KOTO has a radio show opening on Saturday nights from 9 to 12. They let me have it for the next three years. My call sign is: "This is the Uncle O Saturday Night Dinosaur Show, spinnin' them dinosaurs out for all you dinosaurs out there. No shuck, no jive, we're stayin' alive."

The show usually starts with Juice Newton's *Fire Down Below*, or Aretha Franklin's *Respect,* or the Rolling Stones' *Sympathy For The Devil*, or Little Feat's *Dixie Chicken*. For three hours I weave rock'n'roll with jazz with blues with R&B, gospel, country, classical or whatever fits the musical mindset of the evening, in the corner room of the Miner's Union on the sunny side in the dark. Off-season there's no place to go, so occasionally nightriders, back street cruisers, or friends looking for something to do stop by, and a party develops. Whoever brings drugs shares them. I cue up the LPs and keep the flow going.

Beautiful blond Teresa, with huge hoop earrings and a rack to die for, does the chickie boohoo show before mine. Brad takes over at midnight, with a cabbala show for late night junkies.

This is my most reasonable version of Telluride, one where the town belongs to the people who work and live in it, and not to the wealthy and super-wealthy interested only in erecting monuments to money and their own inflated egos, people who fuck up wherever they come from and now are intent on influencing local politics with twisted politically-correct horseshit. Telluride is advertised as a high-dollar conscience-salve playground for people who have more money than sense.

"Private property no trespassing violators will be prosecuted" signs now dot the high mesas where we hunt grouse, venison and elk, a sure sign the choke of ownership heralds the end of an era. Our solution is road hunting, not ideal but effective.

The timing is right. I'm 34 years old, living with a good-looking brunette Cajun swamp princess, in a surface slick situation which may slip away soon. I ask Sandy if she'll marry me, not because she's the love of my life but because it's the right time. She accepts.

We borrow $2,000 at the local bank and get married at Alta Lakes above Telluride. The night before the wedding, at the Sheridan Bar, my father asks why I'm getting married. Because I've done everything else, is my reply. Then he asks why I'm marrying a foreigner, meaning a woman who isn't Ukrainian.

Steve Steed and Tom Spyke dig a pit outside the rock-and-beam building at Alta Lakes, run an oak fire to coals, and cover a spiced sheep carcass wrapped in wet burlap in the coals, which they cover with rocks the night before the ceremony.

Dr. Andy Goldman, who runs a fresh seafood business in Montrose, brings iced oysters. Champagne and beer float in the lake to cool. A huge table with sweets,

Art, Crime & Lithium

treats, sandwiches, canapés is laid out in the huge hall inside.

Ronn and Charlie Alexander and their son Seth arrive from California in a 1951 pale green Buick coupe.

Ray L'Hommedieu and his then-wife Donna arrive from Rochester, NY, in a VW.

My mother packs around an oxygen bottle in case the altitude gets to be too much.

My father complains he isn't "in his own sauce." I explain this has nothing to do with "his sauce", and put a bottle of vodka in the freezer for him.

Sandy's mother passes out Vicodan to whoever looks like they might need it. Big Steve keeps an eye on her.

Richard Unruh, local womanizer, ambulance chaser, disc jockey and sometime minister, rides up on a black mare with a silver saddle, carrying a Bible, to the meadow by the lake where we gather. He dismounts, makes the necessary invocations, and we're married September 9, 1979.

Every marriage Unruh performs goes sour, it turns out.

Early next morning I'm driving around with Ray, looking for parts for his VW so he can make it home to New York in time for work.

Lamont has financial problems at Telluride Sports. When creditors call, I tell them he's skiing in Italy. He owns four lots, with a miner's shack 20 miles down-valley in Placerville. We make a deal. A realtor pal of Lamont's arranges for paperwork-magic with the GI Bill.

Miner's Shack

I sign the papers in Montrose, October 17, 1979, the day the Pirates win World Series game 7 against the Baltimore. I drink myself into a tequila stupor celebrating home ownership, marriage, partnership and a mortgage. Sandy drives us home.

The place is a wreck in progress, a leftover miner's shack on First Street in Placerville, CO, about 20 miles down-valley from Telluride, a hundred yards from the San Miguel River, down the street from the post office and Mary's Market. The shack faces First Street, with red rock directly behind and straight up a mountain. Midwinter sun shows at 1 p.m. and sets about 2:30.

Low ceilings permeate every room of the shack, with the exception of an addition Lamont built. First order of business is to Sawzall offending trusses so I can walk through the house without hitting my forehead.

Effluent from the toilet has a disconcerting habit of coming up in the bathtub/shower combination, when the decomposing 55-gallon drum that serves as sewage collector overruns.

An Ashley stove serves for heat. An ancient Kelvinator refrigerator hums, keeping food and beer cold. We have water in the kitchen and bathroom. The kitchen stove cooks meals with propane. We have a bed and bay window in the addition.

The place is a piece of shit with backcountry charm, our home.

My venerable SAAB gasps its last, and fills a slot on the third row of Darryl Elder's Hog Farm wreck-fence

Art, Crime & Lithium

outside Norwood, Colorado. I buy a turquoise 1957 Ford F100 pickup.

Firewood to last the winter is paramount. I buy a brand-new Husqvarna chainsaw at the hardware store in Telluride, and cut ponderosa rounds weekends on Horsefly Mesa with Donny Beaumont. It takes both of us to muscle the beefy rounds into the turquoise pickup. We fell huge standing dead trees, cut rounds, roll them into the pickup bed. The radio plays a Colorado football game, with a 12-pack on the seat for nips between trees. Contrails of cross-country jets litter the blatantly cerulean sky, sawed rounds smell of high mountain incense, the nip of fall is in the air.

Rounds roll off the pickup like muscular bank deposits. The next day, and for the next few weekends, we're at it again on the mesa. Ponderosa is split and stacked once we amass sufficient wood to last the winter. We share work, loads and benefits.

Sandy and I are toasty and secure by first snow. The turquoise Ford is loaded with ponderosa rounds, packed with sand, hosed—and freezes solid. The rear wheels get studded snow tires. Getting to work in the mornings up Keystone is a dicey affair in fresh snowfall. I put the pedal to the metal around the county shop at the base of Keystone and keep it floored all the way up, sliding sideways on the last turn before the revelatory splendor of the valley. The slide at the last is chancy. I drive to town at daybreak, getting first tracks through fresh powder, and never encounter anyone coming down the hill at that time of morning.

Winter passes quickly. I get the skis out daily at Telluride Sports, do repairs and go skiing. Sandy and I play house. The house is warm.

Lamont hires Paul Calvert, "The Wizard", to help with the rentals and repairs. Paul is a guy who intrinsically understands what makes things work.

O.Z. Lysiak

All that winter Lamont swears he'll take us to the big ski trade show in Las Vegas at the end of ski season, but goes back on his word and leaves us in charge of the shop.

Soon as he's out the door, we have his two-man kayak and paddles down from the rafters—along with sleeping bags, pads, all the camping gear we might need for a run down the San Juan River. We lock the door, rig the double kayak on top of my Ford, throw the equipment in back and leave for the Navajo Nation.

At La Sal Junction a semi blows the kayak off the roof. Slowing the truck down takes a while, kayak scraping road surface. We re-rig and press on to the put-in at Bluff. It's raining. The local laundromat, complete with Navajo women in colorful skirts, provides sufficient dry space to repair the kayak with duct tape and line.

Emboldened by our good fortune, we put in at Sand Island. Unfortunately opaque, silted water is extremely shallow. We struggle for forty minutes, sweating and cursing profusely, until we reach the current and point the nose downstream to Mexican Hat.

Paul is lighter and in the bow. I steer from the rear. A forceful roar gets our attention as a series of six-foot sand waves form downstream. We head directly for the waves. Paul gets doused, screams for me to get us the hell out of there. Hysterically laughing, I crank the kayak to someplace that isn't covered in waves. We need to get off the river and out of the kayak. The sun is setting. Paul spots a beach. We peel off wetsuits and dig out gear, agree not to bother with cooking, instead pack a serious stash of Snickers for fuel and LSD just in case. Paul is pissed off, having endured the dunking in the bow. I can't stop laughing. Pretty soon Paul laughs too.

Firewood gathered and lit, we hunker down and warm up. Multicolored sunset eases into night with brilliance. The Navajo Nation is on the opposite shore. We're

Art, Crime & Lithium

in sacred country, bones and history of the Navajo around us and beneath our feet. The roar of sand waves resounds a short distance downstream, reminding us what we're in for tomorrow.

The most efficient way to deal with sand waves is head on. To Paul's chagrin we spend the next day dunked, laughing our way down the river.

Late into the third day the canyon narrows, the flow of the river increases. We find a tight campsite on a ledge, high up a sheer rock embankment, one end blocked with rocks from what we assume were Anasazi times.

Low on water, we scout vertical crevices for flowing fluid and fill a large clear plastic bag. Tiny squiggly creatures swim in the bag. I dose the water with several hits of LSD, figuring that should take care of negative amoebic possibilities.

A drink of the dosed potion and we settle in on the ledge, carve a backgammon board into the soft rock, stones and sticks for pieces, fashion dice from candle wax and light one of the candles at dark.

The game goes on to the river's roar. Night sky peeks in through the jagged cut as if deities slashed the canyon with an eons-ago can opener.

Daylight brings a new lease on life, eases us into reality. The critters in the LSD-dosed water swim on, impervious. The squirts haven't overtaken us. The remaining miles to the take-out at Mexican Hat are an easy cruise. Paul stays with the kayak. I hitch-hike to Bluff for the pickup. Lamont is understandably disappointed about his kayak, but doesn't need to make such a production of it.

Dirk DePagter, a sixth generation Dutch builder and world traveler, advertises on the grapevine for mindless nail benders to help with projects in and around Telluride. I know my way around a hammer from working for John Woodjack at the Renaissance Faires, and talk my way into a job at Dutch Masters Construction.

What I don't know is that custom-home construction and gusseted set-building are worlds apart. I buy a framing hammer, a square and a tool belt, wish Lamont all the best, and become a construction worker. I already own a pickup truck.

First job, I nail together a garage wall. I uniformly nail the uprights on the wrong side of the layout marks Bill Gordon carefully makes. DePagter is cool. I take the wall apart and re-nail it on the correct marks on my way to being a bona fide carpenter.

Dirk and I come up with the concept of "immigrant engineering." He's a Dutch immigrant. I'm a Ukrainian immigrant.

Faced with getting a glue-lam ridge beam, a heavy piece of composite wood, up to the third story of the project without hiring expensive equipment or a lot of workers, we rig a block and tackle at the high point of the building, run a heavy-duty climbing line through the block, down to the hitch on my pickup and around the beam. With Dirk on the third floor to guide the beam and me at the wheel, I ease the transmission into compound low and drive forward. The beam rises rapidly until it balances in a window opening tipped forward and drops on the third level sub floor. When the beam drops, a corner of it forces a triangular hole in the floor, a small price to pay for a well-conceived and executed process.

DePagter scores the contract to install Victorian streetlights on Colorado Avenue. I jackhammer Colorado Avenue down one side and up the other. It's November, and the shallow ditch freezes overnight. Dirk rents Ray Fancher's ditch-witch, a huge contraption we hope to dig the ditch with. The ditch-witch is reluctant to start, so we chain it to my truck and bump-start it by dragging it down Colorado Avenue. When the dirt is too frozen to dig, I pour a couple jerry cans of gasoline in, flick a match and step back. The flames often reach past the second story of Main Street buildings. They turn the trick, and we dig ditch, lay cable and build forms to support the lights. Once poured, the light bases are wrapped in plastic and heated so they cure properly. Those lights and bases remain on Telluride's main street today.

DePagter and I trade his leftover building materials for my fossil ivory, which I acquire from traders and Renaissance Faire connections. Dirk fancies himself a historical type, and the exchange works to mutual advantage. He loads a trailer full of construction leftovers, one with a piece of tempered glass 17' long and 4' high which I carefully stash around the yard until I build a wall to handle it. I trade Eskimo artifacts he treasures. I build with what I get from him, and he builds his historical treasure trove with what he gets from me. European, Dirk smokes hash—sometimes his, sometimes mine. We snort coke. If you don't do coke in Telluride you're regarded with suspicion.

DePagter is a cheap son of a bitch and a good guy, not mutually exclusive. I don't know if it's a Dutch trait or if he earns it by other means. We call him the generic Jew. I bump the value of my stuff up because I know Dirk overvalues his stuff. In the end we work it out so everyone goes home happy.

Dutch Masters Construction builds commercial buildings, condominiums, "condo bondage" in the parlance of the mindless nail bender, anything with an overabundance of sheetrock and oak trim, and custom homes. We work rain, shine, sleet and snow.

The heart of the Dutch Masters crew—Tommy Farrell, Bill Gordon, Buck Lowe, Dirk DePagter and I—meet at the Last Dollar Saloon every Friday afternoon for euphemistic "safety meetings." We drink beer and raise hell until dark, when our coke anaconda rises and we're off in search of whatever part of an ounce of blow we can afford. We score the blow and the party leaves for Gordon's office above Colorado Avenue, where we snort our brains away. The anaconda takes a firm and serious grip when we hit the street for whatever the night brings. Occasionally I call Sandy to come get me because I'm too fucked up to move. We get along swell back then, and she makes the drive to town.

The crew designs company T-shirts with Dutch Masters Construction over a pocket on the front, and a rendition of an asshole copied from a Kurt Vonnegut book on the back with the motto "WE LIKE IT TIGHT".

We're young, capable and tough, with a sense of humor. 25 years later DePagter decides he'd had enough of digging holes and taking care of them for rich whiners, and becomes a real estate broker. Gordon builds a gasoline station at Society Turn on the outskirts of Telluride. Farrell works for the San Miguel County assessor's office. Lowe dies of cancer in Tucson.

I make eight dollars an hour at Dutch Masters, and ask DePagter for a raise. He won't do it. I go to work for Steve Steed, at Steed Custom Homes, at $10 an hour the next day. Steed's main man is Tom Spyke. The three of us hunt and fish together. Our hunting seasons open with pigeon in early fall, then grouse, deer, elk, duck and rabbit, and high-mountain lake crawfish in summer. Money isn't something we have an abundance of, but our freezers are full and we have something good to eat and share on the table. In years of hunting with Spyke, I never shoot a deer or an elk. Tom learns hunting from his grandfather in Michigan, and always fills our tags, so what is required from Steed and myself is the ability to quarter, skin, pack and butcher a carcass. Adept with a shotgun, I earn the nickname "Eichmann of the Ducks." I hunt ducks on the way to work, at work, and after work, good with pheasant also.

On wood-gathering forays to the 11,000-foot beetle-killed spruce forest, Sandy sometimes comes along to hunt fall mushrooms while I fell, buck and load fragrant gray, pink and yellow beetle-killed spruce. On these forays I bring along a .22 rifle, anticipating grouse. Invariably, a

Art, Crime & Lithium

grouse sticks its head out to see what's going on. A crisp .22 invite to dinner, and it tumbles out of the tree and home to our dinner.

The road to the wood site goes past the turnoff for Wood Lake, and climbs up the dirt track. Often the approach is wet and slippery, and it requires care and audacity to get past the morass. Felling a 100-foot spruce as close as possible to the truck, and the falling tree takes the mirrors off my truck more than once. I load and rig the wood above the level of the cab. With all that weight in the bed, the front wheels hardly touch the road on the ride down. The spare, which I carefully place on top of the load, invariably bounces off and speeds down the hill to the bottom of the creek-bed at the turn for Woods Lake. I climb down and retrieve the hefty 16" mud-and-snow spare. Leaving the spare at the bottom of the pickup bed is an invitation to a flat.

I watch for inky-caps protruding from the side of the compacted dirt roadway, a delicacy to go with the satisfaction of bringing home another load to keep us toasty over the long and severe winter. When I spot boletes, I stop and pick them for treats in the pan.

I know I won't see Sandy naked in winter unless the house is sweltering, so I put in 12 cords of wood every year by the end of August. Spruce and ponderosa firewood is stacked in a 6-foot high fence between the house and the highway to let passersby know I have my wood and plenty of it in, assured of viewing my bride's dusky-dove charms on the coldest nights.

I build a sleeping platform in the raised addition, which frees up precious room below. Sandy practices her swamp-princess sex-juju rituals on the platform, with scented candles and lengthy warm—ups, before engaging in sex. I hang in best I can, nothing special or outrageous, just good old pedestrian sex. I try everything I know and it always turns out the same old two-step.

In between jobs with Steed, I hire on with a local glazier to work on a project: enclosing a three-story glass structure around a swimming pool, at 11,000 feet, on Wilson Mesa. We construct three-story-high scaffolding and muscle 4x8 sheets of insulated double-pane glass by hand. The contractor can't get a forklift to the site because the terrain is extremely steep.

Lifting glass sheets in unusual positions probably causes the hernia that swells my left testicle to the size of a grapefruit. I can't move when I wake up. Sandy helps me to the car and drives to Montrose Memorial Hospital fast as she dares.

Dr. Shannon the urologist looks me over and announces the testicle needs to be removed. I protest. No way this cut-happy chump is going to take my left nut.

"OK," he says, "You die."

He walks away. I don't have to think it over.

"Wait," I say. "Let's go for it."

What I remember of the surgery and recovery are dreams with masses of glass shards, sharp, threatening, flying toward, around and through me.

To add insult to injury, the urologist asks if I'll submit to another surgery to install a prosthetic testicle in place of the one that had been removed.

Not quite light and Sandy asleep in the loft, I cross the highway in front of the house and fish the deep, long hole against the red rock cliff. I cast a black Woolly Booger, watch it sink with the current. Suddenly my line straightens and takes off downstream. I bring the tip of my pole up and put just a little stress on the line. The pole bends over in a horseshoe: a big one on. The fish and I tussle. Daybreak turns light, outcome in question. I take my time and don't muscle the fish. Eventually I wear him out and ease him onto the gravel past the flow, a healthy robust German Brown, a magnificent 19" and a big fat fish. He is actually 19 ½", but why quibble? I hook a finger in

Art, Crime & Lithium

his gills and make my way back though the underbrush, across the highway to the kitchen table, where I lay him down and admire him, the biggest fish I ever caught out of the San Miguel River.

When I don't arrive to work on time, Steve and Tom come looking for me.

"Holy fuck," says Steve when he sees the fish on the kitchen table. "Fuck work today. This is a sign that we need to go fishing. Work will be here tomorrow."

We have trout, stuffed with almonds and apples, for dinner. There are many things I've forgotten in my life, but not that fish or that morning.

We can drive anywhere in the county and never encounter a blacktop road. The back roads are more interesting, and a guy can put a 12-pack on the seat and not be bothered. Cops don't cruise dirt roads.

The San Miguel River is our mainstay, from outside Nucla to the beaver ponds in Ilium Valley. The good holes, stretches and approaches we know by heart. The small trout in Priest Lake above Telluride take Gray Hackled Yellow Body flies, or canned corn ice-fishing in winter. Leopard Creek has a population of small Rainbows. Artificial lures at Woods Lake attract reasonable sized trout, but trail a night crawler behind the lure and you're likely to hook a big one. I hear through the grapevine that such imaginative innovations yield results. Miramonte Reservoir at 10,000 feet is good for crawfish, which grow considerably larger than their swamp cousins in Louisiana. The reservoir also has planted trout, which grow to several pounds but taste muddy, except in early spring when the reservoir is covered in ice.

Our favorite place to fish the reservoir that time of year is on the rocks at the inlet. Once a healthy fire is underway we fish with Velveeta, worms, and spinners, and cook fish under sixteen inches on the fire for immediate consumption, keeping those over sixteen inches for the freezer or the smoker.

Mescal con gusano is the libation of choice. We dress in serious winter gear with Sorels to keep toes toasty. More than once, one of our crew winds up in prayer–mode, head down in the shower, after swallowing the last hit of mescal with the *gusano,* while we discuss who should go to the Sawpit store for more.

It is for just such occasions, an abundance of trout, that I convert the ancient rounded Kelvinator refrigerator in my yard into a smoker. Once the inside is gutted, I cut a hole in the bottom and top for a stovepipe, and shoot a few .22 holes in it for ventilation. The smoke feeder is fashioned from a 55-gallon drum on a stand with 12 feet of stovepipe to cold-smoke brined fish. Three semi-sleepless nights and the trout flake to the touch, delicious. My intention is to stash the delectable smoked trout and dole it out over the course of a few months, but word gets out and the smoked trout is gone in a week.

The trout is smoked with apple-wood Dirk DePagter and I cut and collected from an orchard in Delta, Colorado. The brine is a recipe concocted by Mike Baer. He swears me to secrecy before imparting specifics, after we make a deal for a percentage of the finished product.

After a successful all-night crawfish foray at Miramonte Reservoir, we boil crawdads, lay newspaper out on the table, slice fresh French bread, make butter and garlic or piquant red sauce for dip, lay out all the pliers we can find to crack claws and have at it: good days and great meals, costing barely more than effort, camaraderie and enthusiasm.

Time comes to stop sewage from bubbling up in the bathtub. We dig up the old line and drum, and replace it with a plastic system that works. I'm so excited not to have shit come up in the shower, we build a two-storey addition with a staircase onto the existing one. The upper storey is our bedroom. I tear down the platform we used as a bedroom, and suddenly we have space and headroom in the house.

Art, Crime & Lithium

Technically no longer a shack, the place retains shack-like aspects. The kitchen and hallway have low ceilings, and the remaining original structure sits on a questionable foundation. Adding to structural problems is a packrat in residence. Leaving out keys, cigarettes or anything shiny is ill advised. The packrat snatches everything and stashes it within our walls.

I buy a gram of cocaine, load my .22 automatic pistol with birdshot, do a line and settle back to wait for the packrat to make his appearance. A while later, in the dark, I hear the scurry of packrat feet across the top of the hallway wall, and fire twice. My wife wakes up, asks what's going on. I tell her to go back to sleep, everything's fine. The packrat disappears into the wall. I dismantle the wall, knowing the smell of rat decomposing will waft through soon. I find the rat and most of the stuff he stole.

One chilly night in winter I open the doors under the kitchen sink to find a small skunk looking up at me. I quickly close the doors before the skunk sprays and stinks up the kitchen. He doesn't. I get the same pistol I shot the packrat with, and shoot the skunk with a hollow point. He doesn't let go.

Steve Steed lives up the road in Tiny Town, just this side of Sawpit. He lives in a tiny house built with remnants from the water-system construction project in Telluride when I work for the maintenance department. Part of my job during the new water-system installation is to clean up construction sites at the end of every day with my John Deere backhoe. I clean up ¾" copper pipe used for testing the system, and 4x4x8' Doug-fir dunnage the pipe arrives on. I load booty daily in the back of my turquoise Ford pickup, and deposit it in Tiny Town at Steve's building site.

Steve invites me fishing one August Saturday. I'm not too enthusiastic, since the trout at Miramonte Reservoir are muddy-tasting that time of year. We load our fishing gear, a 12-pack of Coors, which is all Steve drinks in misguided Coloradoan chauvinism, and a pint of EJ downstream brandy. I don't like Coors, since it tastes like mild near-beer. Steve likes it. Drink enough, you'll get a mild buzz. That's where the EJ brandy comes in as a kicker. We're skunked, and make for home once the wind picks up. More vehicles than usual are parked in front of our house. I walk in, and most of the people I know in the area are gathered, yelling Happy Birthday!

    Sandy gives me a puppy for my birthday, a Yellow Lab/Golden Retriever cross. He's heavy the moment I take him in my arms for the first time, as close to true love as I feel in my life. I trade my rifle on a 12-gauge pump shotgun. Butkus is four months old when I take him to the Delta cornfields to hunt pheasant. He knows more than I do. I go everywhere with Butkus for years. We hunt pheasant in fields, ditches, and windrows outside Montrose, Delta, Olathe, Redvale, Nucla, Naturita; ducks everywhere; spruce grouse in the timber above 10,000 feet. The first duck I send Butkus out to retrieve he sniffs and abandons. If the duck is flopping, he'll retrieve. If the duck is dead, he abandons it. I jump in a freezing high mountain December river or pond, drag Butkus by the collar and stuff the duck in his mouth. I tell him to get in the truck, and he'll jump on the hood and try to go through the windshield: a once-in-a-lifetime dog.

Placerville

A beat-up 1955 International Harvester 1-ton dually is for sale for $200, up the hill from Mary's Store in Placerville. I buy it for construction trash-hauling, based on my familiarity with Telluride construction and the need for an independent contractor to deal with overflow. Steve Steed drives my turquoise pickup, with the International chained to it, around Placerville a dozen times before the International's six-cylinder fires. I build sideboards.

It's March, with snow on the ground. Charlie Delorme, an ex-tree-planting pal, invites me to go on a river trip down Labyrinth Canyon on the Green River. The blue 15-foot fiberglass canoe I bought from a local leaving town is rigged on top of the International's rack, Butkus and gear in the bed with a full toolkit just in case in the cab, because driving a 1955 vintage vehicle, just-in-case is more than likely. Butkus and I are going to Mancos to meet up with Charlie and rig the trip. Sandy will meet us at the state park in Green River at the put-in.

In Placerville the skies are cloudy but not threatening, snowing at Society Turn outside Telluride. By the turn for Ophir it's coming down hard, and visibility through the snaky turns for Lizard Head Pass is minimal. I pass a tanker truck coming up the hill, and realize that may be a serious mistake. With it snowing harder, I can hardly see the end of the hood. Driving by feel, having driven this road hundreds of times, I assume I can slide by once again.

An eerie feeling in the pit of my stomach insists I'm wrong. We're off the road, rolled over and sliding down an embankment on the blue canoe. Everything is blank white outside. I'm upside down with the toolbox pressing against my face. My left leg is clamped between the door and steering wheel. Transmission fluid leaks onto my head. I desperately try to get my bearings.

I muscle the toolbox off my face. Then I work my leg free. The oil rag wipes my face clean of transmission fluid. I roll down the window and brush away the snow. Butkus leaps to the open window and licks my face. We're alive, nothing broken, no visible blood. Serious exertion, and the driver's door opens enough to let me out. Butkus barks, leaps and runs circles.

All six wheels are in the air, rack intact. The canoe has a cracked gunwale. The climb up to the highway looks forbidding with deep, soft, fresh snow. We make it. The skies are clearing. I stick out my thumb.

A fancy van with Louisiana plates stops. I ask the guy about Butkus. He doesn't mind. Butkus jumps in. I perch in the passenger seat. The guy looks at my truck down the hill, shakes his head, asks if I'm OK, then pulls a .38 Smith & Wesson sub-nose out from under his leg in case I have any funny ideas. I assure him I don't, and politely request he drop us off at the gas station at Brown's Homestead.

Tom, the owner of the gas station and wrecker, laughs, fires up his wrecker and a hand rolled Maui Wowee. I have a bottle of 160 proof schnapps. We're on our way to save my truck. If we don't and it snows more, which it is likely to, it will be months before we can find it. Lizard Head pass is deserted except for Tom's wrecker and my International, road ice and snow packed solid, more slippery than fresh snot.

Tom pulls his wrecker diagonally across the road, up on spiked blocks with the winch and cable facing downhill

Art, Crime & Lithium

to my truck, and has me pound a 4-foot deadman into the roadway with a double jack. He chains his wrecker to the deadman, and has me clear a path through the snow to my truck. He hooks two cables to the frame and another center rear. The International slides up easily.

We finish both joint and schnapps, and fill the transmission and radiator.

Tom says, "See ya later. Keep it upright."

I put Butkus in front, tools in back, fire up the International and drive to Charlie's.

At Charlie's we put the blue canoe up on blocks, spread the crack, fill it with epoxy and screw it solid. The blue canoe goes on many more expeditions without complaint.

Sandy meets us at the state park in Green River. We rig the canoe, Butkus jumps in, and off we go down Labyrinth Canyon with Charlie Delorme, Soupy Campbell, Dan Peha and a few others guys whose names are long gone downstream.

A geyser erupts every 12 hours, just eight miles down the Green from the put-in, the first place we camp. The eruption is enough of a novelty that we stay to see it twice. This is my first trip down Labyrinth, special because the lack of big water and life-threatening rapids don't attract your run-of-the-mill thrill-seeking river-running idiot.

David Richards shows up at our house one evening, asking if I'll help him with a project, which involves moving telephone poles from one place to another in the dark. David and I do projects, some in the dark, some not, but always involving moving piles of stuff from one place to another. David pays the going rate, but lays out several times that in un-stepped-on Bolivian marching powder to facilitate projects. I never eat dinner on DR (Dead Reckoning) projects because I'm coked up beyond food by the time I get home.

DR is a full-on sailboat skipper, an accomplished woodworker, carpenter, world traveler and scammer. He spent time in a Moroccan prison on a Mediterranean hashish scam. Curly-haired, athletic, David usually is in good spirits and fun to be around. We have all-night darts tournaments, fueled by an openly-available mound of cocaine on a plate at his house, until the birdies laugh at us at first light and it's time to go to work.

First vehicle I buy from David is Big Green, a 1958 Dodge 2-ton truck with dual wheels, a steel bed, power takeoff with lift, ¾" plywood sectional sides reinforced with 2" steel square tubing, and a rebuilt 318 cubic inch motor. Big Green is built to work, the heart and soul of Trusty Trucking and Midnight Salvage. I inherit the name along with the truck.

Since I already know most of the contractors in town, all I need do is breakfast at Sofio's on Colorado Avenue at about 6 a.m. Contractors who need construction trash hauled come to my table and make their deal. I pick up a job or two every morning. Big Green is a lot more mobile than the big-rigs that haul commercial trash bins. I can maneuver and park Big Green in places the commercial outfits wouldn't dream of going.

Eight dollar an hour laborers load expediently. I have them separate burnable wood from construction trash, as well as usable windows, doors and hardware. Burnable wood I dump at local friends' homes. They appreciate the kindling. I don't have to haul it to the dump. Doors, windows and hardware I stack for sale and trade material. Actual trash I haul to the dump in Nucla, at first, and later to Darryl Elder's. Darryl owns the Elder Hog Farm where my old SAAB sits on the junk-car fence, on the third row up with the UKRAINE sticker showing lower right rear.

Old redneck cowboys with pickups, and nothing to do but drink beer and reminisce about the good old days, I hire to cut and pile pinon at a lot in Norwood. Once three cords of prime pinion accumulate, I load Big Green, pay the cowboys $40 a cord, and sell it in Telluride for $120 a cord. The cowboys don't help load the truck. They sit on rounds sipping Coors, and laugh at me loading. Once Big Green is loaded, I call Butkus to load up. He makes one leap, touching the pinion rounds on his way up, and lands atop the load, ready to go. People I pass on Norwood Hill, along the San Miguel River or up Keystone, point in amazement at the big gold dog leaning with the load through curves on top of Big Green, lips skinned back and flapping. Days I get up at 5 a.m., and get home after 10 p.m. with $600 - $700 in my pocket, beat mindless nail bending.

Customers in Telluride often ask if I stack the wood. I pull the lift lever, dump the load and give them "Pickles" Peckarelli's number. He stacks for $10 an hour.

Firewood business is seasonal. Fred Williams, a good pal transplant from Delaware, is a chef—a graduate of the Culinary Institute of America. We need something to round out what we have going, and discuss it over beers at the Last Dollar Saloon. I worked the Renaissance Faires and know organization, booth construction and crowd mentality. Fred knows how to cook. Telluride has summer festivals, a ready-made situation for entrepreneurs with ideas, grit and style. The best thing we know that's good to eat and easy to make is a Philly cheesesteak sandwich.

First festival, we learn that better equipment and organization will make money. The fire in the barbeque pit smokes us out and stings our eyes.

I design and build a modular barn-wood booth, with a floor and rusted corrugated roof that approximates an old-time Colorado mining shack. We hang a Colorado flag and elk antlers, score a commercial grill and six-burner stove and two hundred-pounder propane tanks.

Steve Steed and Tom Spyke help load, organize and build the booth. They pre-build flats down–valley, and color-code correlating corners. Once the floor is leveled and screwed together, putting the modular walls and roof flats together is no problem.

Nights before the festival, Fred and I thin-slice four-ounce portions of frozen top round. A bakery in Montrose bakes hard-crust Italian rolls to specs. Fifty-pound sacks of onions are ready to be sliced and grilled. Lawry's Seasoned Salt with labels removed is our "secret salt".

Onions grilling are the key. You can smell them before you get to the festival. At the festival they're an olfactory come-on impossible to resist. On one side of the grill a pile of onions sizzle. On the other meat portions cook.

Sliced provolone is stacked off to the side, to be placed on the meat and melted just before getting eased into a roll with grilled onions. Somebody continually slices onions.

Two women and a hawker work the counter, "Hot buns! Sweet meat!" our call. Freddy cooks drunk, an unusual individual who works better drunk than he does sober. The drunker he gets, the better he cooks: totally involved, dancing to a drummer the rest of us don't hear. I relief-cook and keep an eye on everything, making sure there's enough when needed. Freddy is the only one allowed to drink working. The only danger when Freddy cooks drunk is getting caught in a hug when he wants to tell you he loves you. Freddy's strong, and his hugs are not to be taken lightly.

If you work for us you follow simple rules: no drugs, no drinking, you work from opening until after the booth is cleaned and shut down. You get $100 a day, a festival pass, all the sandwiches you can eat and a T-shirt with logo. Once our outlay is covered, I provide cocaine and

Art, Crime & Lithium

booze to keep morale up while we make our profit. The other booths run out of juice from burning out too early, while our crew kicks ass and parties hearty.

Subsequent festivals, and there are several each summer, I have an agreement with the town marshal to feed working cops. I make a deal with Dan Sadowski, master of ceremonies, to hustle sandwiches on stage for as many as he can eat. Sandwich customers line up six-deep, and it's all we can do to supply the demand.

The sharp hot separation in my lower back, while loading booth sections and equipment for the ride to the festival grounds, doesn't concern me—until I barely get out of Big Green to fill the hundred-pound tanks with propane at Tom's Brown Homestead Texaco.

Ignition key turned on: flames leap from under Big Green's hood, while I'm backed up to a large white propane supply tank with two full tanks on the back of the truck. My back seems hardly a problem. I slide out of the seat with a fire extinguisher and put my hand under the hood to release the catch. Too hot to handle. I wrap my T-shirt around my hand and open the hood. Flames leap higher, but the fire extinguisher works and I don't blow up Brown's Homestead, Tom's Texaco station, his customers or anybody on the road into or out of town within a quarter mile. The scenario takes a few seconds, although it seems longer at the time. An electrical short arced across the manifold and sparked a leaking carburetor to ignite.

In order to get a non-functioning Big Green with fried wires and all our equipment to the festival grounds, Tom drags Big Green with his tow truck for a toot and a Philly Steak sandwich. And he fixes the wiring after the festival.

Immediate problems are solved, but I can't move. No way I can direct booth layout. I spend the festival on my back in Placerville, with the aid of an eclectic collection of pain-pills donated by friends. The crew goes crazy, fried long before the festival's end, make no money. I give the business to my employees with the exception of the booth, which I keep for a workshop. Nobody wants it. I give the parts away.

Gulf Rigger

Sandy's folks come to visit. Big Steve and I go pike fishing in Gurley Reservoir. We catch a couple keeper "hammer handles", as Steve calls pike, enjoy a sunny afternoon on the water in the blue canoe at 10,000 feet.

Big Steve brings alligator meat for a barbeque. I add grouse and trout. We get along swell. He asks if I'm interested in going to work offshore for McDermott, the world's largest marine construction company, where he is a diving supervisor.

The Seth Thomas clock on the wall nicks sticky seconds off the Louisiana night. Twenty of us wait in the large, gray, enameled room. Hard backed, denim polished, boot-scarred wood benches, faded green imitation-tile waxed linoleum floors, a solitary window and the glare of the overhead light are the only distractions in a room filled with silence.

One after one the men are called. They rise, walk to a room to the left, emerge after a few minutes and resume waiting.

At a quarter after four I'm called. I get up, shove my duffel aside and walk to the room. A stocky blonde woman with chopped, dishwater hair holds a Doberman on a choke chain.

"Assume ze position," she directs with unmistakable Teutonic inflection.

I lean forward, palms flat against the wall, legs spread. She shoves the Doberman into my crotch from behind. The bitch has a good sniff. I keep myself in check and don't chuckle, no time for levity or flinching.

O.Z. Lysiak

I ask the guy on the bench next to mine what that was about. He explains that McDermott, the people we're going to work for on a lay barge on the Gulf of Mexico, instituted a drug-check program before allowing employees to board choppers. Workers were getting loaded, and several had been seriously injured or killed in industrial accidents attributed to dope. McDermott is the largest marine construction company in the world, and doesn't mess around.

We wait for daylight when the choppers can leave, provided cloud cover isn't too heavy. The mood in the room changes with morning. The men talk, anticipation hangs in the air. We're in Morgan City, Louisiana, an industrial town in the bayous a few miles off the Gulf of Mexico, on Route 90 between Houma and New Iberia. It's muggy, sticky, humid, and smells of sweat, tobacco smoke, diesel fuel, bayou slime and burnt bearing grease.

The chopper jockeys show after daybreak. Some wear military-patched leather Vietnam flight-jackets. I'm on the third flight. Hueys warm up and lift off to the thudda-chukka of the blades and whine of turbines.

Atchafalaya Bay spreads below us in merging patterns of beige bottomland silt, black bayou goo, the spectrum of industrial oilslick and blue-green saltwater punctuated with thousands of pure white egrets. Shrimpers and commercial fishing boats trail wakes coming and going as we fly over the Gulf, out of sight of land.

Our choppers land on several stationary oilrigs, refuel twice before the pilots locate our destination. They're either lousy navigators, shell-shocked and burned out, or have a lot of stops to make.

The lay barge is over a football-field long and half as wide, with two 65-ton cranes mounted on railroad tracks running up and down either side. 40-foot sections of 3-foot and 4-foot diameter concrete-encased steel pipe are stacked on either side of the bridge, which is centered on the barge. Black diesel smoke bellows out of the starboard stack as we approach the helipad, home for the next two months.

My foreman Nooni introduces himself, holds out a thumb, forefinger and stub. I make a mental note to be really careful while I'm here as I extend my hand to shake his stub. He directs me to a bunk below decks, tells me to stow my gear, go to the galley, get something to eat, and report to him once I'm squared away.

I'm assigned to the crew responsible for rigging 40-foot sections of pipe onto the crane. The sections are placed onto the cradle at the fore-end of the barge, and prepped for welding. The pipe is welded continuously, then slid off the aft end of the barge onto the floor of the Gulf. The barge works around the clock, seven days a week. Riggers work 12 hours on, 12 off, 6 to 6. After rigging, prepping, and welding, the pipe is X-rayed for flaws and the joints tarred.

We have divers on board who work out of saturation systems, 1000 feet or more below the surface. When it's their turn, they climb into a bathysphere-like contraption and are lowered into the briny deep, where they stay submerged for a week at a time working. Whenever the divers are going below, the riggers help by lowering the umbilical cord, which holds the divers' life support systems. The cord is a foot in diameter, very heavy. We stand a couple of feet apart on deck with the cord on our shoulders, shuffling forward slowly as the sat-system is lowered.

Out of seven guys on my rigging shift, five are black, one from Nicaragua. I'm the only hunkie, the only guy who can tie a bowline, a handy thing to know if you're rigging.

Most of my time is spent on top of the pipe–stack, rigging slings and doing my dance with the crane operator. Once I have the slings in place I look up at the crane operator, grab the hook, secure it to the slings and give him the signal to lift. Then I dance off the pipe to keep from getting bashed. Once the operator and I get our timing down, it's no sweat. A glance is sufficient.

Red is the only black guy on our crew interested in learning how to tie a bowline. He's always after me to teach him knots. Red gets the bowline, splice and trucker's hitch down pat. We spend time together rigging and working on knots. He never calls me by my name. Once I'm assigned the nickname "Big", it's always "Hey Big, heah," or "Yo Big, gimme a hand," a riggers' rite of passage. I live in a different world, by a different name.

After a shower and dinner, I go on deck to check out the stars. The Gulf is lit up like Sunset Boulevard on a Friday night, for miles in every direction: oil rigs like blazing power towers, barges, ships, lit and humming. I can't make out the stars for the glare of industry.

Red is at a corner of the barge with a hand-line, fishing. Before long Red has me rigged up with braided yellow nylon, complete with a 1 1/2" nut for a sinker. We pull in a couple of snapper and a redfish that night. According to Red, the fishing is best whenever we're close to stationary oil-rigs. Fish like structures.

The cooks fry the fish for us in the galley, but it tastes like the steak grease on the griddle that everything tastes like. Unless it's boiled, whatever we eat tastes like steak grease. You can eat as much as you want if steak grease is your pleasure.

That night I find out that the guy I replaced was stored frozen in the meat locker.

"The dead guy," Red says, "Got cut in half by a pennant line. They stuffed the halves in some plastic garbage bags, and froze his dead ass in the meat locker until the choppers you rode in on came around. Wouldn't send no chopper out just to haul a dead man. Word on deck is, he was a doper too stoned to move."

There's nothing to say, so I go on fishing but take what Red has to say under advisement.

Later that week I get a chance to see what pennant lines are all about. The barge is steered by two enormous winches. Tugs come out to the barge, hoist 40-ton anchors out on the Gulf to a predetermined spot, and drop the anchors. The anchors are connected to the winches by 4" braided steel cable called pennant lines. The lines are piled on deck, and when the anchors are dropped, scream off the deck with the velocity of a fighter jet coming off an aircraft carrier. If you stumble, you pay.

I get to the galley late. All seats at the dining tables are taken. This is the deep South, so whites eat with whites, Cajuns with Cajuns, and blacks with blacks. No use eating with Cajuns, because they speak patois from the swamps and bayous.

Nobody makes room for me at the all-white tables. Red sees my predicament and waves.

"Yo, Big! Heah, over heah. Come sit us with us," he says.

I take my tray and sit next to Red. The dining room goes dead silent for a few seconds, but it seems like weeks. I learn some peculiar things eating at the blacks table.

For one thing, if you call a black man a "nigger" on deck, it's an invitation to confrontation and possible mayhem. When you sit at the black table every conversation is liberally spiced with "and then this nigger this" or "man, you ain't nuthin' but an ass-kissin' nigger." I didn't push my luck and try out my new status as a member of the brothers' table by taking liberties I might get shot for in the Philly neighborhood I grew up in.

Next day I'm transferred to the night shift, issued a whole new set of gear and given a new job. I see Red and the bloods only during shift-change after that. We manage to shuck and jive but the harsh political realities of life in the South keep us separated.

My new job is polishing beveled ends of the 40-foot long, 3-foot diameter pipe before it reaches the welders, stationed in the pit where the pipe is lowered by cranes onto rollers. I'm issued a face shield, elbow-high leather gauntlets, a leather apron and chaps. My instrument is an industrial grinder with a wire head, which I wield for 12 hours straight. At the end of each shift I sit at the edge of my bunk and pick out pieces of wire imbedded in my arms, chest and legs before I can lie down to go to sleep.

Positive aspects to this job exist. First of all, nobody messes with me. Second, I'm getting in better shape with each shift: physical and mental stamina increase. Third, and maybe best of all, is seeing sunrise every day. Sunrise on the Gulf is a delicious affair with clouds, colors, and configurations that stagger the imagination. With sunrise comes the end of the shift, the end of drudgery and repetition.

During my tenure in the pit I figure I'm capable of enduring nearly anything, and if a better opportunity comes along I'll take it. Now, risk is a given. If I have to risk life and limb to pay the rent, I may as well get paid well—a line of reasoning which leads me into a different line of work.

I read, or watch football games or movies in the theater on board. Triple-X-rated flicks aren't common, but the boys manage to slip one in occasionally. Seems they were regular fare on board, until some coon-asses went home and tried out the tricks in the flicks on their wives. The wives complained, and that was nearly the end of that.

My shift foreman asks if I'm coming back. The ability to tie a bowline means something here. I tell him I don't know for sure, but I'm lying. This trip pays the bills and then some, but breathing diesel and eating steak grease doesn't appeal to me over the long run. Coming off my shift, two days to go, I trip on a bolt and twist my right knee, which swells enough to cause concern. The first aid techs wrap it an Ace bandage, ice it and give me two aspirin. Noonie wants to know if I can work the next shift.

It's time to get off the barge and go home. Red and I are on the same shift change, and wait for the choppers to Morgan City.

"Yo, brother Big, ya'll need a ride to N'Awlins?" asks Red.

"Much obliged, brother Red," I reply. Not one of the other guys offers me a ride.

Red leaves on the first flight out. I'm on the third, and hope there's enough fuel on my chopper to make it. McDermott chopper-jockeys are like rental horses; once you point them toward home, they don't falter.

We land without incident. I go through X-ray to clear for stolen tools, walk into the industrial sunshine of Morgan City. Red has a cold twelve-pack of Jax. The doors to his maroon Mercury Marquis are open.

"Get in, Big," Red said. "We're giving our brother from Nicaragua a ride to N 'Awlins." Our Latino brother sits in back, ready.

Red hands me the beer.

"Rip that sucker open, Big, and let's have us one," says Red.

I do, and we do, and off we go. A few miles down the road, into my third beer, watching verdant, lush, humid countryside, I feel tears roll down my cheeks between sips of cold Jax.

"S'matter, Big," Red asks.

"Nothing, Red, " I reply. "Just look at them trees, brother. Look at all them trees."

Sandy is waiting in N'Awlins. Absence makes the heart grow fonder. McDermott doctors examine the knee, and take X-rays in New Orleans. Arthropods later do an arthroscopy at Montrose Memorial Hospital, two very small incisions on either side of the knee, and I'm out the door a couple days later. McDermott covers the bill, six months disability. We fly to Louisiana to visit Sandy's folks.

O.Z. Lysiak

Big Steve is at the wheel, a little after 3 a.m. on a country road in backwoods Louisiana. We cross the Tchefuncte and Atchafalaya on our way to Bayou Lafitte for a day of fishing black backwater.

A heavy smell of burnt sugar and ash invades the car. Flame curtains spark, streaking skyward, sear the night. Pungent brown smoke veils the road as we emerge from a heavily forested section of highway.

"Burning the cane fields," Big Steve offers in way of explanation. Not much to say at that time of morning.

Big Steve is born and raised in Ponchatoula, a town on the north shore of Lake Ponchartrain, with a 17-foot alligator in a cage in the middle of town. Steve grew up in the swamps and backwater, a big guy with a big heart and a big attitude towards life.

Steve and I fish, drink beer, tell tales - the taller the better. When he comes to Colorado we fish for trout or crawdads. We fished for pike in Gurley Reservoir before it was drained and the pike killed off, a shame because pike fishing was fun.

Mike Baer and I get together on a buckle project for Big Steve. I cut and polish a fossil-walrus cabochon and commission Mike to fabricate a sterling backing with an inscription: "Daddy was a deep sea diver, you could tell by the length of his hose." I send it to Big Steve.

A few days later I get a call. "What do you know about the length of my hose, ya bald-headed Polak?" Steve laughs. He later told me he was offered a couple grand for the buckle by some of his cronies, but wouldn't sell it.

Steve threatens to take me out into the bayous after gators, but never gets around to it: a grisly deal - you rig up a shark hook with some rotting meat for bait, hang it over the bayou out of the water so the gator comes up after it. When the alligator goes after the bait, the branch it's rigged to breaks off and the gator's hooked. Next day you show up in your pirouge and administer a .38 caliber to the brain. Then it's shoes and handbags for the wimmin, and gator steaks for the chirrun, don't'cha know, sha.

We cross on the clatter of an old wooden bridge. The air smells of salt, tar and diesel. First light streaks through tall, elegant, gray cypress hung with pale chartreuse Spanish moss, over yellowed swamp grass and morning-tipped gossamer mists of Bayou Lafitte, quite a contrast to the burnt cane fields of a couple hours ago. Steve chats patois with locals, gets a tip as to where they're biting, and fires up the big black Merc outboard. We ease out of the landing, get the boat on plane and skim over the bayou, searching for largemouth bass.

Hula-poppers on fly rods are the rig of choice, but nobody's hitting on the surface. We try again, in another spot with more dense cover, but that creates problems with tree bass. Tree bass, to the uninitiated, are snags encountered while fly-fishing in bushes and trees. Sometimes it happens back casting, sometimes in the presentation, but it's always frustrating and a pain in the ass. Retrieving hula-poppers is a chore in the swamp, especially if you're a white boy not entirely certain about putting a hand into that black water, much less getting out of the boat.

Steve tells me he'd wade in the swamp up to his chest, playing, when he was a kid, with water moccasins and alligators. Humongous colorful spiders hang down from intricate webs in bushes and trees. There's vegetation that'll give you a nasty itchy rash. I'm not getting out of the boat.

Steve hooks a baby alligator in the neck, reels the screaming little critter in. He enjoys my discomfort, brings the baby gator into the boat, removes the hook and holds it up while the reptile hollers for its momma. Finally Steve tosses the gator back in the water, laughs, and we keep fishing.

Hula-poppers aren't effective, so we switch to spinning reels and multi-colored plastic worms on a Texas rig.

By early afternoon we have a mess of largemouth and bream.

One the way back to Covington, Steve introduces me to his cronies at roadhouses where we enjoy a few cold Jax after a good day fishing and a better day sharing, despite the nasty aspects of swamps and bayous—beautiful in their own way, and needing understanding to be appreciated, much like the desert. I'm still not sure about sticking my hands in that black backwater, but with time even that would take care of itself.

Opportunity

Hauling cinderblock and rock in Big Green, on a monument-to-money job at 11,000 feet on Wilson Mesa, I meet Claudia and David Hoffman. Their Chicago architect designs a modernistic, glass emphasized, white curved structure out in the boonies. It looks like a modern-art hospital from the outside, but is spacious, comfortable, and cool as can be inside.

Claudia and I discover we share common interest in Alexander Calder. From Louisville, Kentucky, she meets husband David in Chicago. David is a successful lawyer who moves to San Miguel County to chill out, ski, and breed show-quality Kuvasz dogs. David is short, bald, Jewish, brilliant, tenacious and fond of good booze. Claudia is a looker, smart, elegant, fragile, reclusive, devoted to excellent food and keeps a flawless house. She owns a narwhal tusk and an eclectic art collection, tribal weavings and basketry. Claudia wears haute couture designers. My mobiles find their way into Claudia's collection.

Claudia stops by my studio in Placerville. She brings a friend, a gallery owner from Chicago. Claudia asks if I'll build a Calder clone for her. The gallery owner tells her to buy a Calder if she wants a Calder. If she wants an Oleh, she should buy an Oleh. Claudia can afford a Calder.

Chris Johnson lives a scammer/artsy lifestyle up the hill in Placerville. Chris occasionally is a purveyor of indica, hashish or marching powder, and generally minds his own business in doper-friendly good 'ol boy fashion.

From Southern California, he's hiding out in the mountains making a quasi-legal stab at making his fortune. We cut ivory and turquoise cabochons on his lapidary wheels, and make a hellacious racket in the canyon above his cabin blowing off shotguns, rifles, and pistols.

Geoffrey, from Phoenix, Arizona, comes to visit Chris. Apparently Geoffrey and I had been at the Renaissance Faires at the same time and know the same people. Geoffrey walks down the hill from Chris' to our house for a friendly visit and a chat.

He gets right to the point, privy to a serious pot connection, and offers me an opportunity to become part of the operation. What I have to do is drive to Arizona, load up whatever I can handle on a front, and drive home.

David Richards sells me his mother's 1972 Dodge Charger, a clean runner with a reliable 318 cubic inch engine. I call Billy Boyd in Norwood. Billy grew up in a junkyard in Galveston, and raced his own hotrod at the Winter Nationals when he was 12. I explain I need for the car to look like it's empty when loaded. Billy installs a brand-new set of heavy-duty Gabriel Hijackers.

Through Nucla, across the Utah line to La Sal Junction, Monticello, Blanding, Bluff, Mexican Hat, Monument Valley, Kayenta, Tuba City, Cameron, the Navajo Nation, Flagstaff, Camp Verde, Black Canyon City and New River, I'm in Cave Creek at daylight.

Geoffrey, his wife Barbara and their buxom blonde teenage daughters, live in a compound they share with 50 breeding pairs of macaws—hyacinth, military, blue, gold. A couple of junkyard dogs roam the property to make sure nobody unwanted makes their way in. The macaws make an ungodly racket, awake at four in the morning.

Geoffrey prides himself on making concho belts Sotheby's sells as genuine Navajo from the late 1800's. He also has a collection of pre-Columbian pottery he acquired from a previous lifetime as a grave-robber in Central America.

Art, Crime & Lithium

Geoffrey guides me through the barn doors into the shop, so the Charger is out of sight while I'm here. We wait until dark to load his truck from a semi out in the desert under power lines. At the compound I load my trunk with around four hundred pounds.

In Colorado by daylight I run the Navajo reservation at over 100 mph. Over subsequent runs I discover the reservation is a reasonable route during the week. Cops, Navajo and state, come out on weekends when pickup-mad Indians raise hell on the res.

I drive the route through Gallup and Hwy 666 only once, stopping to buy a fresh tape at Wal-Mart. Driving out of Gallup, I have cellophane in my teeth, struggling to get it off so I can plug the music in and get down the road, when flashing red and blue lights go off. Nice officers pull me over and ask why I'm driving erratically. I explain about the tape. They wave me on, with 400 pounds of primo Mexican red-hair buds in the trunk.

In business for myself—except for Mexican entrepreneurs who own the product, Mexican farmers who grow the product, truck drivers who move the product across the border, border guards who exact bribes for turning a blind eye and cops who demand their fair share to leave distribution alone. I get the opportunity to make money because legality and morality are fickle, mercenary sisters prone to whimsical changes for a buck or a change in the weather.

My father denounces drugs in a discussion. A discussion with my father means I listen while he benevolently imparts genius on me. He is an alcoholic. When I tell him alcohol is a drug same as heroin, cocaine, LSD or marijuana, he takes offence and claims it is not. The same mistake is made by generations of alcohol consumers and abusers based on the "legality" of the intoxicant. Alcoholism is a disease. Alcohol is a drug.

Barbara gives me plastic bags filled with of pieces of highly colored feathers to use for mobiles. That plastic bag full of feathers starts me on a mobile run that lasts decades. Feathers become my mobile-sail material of choice. I make mobiles out of glass or rocks, or sheet metal or whatever is available but macaw feathers are my first choice.

Back in Colorado, I nurture a small network of trusted friends. They pick up what they can market. Once they pay, they pick up more. The deal I have going with Nancy, an ash-blonde looker friend in Aspen, is simpler. I show up, get paid and am back on the road immediately. She indicates there's a .38 Airlight in the drawer, and if I have to shoot somebody make sure they fall inside. Women like this are too rare. We establish a relationship based on trust. A mutual friend introduces us. Black market networking is the name of the game . Bob Dylan's lyrics nail it: "... To live outside the law you must be honest."

Before going to work with Geoffrey, I fly a load of Arkansas product to New York. A friend of Sandy's is a grower in the Ozarks. We meet in a motel in Ft. Smith. I repack the load, approximately 100 lbs, in to hard suitcases, spray the channel around the lids with Right Guard, liberally sprinkle cayenne in the channels and close the suitcases. At JFK I watch the carousel until it's nearly empty, snatch my luggage into a waiting taxi. The driver is Polish, a good sign. I greet him in Polish and give the address on Long Island where I'm expected. Chris marries Afghani Franny, and sets up housekeeping on Long Island. Fat Robert, a family friend who tips the scales at over 400 lbs, is the man in the know for expedient product deals. He makes the deal for my product.

On my last trip I arrive on Long Island at the same time as three other loads. Prices drop like teenage panties at the drive-in. Three thousand miles, and I'm faced with absolute bottom-line price. I call Geoffrey. He says not to worry, bring what there is and get home safe.

Sandy is happy at home but endometriosis pain she suffers deters from any enthusiasm she might derive from sex. Orgasms for Sandy are nonexistent.

Art, Crime & Lithium

For years Sandy and I are inseparable, devoted. Of course I look at other women. It doesn't matter where you get your appetite as long as you eat at home. Sandy knows I'm coming home. Nowhere else I'd rather be.

Then the discontent begins. At first it's small things. She gets angry when I say 'fuck.' I've been saying it all my adult life, and as far as I'm concerned there's no need to change. It's bona fide vernacular. Then it's the way I dress. Then it's my approach to sex. I bang away at her with no result other than fatigue. According to her, I can't do anything right. Suddenly she's in charge of every aspect of my life, and nothing I do pleases her. It doesn't matter what it is, it's always something I do wrong that pisses her off. I figure it's a phase and will pass in time, but she is making the turn for respectability. It isn't something I'm at all interested in doing.

When I bring cocaine home, Sandy gets frisky. She'll stay with me toot for toot when we're doing the cocaine, and then whine when I fall asleep after we're done. I spend hours on my knees trying to get her off. Sandy complains that all I ever want to do is fuck and not make love. I have no problem with that.

Love was never a requirement for sex, as far as I'm concerned. Lust is plenty, strange is excellent. Hopefully tenderness occurs on a daily basis, and is given freely and generously. When you growl and snap at somebody all day long it's damn near impossible to conjure tender feelings or a light and loving touch. Love's no reason for despair. We dissolve in definitions. Whether you fuck or make love exists in the chemistry of the moment, not in delusions larger than life.

We hold desperately on to the good years we invested in each other, ignore the reality of the cracks in the marriage. She wants me to see a counselor. A few minutes of psycho-babble and I tell him I'm no good but really good at it, and leave before the second gasp.

Then she wants me to get a sperm count. The nice nurse at Montrose Memorial asks if I want magazines to help me get aroused. I politely decline magazines, work up an erection. The result: a low sperm count.

Even with all our problems we still maintain the illusion of a happy marriage, friends and partners. Sandy's happy because we have money.

Sherry shows up at our house one afternoon out of the blue, not unusual since we we're friends. I feed chocolate cake to her daughter, on the kid's first birthday, the kid's unofficial godfather. Her ex and I are pals, and we ice fish together.

Sherry is extremely easy to look at: short blonde curls, blue eyes, slim. She perches on the window seat without a word, not a talkative woman. I run my mouth for a while, nervous chatter to occupy the space between us, sit next to her. We kiss. I take her sweater off. She bends over to unlace her knee-high boots. "Lock the door," is all she says. We carry on for months. She moves to South Carolina, gets married.

Nancy agrees to meet me for dinner outside Hotchkiss, CO. I'm there for a two day specialized EMT class. She's freshly curled. I'm shallow, crazy for lookers. It's late after dinner, and a long drive over McClure Pass for her. I have a motel room with two beds. She spends the night, claims I raped her. I claim she raped me. We get no sleep that night, a moot point as to who was responsible. We both are sore and smiling in the morning. She knows I'm married.

"I'll deny everything," she says.

"If you're on thin ice you may as well dance," reads a bumper sticker pasted to Annie's back bar mirror in Aspen. My marriage is on thin ice. I'm dancing. Seven years of fidelity vanishes in a flash. I break the big promise, guilty, gladly screwing two hot, beautiful, willing, available women, sluts clothed in respectability, delicious.

My guilt lasts a couple seconds, if that. I'm equally if not more of a slut than the women I so eagerly penetrate.

"Making love" is a misnomer, generally accepted as a politically correct substitute for what is nothing other than having sex, screwing, fucking, boning, humping, poking, stroking, clitoral manipulation or hammering vaginal and/or anal canals in the throes of chemical change induced by varying degrees of infatuation.

Genuine lovemaking is a complicated endeavor over time requiring emotion, tenderness, understanding, communication, truthfulness, friendship, forgiveness and ability to share.

My sluts and I fuck our brains out, good to go momentarily sharing bodily fluids with something akin to extravagant sexual hysteria. The plus side of our hysteria is we establish lasting friendships once the heat abates.

Ray L'Hommedieu shows up in Placerville with 19-year old Nurse Juicy on his arm. She punctuates whatever she says by punching his arm or his chest. He hoses her at every opportunity. An extraordinary dishwasher, Nurse Juicy uses the hottest water to wash and rinse with, a germ warrior. Ray drives her to a nursing job in Alaska in his a latest antique VW van. They visit a few days and depart for the North Country.

Ray leaves his wife and two sons in Rochester, New York, because he can't stand coming home to drunk and drugged in-laws. Nurse Juicy he picks up on his way out of town for a road bone. He is working a welding gig in Phoenix when his teenage twinkie develops a need to go to Alaska to work. Ray's a nice guy and a soft touch, and gives her one last ride.

A couple decades later when Ray is on his third wife, a third son aged 25 shows up at their door on the Oregon coast, looking for his daddy. The third wife, an insistent girl, throws a fit because Ray didn't tell her about the liaison or the progeny. Apparently a friend of Donna, his first wife, comes over to see Ray one night just after he and Donna separate. She arrives wearing a fur coat and heels and not a stitch else, looking for a donor. Ray's a nice guy and a soft touch. He provides the donation she requires.

Geoffrey's daughters come to stay and play with us in Placerville that winter. I arrange for ski gear for them and teach them basics on the bunny slope. The first thing they learn is how to get up after falling, a necessary skill if you're going to make progress without whining. After a week they graduate to steeper slopes, improved views, and confidence.

For her seventeenth birthday, Geoffrey's younger daughter Charlie and I ride my new red BMW R65LS to a lingerie shop to get her set up with outfits to work her moneymaker. We go to lunch at a fancy Chinese restaurant, where I get a fortune cookie that reads "What's vice today may be virtue tomorrow." Passing on obvious implications of the fortune cookie, I get her home intact. She is my favorite. For her high school graduation I take her down Cataract Canyon, some of the wildest wild water in America.

Geoffrey calls for help. Barbara is on a vodka bender, lurching around the compound with a loaded pistol, threatening to shoot him and take all his stuff. I call to see how bad it actually is. Following a brief chat, I have Charlie rent a truck so we can get Geoffrey's stuff out of there before Barbara completely loses her mind. Then I catch a flight for Sky Harbor, rent a car and race to Cave Creek expecting to find at least one dead body. They make up by the time I get there. I'm on the next flight home.

Geoffrey arrives late in the year, unusual for him because he doesn't like driving in slick weather. He brings a kilo of cocaine, requesting I take it off his hands as a favor to his buddy Junior, the Mexican connection. I want nothing to do with the cocaine. He insists, says he can't go back with the cocaine, and I have to take it because I owe him.

Art, Crime & Lithium

The kilo is sold for cash to Mark, a small time dealer and arguably the most reliable of our local toot purveyors. Reliability in the cocaine trade is unusual. Geoffrey is paid, off the hook with his Mexican connect. The kilo weighs in a smidgeon heavy, so I march around for a few weeks.

The downside is when Mark shows up, emaciated, at our house with a loaded .45 in his pants and blood staining the ass on his jeans. I take the .45 away. He's a mess, crying, pleading for help, a cinch to run his mouth. The trick is to get him out of town and not incur any undue attention.

I call a doctor at our local clinic, explain the situation without giving too much away, and ask her if she has a facility to recommend. She mentions Los Lunas in New Mexico, south of Albuquerque. I call Los Lunas and ask how to proceed. They say to let them know when we're coming in, and they'll send a car to pick us up. Basic detox is a month, and costs $3000.

I call Billy the mechanic to come clean out Mark's house. I call the airport in Durango and order a twin. Flying commercial won't cut it. There's a blizzard in the making.

I ask Mark if he has drugs on him. He swears he doesn't. I shove him in the back seat and gingerly four-wheel drive for the airport in Durango. A full-on blizzard rages over Lizard Head pass. On the backside of the pass at Rico, the snow doesn't slow. Just before Dolores Mark pipes up and asks if I'd like a bump. Throw it out, I insist. He won't. I roll the window down and insist Mark get rid of the cocaine. He refuses, crying, wailing, slobbering and freezing in the jump seat, out of his mind. Throw it out, I bellow. I laugh at him, a grown man in America who looks like a Biafran without a clue, bleeding out of his ass. At the turn for Mancos he tosses the cocaine out the window. I roll the window up, turn the heat up high.

The Los Lunas driver hustles Mark into the station wagon. I leave him standing like a calf led to slaughter. It might be funny if it wasn't tragic: fine line.

The twin drops me off in Durango. Nobody is busted or put in handcuffs or goes to jail or is shot. Mark lasts 30 days and emerges better than he went in, without cops or courts or recrimination or intimidation or any of that legal/illegal shit. We take care of our own. Mark's wife divorces him shortly after. She's not the problem.

The cocaine incident puts a crimp in my relationship with Geoffrey. Illegal or not, cocaine use on a personal level is your own goddamned business. Cocaine on a commercial level is an entirely different ballgame. I'm not interested in cocaine commercially. Geoffrey put me in a dicey situation. The time is ripe to move on.

The Next Step

The opportunity presents itself when David Richards calls me, requesting I help him clean out a buddy's place on the outskirts of Telluride. Apparently his pal had been arrested with a couple of kilos of cocaine, and is concerned about adding to impending charges with what could be discovered in his house.

It's dark. The door is locked. We take out part of a wall to the garage, skirting the yellow crime-scene tape, and gain access. Anything incriminating we load into a truck. There may have been cocaine residue in the carpet but not enough to constitute a felony when we left.

Several weeks later I answer the phone and a strange voice asks me if I want to go to psychopath day camp. His name is Gerald Joseph Hylan, of the Chester, Pennsylvania, Hylans—a good, hardworking, middleclass Irish family. His mother calls him Jerry when they dance around the kitchen. He likes to be called Knute. Knute's distinctive physical feature is his pure white hair. He wears dentures, which gives him a slightly crazed look, understandable since he is one part psychopath, one part sociopath, and one part good Irish son from the neighborhood. Knute and his folks together look like an Irish albino trio. His only saving grace is he's funny.

Knute is on his way to the Special Operations Center, a mercenary school and anti-terrorist center in Alabama, and invites me, all expenses paid. David Richards is coming. I tell Sandy I'm going. Knute, David, and I load a couple footlockers with weapons, and catch the train from Grand Junction for Denver. In Denver we board a plane for Atlanta, no problem with checked luggage full of weapons 25 years ago.

In Marietta we're outfitted head to toe in the latest camo military gear, boots, socks, jackets, hats, knives, like an elite death squad.

Psychopath day camp is a two-week course in small unit tactics, firearms expertise, rappelling, clandestine communications, battlefield trauma management, high speed driving, explosives expertise and hand- to-hand combat.

Knute asks if I'll go for a ride with him to the Battlefield at Horseshoe Bend, a historic site where Andrew Jackson employed mercenaries to slaughter an encampment of Creek Indians. The Creeks built a barricade. Jackson employed an enemy tribe to hit them from behind, off the river in canoes, a massacre. I make a mental note.

On the river road he grabs the rental car wheel, throws it hard left and grips the handbrake. The car does a 180 and slides to a stop. I'm intrigued.

We shoot 500 to 1000 .45 rounds daily. At the end of two weeks I'm a good shot with either hand. One eighty's, three sixty's and J-turns are commonplace with a rental car, firing a loaded .45 at metal targets on the move.

Rental cars returned with bullet holes are not a problem in Georgia. We learn long line antennas, clandestine communications and how to determine if a phone is tapped. Jumping off a 60-foot tower is an everyday occurrence. Taking guys out with hand-to-hand or a knife is big fun. The mercury switch on a toilet roll that evaporates a guy on the shitter with a charge in the tank is particularly intriguing.

David Richards leaves for home after a few days. Chris Schaffer, a friend of Knute's from college days and clandestine operations partner is in the class. Chris is an opera aficionado, art appreciator, diver, and bona fide ship captain with his own 130' schooner.

Art, Crime & Lithium

We survive November's final field training exercise in brambles, thickets and swamps—without snakes, because it's too cold and drizzling—and graduate at the top of the class.

In Telluride, Knute and I enroll in an EMT course, able to either kill'em or kick-start'em. Shooting practice occurs indoors, with Beeman air pistols approximating the weight of a .45 automatic. Weather permitting, we shoot outdoors by the San Miguel River or outside Norwood at Darryl Elder's junkyard, where we shoot out headlights, taillights and highlights of stacked junkers.

Knute always has cocaine and *Herradura anejo* available. He rants, raves, and pontificates endlessly. I can't tell if it's the blow or the blowhard. It doesn't matter. We go to EMT classes, study the material and take our turn at practical work in the emergency room at Montrose Memorial Hospital.

One evening after class, we're doing lines over tequila when the phone rings. Knute answers, listens, and hands the phone to me.

"Here, you talk to him," he says.

The voice at the other end says he needs someone on the coast, immediately, who can deal with explosives and blow up a boat if necessary. He asks if I can do it. He'll pay $5,000 for me to show up and check it out, but I need to be there ASAP. Okay, I'm on my way.

Knute gives me contact numbers, advises I break only one law at a time, and suggests I get a rental car in case anything goes wrong. That way the rental car company is responsible.

I'm going to meet with Mike Carter, veteran scammer who's done a couple stretches in the joint, which hasn't deterred him. According to Knute, Carter is okay; he pays on time.

A local miner gives me a case of dynamite, fuses and detonators. I tell him I need the dynamite to reduce boulders to pebbles on a friend's property. He runs me through the drill, shakes my hand, wishes me the best and reminds me to be careful. Locating and procuring plastic explosives in the time frame I'm dealing with is not feasible. I decide to go ahead with what's available.

I drive over Dallas Divide in a snowstorm to the Montrose Airport, with Sandy, so she can drive my truck home. I rent an innocuous Virgin-Mary-blue Ford sedan at the airport, carefully slide the fuses and detonators under the passenger seat and put the dynamite in the trunk. I kiss Sandy goodbye and tell her not to worry. She gives me a rueful look as she drives off.

Off the interstate in Green River, UT, I make a payphone call to California. Carter says my code name is Boom Boom Mancini, and to call once I'm in LA. I make the turn for the interstate west.

I never once wonder why I'm doing this; it makes all the sense in the world to me. I read Robert Louis Stevenson's *Treasure Island* as a child, and knew I was going to be an adventurer. I also knew I was going to write. I knew it early on. I want to write one killer adventure story. This is my story, opportunity presented over tequila, cocaine and a phone call: classic.

A fingerling moon grins through high veiled clouds above the Goblin Valley in the San Rafael Swell, a desolate piece of desert stretching over hundreds of square miles. Interstate 70 cuts right through it. Light snow swirls in the headlights, the green glow of dashboard instruments my connection to immediate reality, not another vehicle on the road, not a gas station for more than 100 miles. Hours ahead tumble visions and revisions of reasons, questions and possibilities. I keep the Ford at a steady legal limit, mindful of the breaking-one-law-at-a-time rule, deep in it. All there is to do is show up, keep my word and do my best. Thinking about dicey situations ahead of time is always the worst. Light of day hands-on is the difference. A left turn onto Interstate 15 south, I pull off at Parowan and find a room.

Art, Crime & Lithium

Too wound up for breakfast in Utah, I'm hot for a Philly Steak sandwich in Venice. The Great Western Steak and Hoagie Company, in a brown booth off Lincoln Boulevard, makes the best steak sandwiches west of Philadelphia, close to everything important, with a bank of payphones in the parking lot. Mike Carter directs me to a bar in the vicinity of the Queen Mary in San Pedro, for a meeting tonight at seven with his partner Gary, a boat skipper. I find a motel in San Pedro, get a shower, turn the LA news on and relax. At quarter to seven I slip the shoulder holster with my .45 automatic on, get into the brown navy flight jacket Big Steve gave me, and walk down the street to the bar. Gary's not hard to spot. We have a drink, talk preliminaries, and drive to his ship through foggy industrial San Pedro streets and alleys smelling of tar, diesel, and ocean salt.

Gary wants to know if I can rig his ship to blow and sink in case the Coast Guard pulls him over. There are other ships and always more loads, but good crews are hard to find. If the crew is in the joint, nobody works. The ship has to go down quickly, and the load can't spill. I have an hour to rig to his specs. He has a schedule to keep and needs to get out there.

The ship can't be blown up from the inside out because the pressure of the ocean on the hull. I check the physics of blowing a boat with T.O. Browning, a pal in Telluride who knows about that kind of stuff. We can rig sea cocks to blow, which requires time for the ship to go down. The best way is to pack her keel with explosive, and detonate with a remote. Once the keel cracks she'll go down immediately. We don't have time to do that that. The best we can do at the moment is to tape dynamite to the base of the sea cocks with a 10-minute fuse, no guarantees. I give him the explosives. He pulls out a hefty bindle, lays lines out on the TV, taps out a pile to keep me awake on the road, and leaves with places to go and people to meet.

O.Z. Lysiak

The lights of Long Beach shimmer and ripple on crystal jack-booted battalions of Gary's coke. Stoned, I call Mike. We'll meet at a Chinese restaurant near the ferry terminal in Larkspur tomorrow evening. Happy to be rid of the explosives, I hook up with Carter in Larkspur. We get into a large gold Mercedes. A few rights and lefts and Mike stops, gets out and asks me if I know where we are. Across the bay from Richmond, is the obvious answer. Mike points out the entrance to San Quentin down the street, mumbles something about the cost of doing business, veteran felon wisdom. I suggest he cut the bullshit out and get on with our business at hand. Back in the Mercedes and on the road. It rains harder, wipers slap back and forth giving barely minimal vision. Mike tries small talk. I'm not having any, gripping the .45 for comfort, edgy as a broken bottle in a bar brawl.

Mike steers the big sedan with a steady hand through the coastal range to Mendocino, pulls into a long wooded driveway and stops. The rain has slowed to light drizzle in the redwoods, with openings in the clouds showing stars. I smell ocean. Mike points to a redwood water tower, my bedroom tonight. Up the ladder, I pull my flashlight out of the pack, lay my sleeping bag out, roll Big Steve's jacket into a pillow, slip the .45 under it, and fall asleep before my head hits leather.

Morning fog envelops the redwood forest surrounding the house. There's a small clearing off to one side, a huge redwood deck off the back, and a redwood walkway leading to a redwood hot tub off the other side. Outbuildings, including the water tower, are scattered in the redwoods. Dewy silence surrounding the round house hangs over the shaggy-barked forest, creating a scenario of diffused light in massive vertical presence, spiced with the pungency of rotting leaves, spongy fungi and sea-salt on the breeze. Sculptures and carvings are tucked away around the grounds.

Art, Crime & Lithium

The house is tall, expansive, a weathered redwood spiral with a mossy green shake roof. A broad-shouldered walk-in fireplace with a burly log mantle supports the structure. Staircase treads to the upstairs bedroom are driftwood, set in chimney cone rock, with a hawser handrail on stanchions. No definite separations between the rooms; each has purpose and utility.

The crew testing cables and winches reminds me of brown rice warriors from the '70s, with women and children happy on the sidelines, California dreaming.

Mike asks if I swim. Yes. Scuba? No. He gives me a fistful of 100s and sends me to Subsurface Progression, a dive shop outside Ft. Bragg, to buy equipment. I'm going to swim. The diving shop owner tries to sell me the colorful model. Basic black, heavy duty, cash, no receipt, I tell him. He understands immediately. I hand him the money. Smiling, he throws in a kit bag and admonishes me to be careful, because it's rough out there this time of year.

Mike says we're leaving, time to go to work. He drops me off in Larkspur with instructions to buy a night scope and industrial slings, adds directions to the unload site.

The big iron gate on the west side of Hwy 1, high above the Pacific, looks like the place. About halfway between Big Sur and San Simeon, Lucia is a small point jutting out into breakers coming from Asia, crashing against composite cliffs. A welcoming committee of what looks to be Manson-family leftovers appears. I explain I'm here to facilitate Mike's—except I have to call him Charlie now, because that's his secret-decoder-ring-password name—unload. My hand is in my jacket, thumb on the hammer, trigger finger moving steadily to go mode. One of the guys I met at the round house recognizes me and defuses the situation.

The morning view from the rock wall above the cook-shack frames the mighty blue Pacific, rolling in on a desolate stretch of coast on what look to be feathery breakers, with the Los Padres National Forest and the Santa Lucia Mountain Range behind. The sun breaks slowly over the mountains, burning off fog as it grows. Immediately below the rock wall on the promontory is a small, secluded cove with a rock beach, where the swells of the mighty blue explode against boulders of conglomerate cliffs. A small grove of redwoods stands above the cliffs over the cove. Impenetrable oak brush gnarls to the highway. A barely visible trail leads to the redwood grove. Highway 1 is off in the distance to the south. It dips to the ocean in a long glide along the green foothills and begins an immediate climb. This is the only place the highway can be seen from the property. The cove is not visible from the road. I assume we're going to unload here. The view from the promontory is mesmerizing. I'm thankful to have time to appreciate the morning quiet.

Mike comes up behind me, asking if this site will work, although he already knows my answer. This is an excellent place with an excellent chance for success, if the breakers subside and Gary manages to slip by Navy and Coast Guard patrols tailing him. He needs to unload soon.

Mike and I use climbing ropes and aids to descend approximately 1200 feet down to the beach, so we can scout the possibility of securing a cable to one of the boulders below the surface of the cove. We also have to check the feasibility of swimming out to the boulder through the big, nasty swells crashing against the rocks.

Three of us in full neoprene diving gear, hoods and booties, make the descent the following morning. I pack a mesh inner-tube float with tools and parts. Mike and Rodney, both experienced abalone and urchin divers, swim out first.

There's 90 seconds between the third and fourth waves of a set, barely enough time to struggle through the surf and swim for your life to beat the crest of the next incoming. If you don't beat the crest, the wave carries you in and smashes you against the rocks with the force of the Pacific behind it. If you do beat the crest, you swim down the backside of the wave and over the next one. Not realistic or sane, but possible. As I search the cove and waves for clues, peregrine falcons who nest in the cliffs dive, play, and swoop above me. Occasionally I spot a seal or a sea otter swimming in the cove. The waves aren't too big for them. They're having fun.

Mike goes first, oxygen tanks and cable on his belly-board in front of him, and makes it. Lee is next, oxygen tanks on his belly-board. He makes it. I'm last, with an inner tube covered in nylon mesh on my belly-board holding tools, clamps, bolts and nuts prepared last night. I crest the incoming wave with seconds to spare, and relax all the way out to the center of the cove where Mike and Rodney are fitting their tanks and regulators. They dive. I tread water and wait. Mike comes up first, pushes his mask up onto his forehead, the regulator out of his mouth. He's got a big smile on, wants me to swim in and bring out the cable lead line.

I swim in on the belly board, wait until the wave going in crests, ride in on the backside and surf the rocks. Once the line is secured, I time the sets, beat the crest and swim to where Mike's waiting. As soon as I can make out his face, I know something's wrong. He's shaking his head and gesturing with one arm toward the shore. I turn around. The line has worked free and is floating towards shore. I abandon the belly-board and stroke frantically to catch the line.

What I don't realize in my frantic chase is that I'm on the incoming wave, swimming in front of it. As I'm about to grab hold of the line, the face of the wave drops and I plummet to the rock bottom of the cove. There's a split second to see an enormous wall of water crashing on me, forcing me onto the rocks with the intensity of gravity gone berserk. The rushing salt-water envelops and flattens me. I push off the cove bottom hard as I can, tumbling insanely, out of control. A second or two later I hit the rocks, wind knocked out of me. I'm breathing Pacific

Ocean while I'm in it. A few knocks, wallops and scrapes later I sputter in the surf, vomiting salt-water and bile. I'm numb and shaking. Nothing feels broken. Everything comes back into focus. Something's wrong with my upper legs, although they don't feel fractured.

The lead line is in my hand. I wrap it around my wrist. I look out to Mike and Rodney. They're two small bobbing figures out in the cove, waiting for the lead-line so we can finally set the anchor and hook up the cable. They don't know what's going on. If I don't get off my ass, my heart will die right here. If I don't move this instant, I'll never swim that line out to Mike. The line is tied securely to my wrist. If it comes off, I'll know. Fins are on, and I'm ready. I don't time the waves: no need. I beat the crest and swim for Mike and Rodney, bobbing with the otters.

We swim in at dusk. Climbing up the rope to the redwood grove, I can barely move my legs. The dinner-plate bruises on my thighs trigger a double take, the numbness from the shock replaced by pain.

Next night I'm loadmaster in a raft, in the cove with Homer. The motor and radio operator, he rides the raft down the cable. I ride the cable.

I spin in three-quarter time as the platform disappears. Shore-bound breezes whistle softly through the trees. I'm suspended in the night along a smuggler's cable, checking out the dazzle of the November sky, Attila the Hun and Tinkerbell in one body. The crash and roar of the mighty cobalt Pacific explodes below me. I pass over the cliff. Multiple overcoats of who I'd been lift off. I hang, fresh as a newborn waiting to be baptized, in the cold dark waters of the cove. It's over in a flash. I break the surface to Homer's grin. He gives me a hand into the raft.

All night long we load product from Gary's ship into cargo nets, onto rafts and up the cable. Dawn spreads like a tentative but eager thigh. We're exhausted, hypothermic, barely able to move our fingers, shivering. Gary and the ship are long gone. Work done, the load is on the road. Mike wants us to rig the raft to haul out on the cable.

Our radio conversation is brief. We can barely move our hands, can't rig. I want him to come down the cable, get Homer and me out and rig it himself. If not, we'll take the raft to the nearest state park. I'll hitch-hike to the unload site in my wetsuit, and come after him.

Mike hands me the boson's chair. I'm out of there, over the cliff into the safety of the redwoods. Homer follows. Mike rigs alone. He has a semi-miraculous reputation among contraband believers. This time his quasi-miraculous status doesn't quite work when he cuts the line holding the raft to the cable, and the cable whips wickedly back and forth. Mike lands in oak brush, where the worst he can do is get a case of poison oak, which we all have already.

The sun shines about the same as usual on this unusual morning. The fog is the same; so are the trees, the shack, the crew, the mountains, the ocean. I'm different. Something has happened inside me. Everything is the same, but I see it, feel it and sense it differently, with intensity, a clarity that's quite amazing. The light is more brilliant, the colors more vivid, and what I feel as I stand on the wall over the promontory, looking at the Pacific, is like nothing I've ever experienced: an intense elation, an affirmation and expansion of the faith. It keeps me in the biz for years. I make the majors with the hardball players.

Christmas at our house is extravagant that year, and for years to come, years when money comes in boxes. Benjamin Franklin becomes my favorite American, father of the hundred-dollar bill, my Uncle Benny.

Knute and I ace the EMT final. Middle of December we go to San Francisco to meet the Shaffer brothers, first class tickets. All I need is a change of clothes and a toothbrush.

San Francisco and Points West

Knute knows Bill and Chris Shaffer from Penn State. He lays out background on the flight.

Their father was a spook, FBI or CIA, and left them orphans. Something in their blood, the Teutonic rigidity, makes them Shaffer as crazy as they are. They grew up in London. Chris is a gray-haired scoundrel, loves opera, makes oceanographic films, a full-on schooner skipper. He's a good man to work with, will stay with you through the nastiest stuff.

Bill is a whole different ballgame, no winning an argument with him. He'll run rational circles around you and fuck you when he knows he's got you. If his lips are moving, he's lying. The imbalance in his psyche teeters on a fulcrum with an ugly hog at one end and a frenzied shark at the other, fueled by a speeding brain interminably occupied with who is covering the deception department at the moment. He can't help lying, no self-respect, a dark side lunatic genius in charge who makes deals, a master at manipulating greed. He comes up with the concept of the rolling net, where you never can pin down how much money there is so you never know what you're getting.

In San Francisco a week the brothers call me into their office and propose I help them bring a load of number one Thai across the Pacific. They offer six figures to work with them as a crewman bringing a load across the Pacific to the rendezvous, want me in Manila as soon as possible. I require $10,000 to take care of business at home while I'm gone. Done. They'll get me a lawyer and take care of everything if I keep my mouth shut. If they fuck me over,

I'll find and kill them. They understand, and want me in San Diego in a week.

Sandy's reaction is to have me put the house in her name. David Hoffman had the papers drawn up before I left to work on the Gulf of Mexico. The house is in her name for two years. I give her $10,000 cash and tell her to make it last. Thirty-three below zero, it's the coldest night of the year. I leave for San Diego at daybreak. It's noon before she stirs.

A couple days of meetings at the Intercontinental Hotel: we discuss plans, routes, codes, contingencies, possibilities, probabilities, personalities, and the best places to get laid. Bill and Knute drop me off at a radio expert's condo, where I spend several hours on a crash course on RTTY, which transmits entire messages in a single blurb to another RTTY. The message is coded so there's no chance of it being intercepted, high tech and professional. I like it. These guys are serious. Bill gives me two code sheets, one for the skipper, one for me.

We board in Los Angeles, make a stop in San Francisco and Honolulu before the trans-Pacific flight to Manila. I wear cowboy boots filled with $100 bills for Chris Shaffer to facilitate the scam.

Tom Steider—scammer, felon, and biker with a rap sheet the length of the West Coast—is my traveling companion. Steider, a wannabe skipper for the Schaffers and an old Philippines hand, gets us through customs easily. We have reservations at the Regency Hotel on Balboa Boulevard, but Steider knows the manager of the Holiday Inn. Communist insurgents burn the Regency the night after we arrive. The Holiday Inn has sprinkler systems. Morning headlines read "47 DEAD IN REGENCY FIRE". I give the 15-year-old Filipino hooker from the Firehouse on Malbini Street $100, and send her on her way with my driver.

The Holiday Inn has a massage service with a female masseuse who inquires if you want her to give you "sensation." Manila is an ultimately civilized place with a lovely attitude toward sex.

Playtime's over. Chris calls for a meeting at his hotel, gives me airline tickets for a flight to Kota Kinabalu and another for Labuan in Malaysia the following day. I haven't heard of either place. His advice is to keep it in my pants, because Muslims don't fuck around.

The ship I'm looking for is the *Six Pac*, a 165-foot steel rig tender, black with a white superstructure. The skipper, an Englishman named Terry Restall, is expecting me.

Bold red letters on the boarding pass declare "SMUGGLING DRUGS IS PUNISHABLE BY DEATH."

Every cab outside the Kota Kinabalu terminal is a Mercedes. Malaysia is rich in rubber and crude. The cabbies will take your money but won't lift your luggage. My attitude is jovial, since I'm doing nothing illegal. Intentions don't count when you're playing hardball. You can't be arrested for what you think unless you blab.

The turbo-prop to Labuan is bumpy in a downpour over Sabah, on Kalimantan Borneo between the South China Sea and Sulu Sea, heading for the Balabac Strait.

She's easy to spot: black hull with white superstructure, at the end of the first pier. Ships of all sizes and flags inhabit the port, which exudes an industrial feel with the smell of diesel, tar and paint. Two enormous cranes ride rails at the end of piers flanking the one I stand on. Oil-slicked harbor wavelets slap softly against hulls and concrete.

I tell Terry Restall I brought a code sheet and RTTY wiring Polaroid photographs when he asks if I brought anything from Chris. He wants to know what skills I brought. Firearms, explosives, emergency medicine, welding, carpentry, rigging and I speak a few languages. I'm appointed ship's medic, armorer, and third engineer.

Restall has six AK-47s aboard, with 3000 rounds of ammunition. The South China Sea is famous for pirates.

Art, Crime & Lithium

Tentative hints of Malaysian daybreak appear on the starboard horizon, soft, with a straight razor-fine slash of magenta. The lights of Labuan and the harbor shimmer and ripple in riotous, oil-slicked patterns. I'm on the bow, watching for anything the radar might miss. Subcutaneous bumper-cars run berserk along my arms, chest and shoulders. The South China Sea, the Sulu Sea, and the mighty blue Pacific lie beyond the darkness.

We clear the harbor and make for open water. The swells pick up. I assume a saltwater sailor's squat stance, legs spread and arms out for balance. I immediately look for a bucket because, once swells begin, sea-sickness isn't far behind. In a short while I'm heaving up regularly. My puke-bucket comes along to the bridge, to the galley, to the engine room. On deck I heave overboard freely.

The Brits on board gain my respect with a stiff-upper-lip way of dealing with adversity that puts Americans on board to shame. Where the Yanks bitch and moan, the Brits shrug it off and smile their way through it. When the weather turns disgustingly ugly, the Brits take it on as a matter of course. Their incorrigible attitude helps us all get through it. The Yanks complain about weather, which they can do nothing about. They complain about food, work, whatever. If there's an opportunity to bitch, they take it. I hang out with Brits. They're a lot more fun to be with.

Food is the last thing on my mind after the second day out. Seasickness takes over my life in a storm off Palawan. The South China Sea assumes a nasty attitude. The waves don't have much room to form and bounce off the coasts of China, Vietnam, Kampuchea, Malaysia, Indonesia, Sumatra and the Philippines in a nasty, short, steep chop. I tend to my duties as third engineer with bucket in hand, live life according to the biscuit, meaning all I can get down are dry biscuits with an occasional Coke or orange for hydration. Grim for days, I know from experience I'll wake up fine soon.

The weather stays nasty along Palawan past the

O.Z. Lysiak

Mindoro Strait, clears up off the Lubang Islands as we make for Manila Bay. I wake up sea legs solid, smile wide as the horizon.

We sail into Manila harbor in the dark. I heave AK's and ammunition overboard.

On the bow, watching for anything the radar might miss, I take the opportunity to chuck my bucket overboard.

The scurry of Manila lights the harbor. The smells of Asia fill the night. We drop anchor and settle in among ships of every seafaring nation in the world. Balboa Boulevard runs steady streams of headlights, much like New York or any other major port city in the world.

We make a direct run for the coast of Kampuchea, no distractions, urgency on board palpable. We rendezvous with our counterparts on a drizzly night in the Gulf of Thailand, tie off and commence the load transfer. Thais are anxious to be rid of the contraband, and heave the oversized dufflebags on our deck. They pile up quickly, and some fall into the sea. We lift the dufflebags overhead and heave them into containers. The bags have no handles, so we're rubbed raw with canvas on fingers and knuckles, bleeding. The Thais see we're struggling but keep up the contraband barrage.

"SLOW THE FUCK DOWN, YOU COCKSUCKERS! SLOW THE FUCK DOWN," I scream at the top of my lungs.

The barrage stops, silence overwhelming. Nobody knows which way this is going. If they want a firefight, so be it. Fuck the paranoid gooks.

The Thai skipper speaks to his crew from his bridge. Everyone relaxes. We clear dufflebags and load them into containers. The rest come at a relaxed pace. The load transfers quickly, smoothly.

The Thai skipper speaks with Chris, comes to the rail and points to me. I approach the rail not knowing what to expect. For all I know Chris told this guy he can put a bullet in my head. The Thai is dead serious, looks me right in the eyes, smiles, reaches under his tunic, hands me two flat identical small painted wax dragons, the size of a jumbo Hershey bar, back to back in relief.

"For luck," he says, and climbs the gangway into his wheelhouse. The Thais urgently cast off, engines roar, and they vanish in the drizzle.

Our focus now is crossing the Pacific, getting to the rendezvous. The first order of business is to repackage the entire load into smaller, more easily handled packages. Real sea-going scammers think shore crews incompetent, much as US Marshals think DEA agents are shit. The skipper thinks it will be one less thing to go wrong. We set up a production line, cut the dufflebags in half, pack in as much product as possible, fold the ends over and band the whole deal. As we go through our process we weigh each package on a hanging scale.

On stormy days the Pacific is black, gray, relentless, swells 40 feet. The ship strains up one side, surfs down the other, slams in the trough before the next mountainous swell, creaks, crackles like she's breaking up, slams and shudders, day after day. Sleeping is tough, elbow jammed into a corner of the berth, knees and toes jammed wherever they'll fit, listening to the slam, shudder, creak, hoping the next pitch doesn't toss me across the floor. When it does, I crawl back and lock in. Nothing ever stays terribly bad or wonderfully good for very long. Storms pass in their own sweet time.

Gary delivers Chris to the rendezvous north of Hawaii. The load is ready, rigged, our months of work stacked and lashed.

This time the load transfers reasonably, with a couple Zodiacs in broad daylight. We hustle contraband from the *Six Pac* to a vessel approximately half her size, cram the fish-holds full, the cabins, the head, three quarters of the galley: solid number one Thai, deck to ceiling. We even jam product into the aft tanks and fit blue tarps over them to make them look like they're filled with water, in case somebody scopes us from the air.

On the last trip from Gary's ship to the *Six Pac* for the final bags, Chris takes me aside as the boys load the Zodiac, says I'm going in with the load and to say nothing about what the load weighs.

I am ecstatic, back with my pals, a few days from the coast. I think it exceedingly strange what Chris has to say about the weight of the load: more deception, bullshit and lies. I'm a freethinking scammer and do what I goddamn well please, with my own now, the crew from the cove where I was baptized in black. Besides, I'm being paid to bring the load across the Pacific, not bring it in—a major difference.

What I don't consider, in my moment of joy, is that I'm committed to run the Navy and Coast Guard blockade. I stuff passport, sleeping bag, foul weather gear, sweater, and change of clothes into a sea-bag and sprint to the raft. From on top of the pile of contraband I turn to take a last look at the *Six Pac*.

Gary lays out a racehorse line. We grin at each other. He asks what the load weighs.

"Forty-two thousand, one hundred seventy-eight pounds: 21 tons and change," I say.

"More than Bill Shaffer advertised. There's something going on here, a deal within a deal. Let's keep this between us. Go find yourself a place to bunk wherever you can, and check with me later. You'll take the midnight to eight. We're running without radar, because the lazy fucks catch you by zeroing in on your radar. We'll use a night-scope and scan the horizon every fifteen minutes on your watch. The radios are tuned to Navy and Coast Guard frequencies, on 24 hours a day. We monitor these guys every day, 365 days a year. We know their names, voices, how their last date went, if they have a cold. If you hear or see something unusual, wake me; I'm in the cabin behind you. And don't worry about making the run in with us. We've been watching the Navy and Coast Guard for years now," Gary replies.

The California coast breaks out of the fog. Cool tears of joy streak my face. My body tingles, crawling with wave after wave of emotional ants marching under my skin. We pull into the cove after dark, the one where I was baptized in black.

Jack Locke and I work a Zodiac that night. He's the boat-jockey and the radioman, and I'm the loadmaster. The crew drops an anchor off the stern while Gary works on the bow anchor winch. Jack and I run a half-dozen loads. We come back aboard because there's nobody tossing packages at us. Gary is frantically working on the bow-winch when the ship slams onto a rock with a bone-jarring shock. She lifts with the next swell and slams again. All hell breaks loose. Jack and I sprint to the stern. The line holding us fast is a braided hawser. The ship slams on the rock again. I have the rigging knife on a lanyard around my neck under my sweater, pull it out: line severed. Gary calls Jack and me to the bridge. We're going back in tonight to finish. He hasn't slept in three days, needs to get some sleep. Gary wants us to steer the boat straight up and down the coast until he wakes up.

We run load after load, done before daybreak. The unload runs smoothly. Jack runs the Zodiac over to the hook one last time. A bosun's chair waits. I shake. We work the entire night without wetsuits. I load in the chair and Jack radios the platform. I'm jerked out of the Zodiac, hanging onto the precarious perch, spinning above the crash and roar of the Pacific, shaking, as a soft gray dawn eases over the fog. I hear Gary's ship rounding the headland, and catch a glimpse of her making her way up the coast—like nothing happened, like this is all a dream. Hands grab my shoulders and pull me onto the platform.

Mike holds me up. I can't stand on dry land after four months at sea. The mighty blue Pacific's rhythms have a hold in me. I know I'm on firm ground, but the deck rolls on inside. Uncertain but elated, I stagger slowly along the trail, feeling for each step. The sun is out, shivering gone. Soaked sweater and shirt abandoned, I luxuriate in the warmth of California's morning rays, a million things running through my mind on fast-forward. This morning the trail to the cook-shack is soft, a chameleon, alive, dream-like, changeable. The remainder of the walk up the hill is shaky. The Pacific continues her foam-crested aquamarine swells without and within, while the pale yellow morning fuels an aura of ethereal unreality. The wall is familiar, rock warm, inviting. I crawl up and look around, momentarily solid, one with the rock, with the relief of having come full circle alive, with the elation of accomplishment, the palpable reality of change, back at my spot. Gary's ship is a speck on the horizon. The cove continually erupts with the fury of the ocean's indefatigable rhythms. I can barely hear the crash and roar. I'm soaring. This is where my life begins, this cove, this wall, the baptism, the expanse of this experience. Everything remains the same, but everything is different. Chris brings me out of my reverie, on our way to San Francisco.

I call Sandy from a phone booth on the coast. She wants me to pick her up. Four months at sea and she wants me to come get her. Absence, especially on a money scent, makes the heart grow fonder.

She wants to know if I'm going to keep doing this. As long as they'll have me, I tell her. When I worked offshore I took the same kind of physical risks, but made nothing. I'm finally making some real money. There was as much possibility of my getting killed or hurt then as there is now. I didn't hear her whine about it then. I'm good at this, and I don't have to kiss anybody's ass to do it. I've done stuff now I never imagined possible! This is the first time in my life I have money. I got an opportunity, and did well. I'm going to continue doing well. The possibility exists that I'll go down sooner or later. I'm prepared to deal with that. If I get busted, I'll keep my mouth shut, ride it out and deal with it from there.

Remodel

The remodel I envisioned begins, process simple enough: a crowbar, a sledgehammer, some cables and clamps, and the old walls come down. I hook a cable through the windows and drive down the road in Big Green. They come along. We load and haul over and over, rake and sweep the site clean of ghosts and memories. Butkus and I drive Big Green to Dolores for logs. The sawyer at the mill, an old cowboy in the crusty but benign mold, saws better drunk than sober. I bring a pint of Jim Beam and a Budweiser 12-pack. My load is ready in a couple of hours, with less than an eighth-inch variation in the ends of 20-foot logs. The Dolores mill has good logs, standing dead-dry beetle-kill. We do several loads. While the sawyer plies his trade and applies libation, Butkus and I drive to the reservoir. We swim to the middle. I grab hold of his tail and he pulls me in.

When the truck vapor-locks, we wait for the pump to cool off—unless we're high up in the passes, where there's snow. Then I mash a snowball up against the electric fuel pump until the snowball melts, and on our way.

Working friends camp on the property, peel logs, form the concrete floor, sit around the campfire telling lies, and drink whiskey. The concrete floor is poured and finished. The walls go up, log by log. Stanley and Soupy set the logs. Marcus creates precision, beautifully dovetailed, joints. I lay the fiberglass insulation between the logs and pound the spikes, pinning the logs together. The homestead rises daily. Butkus and I truck another load back from Dolores. The material rolls, the project flows.

Slowly, steadily, meticulously, the house takes shape. It should last several hundred years. The crew is pleased with the job, and so am I. Every Friday I pay the boys in Uncle Bennies. We're old friends. They snicker when I pull out the roll of bills.

Knute stops by, admires the project, and says we're getting paid in a few days. I'm to meet with Mike in Orange County, Saturday, and him later at the Westwood Marquis.

Sunday at John Wayne Airport parking lot, Mike hands me twenty grand in Uncle Bennies in a paper bag for my part running the load in from the rendezvous. Scammers working for the brothers are paid eighty grand for the same run. Mike has no specific answer for the load's disparity, side-stepped by Bill Shaffer again. Supposedly part of the load belonged to the Thai skipper, only we can't talk with him: four tons unaccounted for, eight million dollars.

Knute and I meet at the Westwood Marquis. I check and load the .45 I'm carrying. We're going to pick up a serious boxful of cash. People have been robbed and killed for less.

A mound of money covers the carpet in the bedroom of my Westwood Marquis suite. I've never seen this much money in one place at the same time. It isn't all Uncle Bennies, so we're not done counting until well into the evening. We split the money up, and stash it in the air-conditioning duct in the ceiling, overpaid nearly $3,000. Whoever counted this box last was careless.

Knute is off for Lausanne in the morning, to cavort in the Alps with Bill and his girlfriend. I'm flying home with all the money and all the guns. I order a Lear for Moab at 10 a.m. What we were overpaid covers it.

Knute orders hookers. I've never been this close to women who look this good. I work the 17-year-old brunette over until daybreak, then have her call Stevie, her blonde girlfriend, and spend the remainder of the morning in the sack with her.

It takes all my will to get out of bed and let her go. She's a true artist: imaginative, obsessive, adventurous, skilled and not hard to look at in daylight. She looks as good as a mess as she did perfect. I just can't afford her for long. Reality knocks; I'm on my way home.

The Lear taxis onto the runway. In a matter of seconds we're climbing straight up. The pilot levels the Lear off and L.A. disappears for the brown desert mountains of Nevada. The copilot invites me to take his seat for a scream through the Grand Canyon, capped with barrel rolls into Utah. We fly over Lake Powell, along the Colorado River drainage, over Cataract Canyon, down to the tarmac in Moab.

The house is coming along. Most of the Uncle Bennies we Seal-A-Meal and bury. The rest go in the safe in the floor.

My fortieth birthday is spent with an orthopedic surgeon at Montrose Memorial Hospital in Montrose, checking out the pain in my left hip. The ski season prior, I couldn't step on my left ski to initiate turns like I had in the past. The left ski chatters and the edge won't bite, because I can't exert enough pressure to make it do what I want with expedience. Skiing double black diamonds is history; hurts like hell just to walk on it. The doctor's advice is to wait until I can't stand the pain anymore to have surgery.

Forty years of unbridled enthusiasm take their toll. Butkus and I go grouse hunting in the high country in the morning, slow going. Sandy's reaction is I should give up everything I love to do, listen exclusively to her, drink herbal tea and see an acupuncturist. She's become quite the New Age expert.

Home from Europe, Knute requests I fly to LA and negotiate a Shaffer brothers back-to-back unload. The

Schaffers agree to a quarter million for five guys. No Bill Schaffer deal ever goes as negotiated, promised or planned. A week before the job Bill calls Knute and tells him we're getting thirty-five grand instead of fifty. I stay home and go hunting. Knute rents a Lear and flies to the coast with his crew.

Bill calls because Knute is driving everybody crazy with his ninja bullshit. I ask Bill what makes him think I'm any less crazy. He says I affect people differently. I insist on the fifty grand as originally agreed. He agrees and guarantees. I'm on a flight in the morning. We do a two-night unload in Santa Cruz and Santa Barbara.

The boys are hot to go to a celebration party. I politely decline because I don't know the people, don't know who they are, who they work for, what their connections and affiliations are. I don't know who is following them. I don't know who their hookers work for. I don't know what mistakes are in the works. This can emerge later to some devastating results. What we did the last two nights can get us ten-to-life. I'm not going to the joint because of some cut whiff and high-mileage pussy. None of the guys on the beach can identify me except for our guys. I know where to find them.

I check into The Americana Hotel and call Stevie. She wants new shoes. We go shopping. Shopping with her is not a break from sex; it's an invitation. She picks out a pair of stiletto heels covered in flashy multi-colored stars, and does a calculated, precise, sensuous strut around the floor that has me howling softly and leaves other customers amazed and impaired.

The house is done, furniture and appliances moved in. The space is elegant, lofty, beautifully crafted. Sandy immediately arranges dinner parties to show off her new station in the valley. I go hunting with Butkus until the snow flies. With snow there's skiing. Life is level. I bother Sandy less and less. She sleeps until noon. I'm usually out of the house by six a.m. As long as there's money, we

Art, Crime & Lithium

stay out of each other's way and go about our own business. I miss the old place. The warmth is gone, like the old roof, walls and floor I hauled to the dump, no foundation to haul away.

Knute shows up with half my money, our discussion heated, confrontational, the final straw. He pulls a butterfly knife. I backhand it away and cock a cast iron skillet over his head, tell him never be on a scam I'm on, get the fuck out of my house and never darken my door again.

With the money I made, I acquire an armory in the gun safe. The art collection expands. We buy a microwave, refrigerator, range, furniture, TV's, VCR's, CD's. The collection of rigs in the driveway in front of the house stands as testament to outlandish ownership: Sandy's new car, my new truck, the Baja, my 2-ton dump truck, my old pickup, a motorboat on a trailer, a red BMW65LS in the shop and my new motorcycle stored in California, monthly insurance ridiculous, our house a beacon flashing to the neighborhood something's going on here. I miss the old place. I carry a few grand in my pocket in case I see something I want. A quantity of cocaine is continually in the house. We're deep in the greed trap, which will continue to work as long as I continue to smuggle, living in a house of cards held together with spit and whimsy on a highly precarious balance. We may as well be Republicans.

Local friends work on the house, patio, shop, fence and decks, snort my cocaine, take my money, resentful. We've been friends for years, but now I'm the asshole on top. They don't consider I'm also the asshole who takes the risks, faces the consequences, keeps it together, survives, and offers to share what I accumulate with them. I put people to work when there is none. Money does strange shit to people.

For six months I lock myself in the house, walk around all day with a 9mm in hand. Sandy goes to her bartending job late morning. I don't answer the phone or the door. Butkus stays by my side. In the afternoon I watch a movie on the one channel on our TV. When the sun is out it looks gray and grim to me. Nothing makes sense. I'm empty. Day after day I think about blowing myself away, but it's bullshit. Adrenaline gets going when I raise the gun to my head. Butkus keeps me going. We take short walks along the dirt road in front of the house. He bounces, leaps and talks to me, listens to what I tell him. In the upstairs bedroom I pick up the gun, look out the windows for state troopers or local sheriffs. Paranoia on top of depression sends emotional shrapnel through me, tearing me up, day after day after day.

End of summer Gary calls, wants me in San Francisco in two weeks. I tell him no. If I don't go this time I may not get called again. I don't care. Nothing matters. Apparently it still matters to Gary; he comes to get me. I'm in knots, caught between loyalty, depression, anticipation, fear and uncertainty.

We work a scam on the Washington coast, DEA on to this one. We follow them around and radio ahead to our people. While agents are poised to strike at the dock where they assume the unload is going to happen, we've long since unloaded at a dock miles away, on the road to the money again.

Gary and I meet at a fisherman's convention in Reno. He pays me $25,000, generous, considering I was useless. I ask if it isn't time to get out while we're ahead, instead of giving in to more Shaffer brothers inspired scams. How much is enough? Since we're the best, let's go out on top.

Gary's reply is that we smuggle huge loads because we're artists, and our karma is good because we smuggle green. We're not earning points in heaven for political correctness, I tell him. This is where the romance stops. What we're doing is dangerous, grim shit, for money in the dark. That's all. Thanks for the payday.

Art, Crime & Lithium

Sandy and I remain tolerant of each other in familiar patterns. We sleep in the same bed, miles apart. Christmas morning we're at the kitchen table, unable to explain the pain between us, neither willing to give up what we remember of the good years. Butkus groans on the floor.

With speed and risk as a cure for the blues, I ski through New Year's into spring. No matter how crummy life looks, there are things worth doing. I flash, slash and tuck the runs, exhilarated, terrorizing flatlanders and tourists, running flat out with my ski pals below peaks and ridges, against a flawless Colorado sky. My left hip kills me, wobbly at speed, edges barely hold. I adjust and make do. Evenings I limp around the house. Every day I check the snowfall at first light, hopeful for a powder morning. The lightness of the snow, the rhythm of unweighting the sharp ballet of edges, the exhilaration of speed, tears frozen fast to cheeks, the immense and undeniable crystal clarity of jagged surrounding mountains replace the killing dullness of pain I can't reach and don't understand.

That spring I buy a BMW 733i sedan from a used-car dealer friend in Texarkana, TX. The car needs tires, brakes, stereo, fluid changes, detailing, a tune-up. He offers me a great deal. In the morning it's waxed and gleaming, new Pirellis all around, a Sony stereo with four new speakers, the sun-roof open and the leather upholstery smells like it's fresh off the showroom floor.

I drive to the Limpia Hotel in Ft. Davis, and retire to the bar to sample their tequila. The bartender explains the Davis Mountains, some of the tallest in Texas, have the darkest skies—which is why the MacDonald Observatory was built here. He claims it's worth seeing. The skies next morning are black and blue, nasty. Bolts of lightning rip the skies, thunder shakes the foothills, wind shrieks. I open the sunroof. Rain pelts my hangover. A Van Horn radio station plays Mozart's "Requiem". I crank up the volume. The chorus kicks in. Rain hammers through the sunroof. I'm soaked. Thunder reverberates through surrounding hills, lightning crackles, blinding the darkness. I stop the car, get out, work my wedding ring off my finger, step back, and throw the ring as far into the desert as I can. No turning back. I close the sunroof, drive up the winding, soaked road to the observatory. My thumb strokes across my ring finger on my left hand seeking the familiar gold band, finds nothing but pale skin which hasn't seen sun in over a decade.

The crew is in LA. I call Mike Boren in San Angelo and propose he drive the 733i to Colorado, where Sandy will give him the K100 RS and a couple grand so he can go for a ride. And I'll buy him a ticket home.

I arrive at midnight, get a room at the Airport Sheraton and call Stevie. She's working a double tonight with a friend of hers. They'll be here in an hour.

"THIS ISN'T THE END OF THE WORLD BUT YOU CAN SEE IT FROM HERE," a small hand-painted sign declares, on the way in from the Kodiak Airport when I get off the plane on the island in the Gulf of Alaska famous for the world's biggest bears.

Mike gives me a choice: go to sea or babysit his wife Kathy, pretending we're a married couple scouting film locations on Kodiak, when we're really watching Navy and Coast Guard movements. I opt for the babysitting job. My hip is killing me and I don't want to go out for a week and puke. Mike has a trailer rented in a neighborhood where multiple antennas protrude from other trailers.

A rusted-out inexpensive 4x Toyota is an easy score in the local classifieds. With judicious application of expanding house-foam and a new exhaust pipe, asphyxiation is not a problem. An Alaskan driver's license, and I'm able to purchase a stainless Rossi .357 revolver and a Mossberg 12-gauge double-rail pump shotgun. Kodiak is home to the world's largest bears. I want to even the odds. A visit to the pound and Josh, a 130-lb Newfoundland-Labrador shiny black mix, due to be gassed the next morning, is my new best friend. Now nobody in his right mind will mess with my Toyota or approach the trailer unless Josh lets them. I clean up the trailer and put Josh on a chain outside.

Blonde, busty, tanned, Kathy looks good coming off the plane. Josh likes her. Kathy wants to play trailer trash. I remind her that her husband is my good friend, on the Gulf of Alaska working a dangerous job. Apparently she thinks we're going to fuck our brains out while Mike and the crew bring the load in. Wrong. This was a bad idea when I first heard it. I've had enough. Time to go home.

Kathy insists I take her along when I go to find if the ship is back and, Mike with it. She bolts out of the Toyota and down the gangplank. When Mike comes out I see by his face he swallowed her version. We agree to meet in a couple days. I buy a tent and move out into the woods with Josh, the .357, the 12-gauge and the Toyota. In anticipation of the outcome of the meeting, I book a ticket for Seattle for Josh and myself.

Mike wants me to stay and finish the job. I can't leave, he says, because I'm a security risk. Then I get the best idea I've had in ages. I'm going to kill Bill Shaffer and do the world some good. I leave the Toyota at the Kodiak Airport with the keys and the shotgun under the seat. Mike's smart, he'll figure it out.

Everybody involved in the scam I talk with in Seattle swears Bill left for Singapore after a call from Mike. Gary's disappointed because the scam is going to shit, Bill is in Singapore, and now I'm leaving.

I get home with Josh. Sandy yammers on about how we're going to adopt babies, run a video store out of our home and convert my shop into a framing studio, get rid of our Ashley stove for natural gas and redo the water system. I sneak looks at her like some alien has taken over my wife. I have subsidized Sandy and her coke-whore girlfriends, snorting miles of blow instead of buying groceries or taking care of business. And she's leaving for Tucson in the morning to visit her girlfriend but I'm not invited. Her girlfriend doesn't like me.

Butkus and Josh do a stiff-legged dance for a few seconds, but wagging tails prevail and they bolt up the canyon together.

Sandy meets with Mickey later that day to discuss plans for a framing shop in what is, for the moment, still my shop. When Mickey waited breakfast tables in Telluride I admired her style, long legs, great ass and yummy little tits.

As soon as Sandy's out the door for Tucson, I call Mickey. She's a horny bitch who loves to suck and fuck. I rent an apartment at Last Dollar Development above Telluride, empty the safe down-valley, sell the trucks, cars, boats, motorcycles and guns. I move the art collection into the apartment. Mickey is a treat: willing, unafraid, beautiful, blonde. And she can cook.

The coke-whore girlfriend hotline is buzzing. I encounter Sandy on Main Street after she returns from Tucson. She screams that I'm a no-good bastard and I'll never get the house. To which I reply if she pisses me off I'll rip her face off and burn the house down. A San Miguel Deputy pulls me over on the way out of town, with a warning not to threaten or approach Sandy again. He's been through a divorce and knows.

A recon trip to Bluff I find a house to rent. Done with Telluride, I load what I still have to move in a friend's truck, and take up residence in a small house for rent cheap on the south end of town, behind the Chevron station and the local Navajo bar. A few minor repairs, and the swamp cooler chills the bedroom and most of the rest of the house. Two gigantic cottonwoods shade the yard. The muddy San Juan River is a few hundred yards east. The place is surrounded by an ancient gray picket fence that hasn't seen paint in decades. Butkus takes to the yard, and establishes favorite haunts under the swamp cooler and beneath the cottonwoods. Drunks stumbling home past the yard no longer fall asleep against the fence. Josh took off up the hill one morning in Telluride and kept going.

Every morning before the sun is up and heat waves cook the road surface until it's too hot to touch, Butkus lopes along my ten-mile bicycle ride south along the highway, above the river, to the entrance for the riverbank. He usually disappears through the barbed-wire fence, chasing rabbits in sagebrush on our way home. Today I arrive at the house alone. The old guy with the perpetual white stubble at the gas station tells me that a big, yellow dog was shot today across the highway at the trading post. An uneasy, unpleasant feeling tightens in my stomach.

A knock on the door. Rudy the local cop tells me my dog is dead. He buried him south of town out past the dump. The dog was on private property. He was lying down in the shade at the trading post across the road. The owner saw he was foamy around the mouth, and shot him.

I scream, tears won't stop, hands shake, body convulses, spasms. I vomit viscous yellow bile. Every fiber of my being is twisted, ripped. I howl until my throat is too raw to whisper, wallop my face with my fists until it's bleeding, numb, unbelieving that Butkus, who I love more than any person, any being on this earth, is dead. The cop drives me to where he buried Butkus, fresh earth and a few rocks over the shallow grave. I drop to my knees because my head is spinning. There's nothing left to vomit except pain and regret.

The morning is cool, dry, bluffs on the east side of the river in shade, the angle of the sun rising lights and heats the sagebrushed dusty plain, second by second, softly. It lights the tips of the mountain peaks to the west. What remains of Butkus is in the light. I'm talking,

talking, talking, telling him about the places I went when I left him behind, cringing for every time I lost my temper and hit him, crying when I realize he's dead. I'm talked out, and lie down on his grave. The sun has made its run when I awake. I tell my good friend goodbye and walk to Bluff.

Sandy suggests I come home when I tell her Butkus is dead. A stranger in my own house, I spend my time on the river, fly fishing, noting the daily changes in the fall water's flow, the depth and variation of colors, the intensity of the wind and light, as though I'm seeing the mountains for the first time. Sandy makes herself scarce. I haven't seen her in months. I can't hunt. Thoughts of Butkus make me crazy. I give away my shotguns. When the snow flies and the river's edges freeze towards the middle, I buy my last season pass for the mountain, ski my last runs. The hip is progressively worse. Walking or wading the current is tough enough, holding an edge at speed impossible. I ski slowly on intermediate runs. Forty years skiing end that winter. The quality of my life erodes. I learn about the quality of struggle. I assume the low point of my life is Butkus being killed. Wrong.

Gary calls with a summons for a crew meeting on Kauai. There's been a federal grand jury, an indictment has been issued and my name is near the top of the list. Apparently one of Bill Shaffer's skippers gave it up, and we all get to be somebody because of a sleazy snitch. Gary looks for a country with no extradition treaties. Mike buys a motor-sailor in Australia, off for the South Seas. Jack Locke is going with Mike. Jerry Meyers is already anchored on the other side of the island, with two bon voyage parties to his credit. I'm looking for a perfect bus to drive to Tierra del Fuego.

What we find out is there's no place to run. Computer-linked communications systems cover the globe. We play by seventeenth century rules in a twenty-first century world. We piss off the powers that be with the audacity of the scam. The feds turn to their stock in trade: deception, betrayal and treachery. If we'd been better students of history we might have figured it out sooner. Our scam is over, nothing to do but play it out and get on with it.

Baja

The bus of my dreams belongs to a retired aeronautical engineer in Crawford, Colorado. I give him thirty-five Uncle Bennies, and it's mine. It has a kitchen, bed, toilet, table, bunk-beds for company and a cockpit that rivals a DC3's. Best of all, the old bus has soul. She's painted orange and beige, with black air horns on the roof. I drive to the first tire shop that stocks brand new big-rig rubber, practice on the two-speed rear end all the way home. The air horns are killers.

Crossing the Utah border never felt this good. Nevada feels even better. Anyone looking will have one hell of a time locating me: mobile, undetectable, untraceable, no credit cards—cash, no paper trail, nada. Maxine has plates from her previous owner, good for a year. The plates on the towed Baja Bug can be changed any time. We stick to back roads, take it easy, slow, steadily south.

Route 1 from Ensenada to Cabo San Lucas is a wild ride with no shoulders, through outrageous desert, ducking Mexican Dino buses going 100 miles an hour, dodging scrawny, obstinate, half-wild Mexican cattle grazing on the backside of blind curves on whatever grows in between the broken bottles and cans littering the edges of the two-lane road. Vultures preen, wings outstretched, perched on saguaro cacti one layer back, waiting. I release the parking brake, slip her into gear and we're rolling through Ensenada, the checkpoint at Manadcro, the vineyards at Santo Tomas, San Quentin, to the twisted rocky countryside dotted with leafless *cirio* trees before Punta Prieta, Rosarito, the turnoff for Ejido Jesus Maria, and

Art, Crime & Lithium

the washboard road past the soccer field to the lighthouse above Laguna Manuela. The road is familiar from when I fished Baja winters, looking for desolate spots on the coast without the burden of too much gringo company, preferably none at all.

Christmas, Maxine is outlined with red chili lights flashing, a small Honda generator humming; bass, halibut, cabrilla, corvina, langosta, shrimp, cakes and cookies on a long folding table with a tablecloth under an awning. Fire blazes in a rock firepit. We have enough Pacifico and Centenario to give everybody a hangover for days. Several local Mexican fishermen come over. We celebrate Feliz Navidad until a Chubasco blows in and scatters the party.

Low tide this morning is right after daybreak. At the trailhead, a half hour before the sun breaks out over peaks to the east, I follow a trail along the ridge of the headland. Radical slopes drop several hundred feet off to both sides. Treading lightly through scattered white-bleached seabird boneyards, I begin my descent to where the surge of the mighty Pacific explodes on the cliffs.

Tricky, the trail down takes time through the razor-sharp rocks. Sun warms the ridgeline. The receding tide leaves a glistening flat spot below. Mussel beds, mosses, seaweed and kelp adorn undersea sculptures exposed by the tide.

The Pacific is now about fifteen feet lower, with occasional waves breaking over my spot. Brandy flask and cigars stashed high, out of reach of the ocean, I rig with a soft green, silver-and-blue combo lure imitating breakfast fish, on a four-ounce bullet-shaped lead head with a stainless steel hook.

The black-and-gold spinning reel is loaded with three hundred yards of 15 lb. Stren monofilament. A half dozen casts to warm up, and I reach out to the spot in the bay where white sea-bass feed. I keep an eye on the swells and the footing while feeling for hits.

First hit I lay back and wait, then another and one more. I yank on the rod good and hard. The hook is set solid. The white sea-bass takes off, reel's screaming, line paying out nonstop. I loosen the drag and look to the point, in case he keeps going and I run out of line, down to 50 yards before backing, when the white sea-bass slows his first run.

I lean back with the rod and reel in. A few dozen pumps and he takes off again. We repeat the cycle. A half hour later he's worn down. I lead him ever so carefully onto the mosses below. The swells bring him in gently, and deposit the iridescent denizen onto the brilliant green bed, a nasty, slick climb down lined with sharp mussel shells. I trip and slide watching the fish, glance to the ocean to see if I'm about to be drowned, bashed and battered, eyeball the tail of the bass when I stop, resting on the same bright green mosses.

I slide the gaff quickly inside his gill, roll on my back, and reach for the rocks, rod in hand. How I find strength and agility to get out of there, I don't know. Blocks-long descending waves may have triggered a gigantic dose of adrenaline.

I lay my fish on the rocks where I'd stashed the brandy. First gulp empties half of the flask. I light a cigar and finally have a good look at the fish.

He's silver, with gossamer gray and black stripes, iridescent all over, a rocket torpedo, stretches across the hood of the VW and hangs over both sides.

The slide to the bass cut me up good. Salt in the wounds adds to the quality of the experience. If these are the dues I pay, then so be it! I sit in the rocks with my fish until the tide rises. The butt of the rod slides into gills and out of the mouth of the bass. I sling the fish over my back, pick up my gear and slowly climb to the ridge, careful to watch for snakes catching the last of the sun.

The sun goes down over a placid Pacific in awesome display when I crest the ridge. A slim flash of chartreuse lines the horizon as the sun disappears. Twilight and the lights of Guerrero Negro soften clouds to the south.

Coming home at the last cove before the beach off the rocks at low tide, I pick up a hitchhiker on his way to a party with friends camped below the lighthouse. He invites me to the party. Sandy's grumpy and won't come. I grab a couple bottles of Centenario, my favorite tequila, with the intention of having a really good time.

The faintest hint of light eases over the distant mountains, stars out full force when I stumble home to Maxine. I should be going fishing, but what I need is sleep. A full-on hangover is in the works and nothing besides sleep will cure it.

Sandy wakes me up screaming, took two thousand dollars out of our stash and is leaving me but wants me to give her a ride to LA because she's scared. I tell her to take more money and catch a plane, take a bus, but leave me alone. If she'll just shut the fuck up I'll give her a ride to LA tomorrow, just as soon as my hangover subsides.

The ride to LA is grim, twelve hours of tears and recrimination. We agree she's to sell the house and get my cut to me.

The wait for the border takes hours, in the rain in Tijuana, inching painfully forward with drenched Mexican vendors shoving plaster and plastic painted statues of elephants, Christ, camels, bullfighters, the Blessed Virgin, dogs, fish, crucifixes, ballerinas, Pancho Villa, and JFK at the windows through the downpour. Fellini must be directing this scene. My gut is twisted tight. Finally our turn to cross comes. The guard checks the license plate and waves us through. The VW runs out of gas blocks this side of the US border. I get out in the rain, kick the living shit of the car, screaming, pummeling the sheet metal with my fists, collapse in the street, sobbing. Sandy won't get out. Crying on my knees in the street, I remember two gallons of gasoline in the trunk with the spare. Hood up, pouring gas into the tank, I laugh hysterically through tears. Nothing makes sense. Perfect.

I drop Sandy off at Gilah's in Venice. Happy trails. Back to plan one, Tierra del Fuego.

Maxine is the way I left her. I take a towel and soap, drive to the third cove where there's a cave with a smooth black vat-sized tub carved out of shore rocks over millennia. At high tide the crash of the mighty blue Pacific floods the cave and blows out the beach side. At low tide the tub fills with seawater, makes a perfect spot to bathe. The water is cold today, but I'm numbed on tequila. The foaming salt and gem-quality aquamarine waves soothe away my blues.

In one of those "it seemed like a good idea at the time" propositions I pack gear and haul ass in the VW for Land's End, with a brand new stereo in the VW and a box of tapes, a bottle of Centenario, several cartons of Delicado Ovalados. My favorite tequila deserves my favorite cigarettes. Smoking and drinking go hand in hand. Pedal to the metal, I blow down the highway as fast as the 1600cc engine will crank, plug in tape after tape full volume. If I don't like the first few bars, the tape goes out the window, disintegrates on the road, visible in the rear view mirror, flat brown magnetic spaghetti flashing twisted on the shoulderless highway. Another swig on the tequila, and another tape hits the road. Come Mulege, my tape collection is seriously diminished. I buy Mexican tapes in Loreto. They go much better with tequila. Three Mexican tapes are all I need. I pick out tunes and a few words of the lyrics, rock out to Latin rhythms making what I imagine to be Latin moves, screaming down the patched asphalt drifting through the turns, dodging cattle.

The split in the road after La Paz brings me to Todos Santos, a quiet small town on the Pacific tip of the Baja peninsula with large shade trees lining the streets, palm trees, flowers everywhere, a square with a dilapidated gray fountain, shutters on the windows of thick-walled old adobe buildings: quiet, with a balmy sweet smell mixed with salt breezes blowing in off the mighty blue Pacific, skinny stray dogs sniffing around, and occasional chickens scratching and clucking add to the overall afternoon peace.

    A weathered sign in the heart of town proclaims Le Bistro over an innocuous, inset wooden door in a wall close to the center of town. The door swings open, and a broom sweeping stairs to the bistro flashes several times before a young woman steps out and looks around. I ask if I can get some coffee and breakfast. She nods her head, and indicates with her hand to follow. The smell of fresh-ground coffee fills the small restaurant, enhanced by the smell of fresh croissant. Tables with white tablecloths and wooden chairs shadow play along whitewashed adobe walls. A brick courtyard, more tables and chairs, a bougainvillea-covered trellis, herb gardens on multiple levels, flowers of every imaginable color and variety under a canopy of expansive, broad-leafed trees with several palms for accent, complete the scene. I order coffee and crepes. Bites of the most delicious crepes my taste-buds have encountered in this life soothe my mouth. The marmalades are homemade, coffee fresh, black, delicious.

    The bartender at the Blue Whale in Cabo gives me a lead to the wrong side, all night clubs where the Mexican whores, working girls, vickies, putas congregate. The first one is an open-air affair where Latino disco blares, hips and shoulders sway, red and yellow lights flash. For a blue Mexican bill with lots of zeros, worth next to nothing, the *pendejo* sitting next to me at the bar gives me my next lead.

    It's drizzling. I drive the muddy back street, wipers squeaking, when a pair of red high heels, beautiful ankles and calves in fishnet stockings, thighs topped with garters visible through a crotch-high slit in a black satin skirt, appear in the beam of the headlights reflecting in a puddle. I notice a drizzle-plastered white bolero rabbit-fur jacket and platinum earlobe-length hair.

I'm stopped on a peso, open the passenger door. She gets in, sits, legs open, crotch to heel tip visible.

Marta smiles with two front teeth browned slightly. Her left eye wanders off to one side, independent of where she focuses her attention. The color of her eyes is pale: not blue, not gray, not anything in particular, with a deep red pupil. Marta's hair is not dyed but pure platinum, white, as are her eyebrows, albino. I'm intrigued by her attitude, bearing and moxie. The teeth and wandering eye add to her back-street charm. Her sad teeth and wandering eye are not worth mention once she takes her clothes off. She has a body angels would kill for, translucent milky skin, artistically proportioned womanly curves, and a platinum pussy to match her albino hair. She moves smoothly, softly, like an animal with implied danger, almost albino anaconda.

She calls two friends and we get a room at the Finisterra. Marta, Luce and Elena don't bother with formalities, and drop their clothes as soon as they're in the room. They're on the balcony, checking out the lights of the town, laughing, three lovely accessible bare asses with tufts protruding from between young thighs, an artistic, sensitive composition lit by the soft light of the room with the glimmer of Cabo San Lucas glittering below. Luce, Elena and I get intimately acquainted on the balcony. Marta waits until we're done. The four of us make flesh mobiles until Luce and Elena leave for the tortilla factory before daylight. Marta and I fall asleep in each other's arms.

Since I arrived in Todos Santos I feel part of me is dying, one personality overtaking another in a palace revolution, the good brother killing the bad brother —or the other way around—celebrating death and life, a funeral, a wake of psychic separation, a cause for fresh possibilities. The religious nature of the heavy Spanish Catholicism

Art, Crime & Lithium

inherent in names of area settlements: Todos Santos, Cabo San Lucas, La Paz, makes me think that the natives, the inhabitants are manifestations of souls sent to guide others without vision or benefit of light. The people here are angels, recirculated souls. I ask the woman who runs the long-distance telephone office if she's a saint. She laughs and says yes. Marta, the albino hooker, has clear vision despite her oblique eye. She sees without eyes. She is one of the most beautiful women I know, not because of skin but because of her heart. She has clairvoyant calmness, like this is all something that's already been written and played out in rehearsal. I'm finally catching on, stepping from dream to dream.

The number 13 has gained enormous importance in my meanderings, both physical and mental. I recognize that a deck of playing cards is divided into four suits of 13 cards each, the year is divided into four seasons of 13 weeks, the Druid calendar had 13 months, there were 12 tribes of Israel plus the one which was lost, Christ and his apostles add up to 13, originally there were 13 signs of the Zodiac, 13 is the combination of seven and six, odd and even, positive and negative, yin and yang. I look at license plate numbers, street numbers, ticket numbers, seeking multiples of 13, scratching at the surface of universality. I feel on the verge of an immense breakthrough.

Passing by the church at the end of the only cobblestoned street in town, I wander in and am immediately overcome by the bigger-than-life crucifix hanging in the vestibule. Thirty years have passed since I stood in a church. A flood of images of saints, devils, martyrs, angels, tortured souls, heaven, hell, purgatory, limbo, guilt, confession, excommunication, flagellation, incense, chanting, redemption, inquisition, deposition, supposition, fear, hits me with the force of a tsunami. I manage to get down on one knee but not the other. Joy and understanding don't live in here. I'm out the door into the light.

A shy halo outlines everything I see, soft, intermittent. Marta has an especially colorful halo, possibly because of her lack of coloration, possibly because she has more moxie than any woman I know. We go out several nights a week to back-street Mexican dance clubs, where gringos fear to tread. Marta knows all the cops and gangsters. We're treated with respect, and given a wide berth in a dark Mexican world which combines religious fervor and fear from the Inquisition with still pounding, bleeding human hearts held aloft: a world of magic, superstition and supernatural reality crammed into the twentieth century like a wide old foot into a too-tight streamlined shoe. Marta loves to dance in skirts slit to the hip. I love dancing with her, hips swaying, close, bodies rubbing in a sweat, to intense Latin rhythms.

The intensity of the literal glow increases daily. I may be an angel who is part of the scheme of things, an angel not only in movies or fairy tales or catechisms, but part of a functioning reality of everyday—like angels who carry AK-47's, angels who find cures. I have visions of prophets, shamans, visionaries, healers: Mohammed, Buddha, Lao Tsu, Jesus, Shiva—all one and the same, come at different times in various guises: people who had enough of the bullshit and laid it down straight, who understood that good and evil are one and the same, separated by a razor-thin line dictated by choice—who understood that we are involved in a never-ending war, that whoever has the most believers wins the day, who shared their insight because of chemistry or psychology or dumb luck, who understood that the spark caused by the struggle between dark and light keeps life going. The most beautiful parts of the day are dawn or dusk when light and dark struggle, which continually happens, always is.

The glow grows in slim ribbons of the spectrum, vibrating absolutely everywhere. Marta understands when I tell her I'm going to Los Angeles because I have something I must do, convinced I have died and am come back as an angel.

Down the stairs and out on the tarmac, I walk in brilliant sunshine towards the gleaming silver turboprop. The plane glows with wide rainbow bands, vibrating. Convinced I'm walking dead, transitional, I'm making the ride to heaven. I finally see how this works. I fully expect to see St. Peter at the top of the stairs in the opening to the airplane. A knockout, tall busty brunette stewardess with a flashy smile, greets me at the entrance instead.

In a Hawaiian shirt, shorts, flops, carrying a small black leather clutch with a thick stash of Uncle Bennies, I take a seat at the front of the plane, which is something I never do since the back of the plane usually survives a crash. There's no need to worry today. I'm dead already! The plane won't go down because it's the shuttle to heaven. If the rest of the angels are like the stewardess, I'm not leaving. The spectrum continues to vibrate.

She straps in across from me, crosses her legs right up to her panties. Out the window below the plane, is the Gulf of California and the islands off the east coast of Baja California Sur. Everything glows, vibrates, shifts from color to color, brilliant. The clouds are heavenly, harmonious. Everything connects, no space, only oneness in entirety, the most beautiful feeling I have ever experienced.

Then it hits me. There is no going to heaven. This is it: right here, right now. The difference between heaven and hell exists in how we see, feel, act. It's been here all along. It will always be here. It's about will, the ability to decide. I decided to sit in front, and a little bit of heaven sat down across from me. I don't know where the vibrating spectrum is coming from, but it is the most beautiful thing I have ever felt or experienced. The heavenly stew keeps the tequila flowing. I realize my fabric is unraveling.

A few hours ago I left for heaven but I'm landing in L.A, city of the angels. This all makes perfect sense.

The taxi driver's eyes bug out when I tell him about the coming battle between the forces of good and evil right here in L.A., after the poor win the third world countries of Central and South America. When they rise up and take the rich to task because corporations are destroying our planet of heaven, polluting the waters of life, killing the forests which create the air we breathe, eradicating the balance of species for money. There's nowhere to run, I tell him. He may as well go home to Guatemala or wherever he came from, and get ready to die there. The angels and the devils will gouge out each other's eyes and disembowel the children. I don't know where this is coming from, but I can't shut the fuck up. My Latino driver hurriedly crosses himself time after time, nervously watching me in the rearview mirror, incredibly anxious to get rid of me. He pulls up in front of the Bonaventure, drops me off and speeds away without collecting his fare. I check in.

Fifteen stories above Los Angeles, holed up on room service, no need to go out, nowhere to go, I have no idea what I'm doing here. Even if I wanted to go home, I can't. So I do the next best thing; have pussy delivered, order Dom Perginon. I'm positive I can't remain alone for long because I'm out of control, losing my mind. I manage to maintain a facade of something resembling normalcy. Hookers are the angels of the streets, sexual and spiritual adventurers of the night, they deal with lunatics of every variety. I pick an escort service number in the Yellow Pages and dial.

Apocalyptic visions race through my mind, gory, gross scenarios of enormous, fantastic battles in black and white, switching back and forth, positive to negative to positive to incredibly brilliant color: scenes of cannibalism, despair, rape, disembowelment, torture, outrageously horrible scenes exploding wave after wave.

Art, Crime & Lithium

When I try closing my eyes, the visions get brighter and more intense. As suddenly as the visions appear, they stop, like a loose connection. A frayed wire is in control of my mind. There's a knock on the door.

A beautiful young Italian woman enters, introduces herself, collects her money, calls in to the escort service, hikes up her skirt and falls back on the bed: an hour of relief for a few hundred dollars.

An entire week passes, hooker after hooker after hooker. The room is a testament to empty champagne bottles and dried, used condoms. An exquisite black whore saves my dead ass, tells me to get the fuck out of here or die.

Gilah offers to have me locked up for psychiatric evaluation. I politely decline her kind offer because I'm convinced I'll go totally insane if I'm locked up. I buy a ticket for Telluride instead. I continually check for combinations of 13 and triple sixes.

Valentine's Day I sign divorce papers in Telluride, pick up my 733i with the P7M13 under the seat. Until closing, I hold court at the Hotel Sheridan bar. The same shitty cocaine is available, from the same boring guys, sitting on the same rickety stools, talking the same old bullshit. The same sluts cruise the bars looking for a free ride. I leave for Tucson with a wild idea about getting a master's degree in something. The synapses in my brain aren't quite connecting.

The money runs out. I sell the 733i, buy a BMW motorcycle and get a job selling used cars. Each month it gets progressively worse, to where I tell people to keep their cars unless they want me to slam them, saddle them with 60 months worth of debt, at which point they'll have nothing but worthless junk after they're done paying it off. Six months after I start, I'm fired.

Helmetless, I'm wearing a hot pink head-rag on my way to a downtown street fair, when a long-haired dope-smoking hippie in a psychedelic VW bus makes a right turn from the left lane and destroys my beautiful motorcycle. I go over the handlebars, miss a telephone pole, and wake up with the paramedics over me. I scream long and loud as the emergency room nurse scrubs the road rash out of my face, arms and legs. No insurance: no painkillers. The paramedics cut my clothes off, so I can't leave the hospital unless it's in the gown I'm wearing with my ass hanging out. The BMW is a total loss. I'm out of a job, clothes cut to shreds on the floor.

I find Sherry after a complex drunk and dial research. Her flight arrives about the time I get home from the hospital with help from my neighbors. When I don't show at the airport, she gets a taxi to my apartment. I'm in bed, nodding, bandaged in pain.

Sherry knocks, comes in, sits on the bed. I explain. She takes my hand and guides it under her suit skirt. No panties, wet. She works her magic, straddles me, not about to be denied. I'm in no condition to protest.

The scabs heal and the bruises fade. I get a job as an outdoor janitor at the Tucson Mall, sweeping the concrete, picking up cigarette butts. I hire a lawyer to see if we can get damages for the motorcycle and the hospital bills.

Sherry works every sex rodeo opportunity. I get home from work, and she's on the couch in a T-shirt, masturbating. I tell her to get my belt. She gets it and gets comfy, face down in my lap, happy to be spanked. Every orifice is enthusiastically penetrated. She is the sexiest woman I have ever been involved with. Elapsed months of playtime, and she feels guilty about having abandoned her kids, flies home.

The visions and vibrations stop. Migraines take their place. A serrated, flashing, diamond-sharp, brilliant segment ripples in front of my left eye. I can't make it go away. It's beautiful, but I know excruciating pain is coming. The segment takes over the scope of my vision like a living screen flashing out reality, although reality exists behind the screen. The only way to quiet the visions and the pain is to force myself to sleep. I wake hours later, pain gone but my synapses fried. There are words I know but cannot reach, concepts trying to get out which won't. I'm semi-mute. A day or two, and everything is back to whatever normal is supposed to be. There's no warning, no schedule, no way of telling when emotions grow fangs and claws and separate the brain from reality.

Three DEA agents knock on my door. The woman leaves once I call her a cunt. I offer the honcho a million dollars to kill the one who needs to use the toilet. His wheels turn, figuring if I have the money. As a last resort, I offer to shoot it out with them. They drop their business cards on the table, and close the door behind them. I pull the H&K out from the kitchen cabinet. I'm out of my mind, out of a job, out of luck, nowhere to run, headed for prison. I consider the beautiful piece. Relief is just a shot away.

Then Sherry calls. She wants to come back.

Moab

I live on delivered pizza, deciding whether to stick the H&K in my ear and be done with it. The prospect of another meal and a piece of ass keeps me going. A card announcing Serena's Tucson watercolor show arrives in the mail, a good enough reason to leave the apartment.

Happy to see each other, friends with things to share, we talk the afternoon away on a vigil for art aficionados. Serena is going through changes, unhappy with her relationship with Marcus. He'd rather fish than fuck. I explain my situation in no uncertain terms. We travel the surrounding desert in her van, camping. She paints; I dabble. She takes her panties off after painting a sunset on the road to Mt. Lemmon above Tucson. I'm thrilled I didn't kill myself. Serena insists I come to Moab and move in with her.

I don't argue, and do what she says. With her help and understanding, I face down my demons. I owe her my life. For months I shudder at the thought of dealing with a world outside Serena's house and yard. I sweep the house, deck and yard daily, maintain equilibrium, keep a lid on the rage. She introduces me to a river-runner friend of hers, Jimmy Ferro, (Dr. James Anthony Ferro, PhD, Psychologist). I trade him mobiles for his time, tell him some of the crazy shit I did, expect to hear I need institutionalization. He laughs and asks if I really did do all this stuff. I assure him I did. Jimmy tells me I'm not crazy, merely bi-polar: manic-depressive, a whole different ballgame. He suggests I read Dr. Ronald R. Fieve's book, *Moodswing*. I find, buy and read it. Dr. Fieve opens

Art, Crime & Lithium

my eyes to the history and reality of bipolarity. I'm missing salt in my bloodstream. I can be fixed by being one with my chemist. Blood tests at the local hospital get me a prescription for lithium carbonate, part of my life for the next 20 years and better.

Serena's oar strokes are deft, soft, responsive to the current. She runs rapids with precision, wile, charm, humor and occasional terror. Rapids conjure terror no matter how smooth you are.

This July morning doesn't stay cool for long, on our first day in Desolation Canyon, in the *Emotional Rescue* on the Green River below the Bad Land Cliffs, the West Tavaputs Plateau and the Uintah and Ouray Indian Reservations.

Sand Wash put-in meanders river-miles behind us as the desert sun climbs, Serena follows foam-flecks of the main current, keeps the *Emotional Rescue*'s attitude perfect in slow carousel-like circles in 3/4 wilderness time. Canyon walls steadily deepen in layers. We descend to the gurgle and slip of the river, the wind's slice through cottonwood and tamarisk, and Serena's near-mute oar strokes.

Serena has paints, brushes, and watercolor paper mounted on plywood, in canvas bags. I have cat-fishing gear. We have a deal. Serena paints and I set up camp, fish and cook. We've done this before. We find a campsite each day, which has shade come morning. Serena waits for perfect light. She paints and I get dinner ready.

We hunt for shade and good places to fish. By dinnertime I usually have a stringer full. It's a tough life, living on fresh catfish and rice, Kenyan coffee and Australian cabernet. When Serena rows I sketch canyons, rock formations, vegetation, critters, capture the immense simplicity of the natural state, like scribbling notes on a moving herd of mastodons as the ice age slips away.

Serena takes the *Emotional Rescue* in the rapids. She has more than 40 trips down Deso as a professional boatwoman. The rapids and Serena are old friends. She has plenty of respect for the roar, rocks, and rushing river. I marvel at her wily, feather-soft style of negotiating rapids, which I try to muscle.

Horseflies and mid-summer heat are oppressive. All we can do is button down and swat. The heat is another matter. When we can't find a shady spot to chill out we strip down, slip into the river and float connected, hanging on to the *Emotional Rescue*, liquid angels in the silt.

It goes by too fast, nothing left to do but pack and leave. I look around the canyon one last time and make ready to shove off. Serena wants another cup of coffee, has to linger, prolong the sorrow. We both know it's time to face the humdrum grayness—phone calls, bills, worries, responsibilities and hassles—of the fabric of our lives.

We sit in the dory in silence, Serena determined to drag it out. The river trip is over. Time to go. She slides the oars into their locks and strokes into the current.

Serena's been running rivers since she graduated from Northern Arizona University with a degree in art. She took to the river like an otter, worked for river-runner outfits out of Moab, became a Desolation Canyon specialist. She ran Westwater, Cataract, the Grand, Gates of Ledore. While she rowed the wild rivers, she developed a set of arms and shoulders befitting a true Taurus woman. Serena refined her artistic vision, and painted her passion.

In Serena's capable hands the *Emotional Rescue*, her wooden river dory, developed into a work of art. Serena sanded and filled and painted and buffed and waxed until the *E.R.* sparkled like a vintage Maserati. She lovingly detailed and lettered the hull. The *E.R.*'s oars, 10 foot Smokers, were sanded smooth and varnished with six coats of UV-resistant premium. The oar stops and wraps were hand-built precise, epoxied and waxed. Everything matched.

Art, Crime & Lithium

As money allowed, Serena added decks and hatches with nothing but the finest brass fittings. Another year the *Rescue* finally got her own trailer. Serena talked about building a boathouse, but that wasn't to be. End of each boating season, she'd swab her out and roll her over. The *Rescue* was a hefty heifer on land, and it was no easy chore. On the water she was an angel: cut through the waves, slipped over rocks, turned with a roll of the wrist. Some years Serena had help, and others were backaches. Once the dory was rolled, Serena carefully wrapped her with tarps she so she'd be ready in spring.

Every couple of years Serena sanded and stroked her and conjured another epoxy paintjob. There wasn't a boat to compare in the Southwest. She was the queen of the rivers, a reflection of the woman who loved her.

The first time Serena took me down the river in the *Rescue*, we put in at the Dewey Bridge below Cisco. She let me row the *E.R.* after a bit. At that point I knew Serena trusted me. We shared a bottle of downstream brandy on a flatwater run, and no big danged deal. As the amber contents of the bottle diminished, so did my good buddy's clothes until she lay in the bow wearing nothing but her cowboy hat and boots, waving to gawking tourists like this was an everyday occurrence, laughing. The Colorado took a big sweeping righthander and we were gone, out of sight, wild in the West.

The *Rescue* was going to need a major overhaul: separations in the fiberglass in the bottom, hull had dings, and it was either a total rebuild or time for a new rig. Serena spent the better part of a year, a couple thousand dollars, and an incredible amount of energy and effort. When the rebuild was complete, the *Rescue* was more beautiful than ever, buffed out perfect. We took one last ride together down the daily on the Colorado.

We put in at Hittle Bottom. Serena had the oars locked under her knees, rolling a handmade. River patterns danced and glistened off the *Rescue*'s creamy, slick hull. The *Rescue* did a slow 360 in excruciating pan of the Lasals, Tukhnanikavits, Fisher Towers and Castle Valley. That's the way I remember her.

The attorney in Tucson sends a letter and a check for $1800, my share of the settlement for the motorcycle wreck. I buy an old yellow Ford pickup. Sandy's lawyer sends papers finalizing the divorce. She gets everything, including the house. I tend bar at the Rio, the local hot spot. Serena and I run rivers together. With more time than money, we use our time to do what we think important: running rivers, creating art.

Suzanne, a raven-haired looker with a dancer's body and massive breasts, shows up at the Rio. Everybody wants in her pants. We have a few drinks, flirt. I offer to give her a ride home. We grope under a streetlight. I know I shouldn't do this. She takes off her brassiere, slips off her shorts and panties and asks why I won't give it to her. I give it to her. Streetlights fade and the sun is up. She leaves pink panties on the dashboard as a souvenir.

Serena is amused. She'll forgive me, but I can't promise I won't do something similar again. I'm a slut and we both know it.

Mike Boren in Abilene gives me his 1952 Silver Streak, a classic rounded aluminum trailer he bought in Key West, so I'll have a place to live of my own, but his dog went nuts locked up in Mike's mother's yard and ate the wiring. I drive the yellow Ford to Abilene, fix the wiring and haul the Silver Streak to the Third World Trailer Park & Sex Emporium on the outskirts of Moab. Trailer parked under a shade tree, I set up a workbench and make mobiles. I hang them in the tree.

The tow from Texas to Utah destroys the Ford's flimsy three-speed transmission. I buy a used four-speed, have a new driveline built and balanced to accommodate the shorter transmission, and go to install it on a concrete pad adjacent to my trailer, cursing the day I bought a Ford. Ray Perera, a biker, oilfield driller, master mechanic and

Art, Crime & Lithium

all around helpful good guy, introduces himself over beers at the Rio, a local restaurant and drinking establishment. I explain the problems I'm having with the goddamned Ford's transmission installation, and Ray shows up the next day and has it up, in and running in an hour. What to me was an insurmountable problem and a prickly pain in the ass is matter of fact mechanics to Ray. We become friends.

Ray is a transplant from Victorville, California: burly, wide, solid, with curly black hair and a smiley attitude. He rides a 1962 FLH Harley Davidson around town and a 1950 Indian Chief Sundays and holidays, and restores a 1939 Indian Four in his trailer on the outskirts of Moab. The exterior of Ray's trailer looks normal enough. The interior of the trailer has motorcycles in various stages of restoration, a couch covered in antique rustic natural naugahyde, a scarred coffee table with a vintage '50s phonograph that plays Steppenwolf's *Born To Be Wild*, the only music Ray allows in the trailer. In the northwest corner of the trailer is a collection of empty beer cans in a cone spreading aluminum towards the ceiling, Ray's contribution to keeping the planet green. To support his motorcycle habit Ray works as a driller in Wyoming oilfields, gone from Moab weeks at a time.

Weekends he's home, we search for old motorcycles in barns and homesteads, in southeast Utah and southwest Colorado. A 1919 Indian chained to a cast-iron front yard fence is our prime discovery on a dirt road outside Redvale, Colorado. An ancient, emaciated, long-retired farmer in his 90s with stark, alive, periwinkle blue eyes, a worn smile, and a field full of classic rusted treasures, answers Ray's knock.

He bought the Indian in 1932, rode it nine miles from Norwood to Redvale in a rainstorm, and chained it to the front yard fence because it ran too goddamned fast. Trees grow through it now.

Ray tries to convince the old man the rusted hulks in his field are treasures.

"Naw," chuckles the old man, "They'd only take away the money."

On the way home I can feel Ray wrestling with how to pry the rusty Indian carcass loose from the past. Stealing it is not an option.

ViviAnn has a Silver Streak model the same vintage as mine, parked across the road at the entrance to our shared trailer park. She's an attractive mid-30s blonde jack–Mormon, who boasts the infamous Ma Barker as a relative. She's an artist who hand-paints erotic nude prints she photographs in the desert around Moab. One thing naturally leads to another, and ViviAnn invites me over to her trailer for a drink, which evolves into a cuddle session complete with erection and innocently enough anal penetration. Oops, oh my. ViviAnn specializes in fellatio with an Oster vibrator. She squeals and jumps with joy when my erection squirts to the ceiling of her Silver Streak. She'll be washing the dishes and I'll come up behind her, slip her sweats down or her skirt up and she's ready to go, hot to trot. ViviAnn in the passenger seat is another reason to find a place to pull over and have at it. She'll lean against the door, pull her dress up, panties down, diddle her quim, hard to ignore. Pull over.

Getting around gets harder by the day as my hip deteriorates. Orthopedic surgeons at the VA Hospital in Grand Junction say I need a hip replacement. The waiting list is seven years long. I buy a cane. A month later they call and ask if I'm ready. The surgeons operate in January. ViviAnn gives me a ride to the hospital. I come out with a horizontal, metal-stapled slice across my left cheek. She takes a photograph.

Ray has his spine operated on, and we both get out of the hospital at the same time. I spend weeks on crutches, and then walk up and down the canyon behind my trailer with a cane. Once we can get around we get together, pool our pain pills, wash them down with Canadian Mist and 7Up and go downtown to see what's what. We'll walk into a bar and hear the murmur scoot out the back door. Of course Ray's reputation precedes him from the time he rode his Harley through the front door of Woody's, a Main Street biker bar.

A Saturday night at the Rio, I grab the dickhead doorman by the throat and lift him off his feet up the wall. He's being obnoxious and I'm not up to listening to his bullshit. Ray talks me into letting the dickhead go before he chokes or the cops arrive. We take care of each other.

April Fool's Day I'm on the Green River, rowing Labyrinth Canyon with Mike Boren in Serena's venerable veteran raft, the *Careena*. Boren runs his mouth the entire trip, since silence apparently frightens him, but burns trash and mashes cans in a genuine effort to keep the cargo minimal. Franck Schroyer, a high school friend, flies out from Philadelphia for a row down the Green. The remainder of the spring, summer, and fall, I row rivers. The water heals.

ViviAnn nags me until I agree to take her on a river trip down the San Juan River. I rig the *Careena* for a week plus on the water, load the Ford, arrange for a shuttle. We put in at Sand Island south of Bluff. First stop for lunch, ViviAnn disappears behind a boulder while I make tuna-fish sandwiches. She emerges from behind the boulder in a see-through filmy white teddy, wearing matching white fuck-me pumps. I choke on my sandwich. Her idea of lunch is apparently different from mine. She spreads an invitation impossible to misunderstand. With a different outfit for every day on the river, ViviAnn has a plan in mind that doesn't include cat-fishing, canyon or wildlife appreciation. Her idea of nature in the wild is to lie spread-eagle naked on the front tube, inducing another servicing. After servicing she rolls over and spreads a buns-up invitation. Three days of ViviAnn on the river, I see her as a cheap flank-steak humped tender. Enough.

She won't lift a finger to help, won't rig or de-rig, won't cook, won't wash dishes. She lies around spread open, angry because I refuse to service her again. We stop talking, with days to go before takeout. The silence feels like lead. I can't believe I got myself into this. Eventually we get to the takeout, I drop ViviAnn off and drive back to the river, jump in with my Dr. Bronners and scrub. No more.

Lake Powell at daybreak is the chatoyancy of moonstones in emerald light, rippling with elongated fingertip breezes, sandstone cliffs immense and graceful behemoths, sculpted by eons of wind and rain moving incessantly to a perpetual drummer we can't hear as we scurry to keep up with something none of us comprehend.

White-tipped paddle blades plow harder every stroke, until a bow wave and a wake appear. I keep an eye out for the ferry, loaded cruisers, blitzed houseboat skippers, water-skiers, overpowered bass boats and wild wave scooters.

The *Orca*, my 18-foot red-and-gold fiberglass sea-kayak, slices through Lake Powell noiselessly, nose pointed at the cut between the islands where Bullfrog Bay and Hall's Creek Bay meet and the channel for Lost Eden Canyon begins.

The *Orca* is a dream when I slide in the cockpit, roll hips for balance, lean back, snap on the screaming yellow spray skirt, touch toes to rudder pedals, take hold of the paddle, shove off and dig in with the first wrist roll.

The afternoon wind picks up. A squall soaks me in minutes. It's a hot day, and the rain is welcome. The wind, on the other hand, turns the lake into a nasty short chop, and makes headway difficult. I struggle with the chop and wind until an expansive beach appears. I land the *Orca* softly, de-rig and make camp.

Art, Crime & Lithium

Everything I need is in the *Orca*. The Thermarest and sleeping bag are forward, behind the flotation bag in front of the rudder pedals; the day bag with sunscreen, sunglasses, maps, mini-binoculars, and lip-screen is rigged starboard. Fishing pole and sailing rig port: first-aid kit and tackle-box behind the seat, secured with shock-cord. The aft compartment, separated from the cockpit by a fiberglass bulkhead, contains tent, kitchen, fuel, groceries, snorkeling gear and waste disposal system.

I set up the tent to get out of the weather, hook up the white-gas MSR one–burner, and whip up a cup of Swiss Miss before cooking a dinner of noodles spiced with freeze-dried veggie soup. I have a brandy flask to nip on, but forgot cigars on this trip.

The wind dies before sunset. I build a small driftwood fire and rig for catfish. The fish aren't biting, but nips of brandy work their magic. I entertain visions and revisions until Orion rotates towards to dawn in the immense Utah sky, and the fire cools to embers in ash.

Coffee first thing. The MSR stove is tricky to light, but I have it down. I have crunchy granola for breakfast with raisins and nuts, handmade by the organic meisters at the co-op in Moab. Delicious, nutritious, excellent fuel, and easy to deal with when you're strapped for space. I'm the engine, captain, crew and life-support system, a Spartan and organic setup. The simplicity of this adventure appeals to me.

With adventure you need to remember that the more you carry, the more you have to deal with, the more you have to maintain. For me it's about the spirit of adventure, not the ease or comfort involved. What I require are essentials and faith in my ability to survive. I'm speaking on my own behalf. People consider me foolish. Thank you. We don't go to the same places. We don't have the same reasons. Leaves me room to move, and I need a lot.

The late Tom "Too Tall" Simmons, a legendary adventurer, surmised I shouldn't have a motorized vessel because of my short fuse and inability to deal with things mechanical. He was familiar with the story of how I heaved a brand-new Johnson 40-horsepower outboard into Lake Powell, after it refused to operate as advertised. It may not have been the best solution, but it was my solution at the time. I immediately had to deal with a whole different set of circumstances about how to get back to the marina, which was over 30 miles away. I had a backup, a 10-hp Honda, which ran slowly but dependably. The Johnson went down in waters close to 200 feet deep, fish habitat by now.

"Too Tall" told me I was a better engine than anything I had to work on mechanically, and the physical exertion would hopefully keep my temper under control. He was right. I'm a good engine.

Cool at daybreak on the lake; my tiny breakfast fire crackles, smokes, spreads pale blue smoldering driftwood incense on morning air.

I watch a spider spin a line between two sapling red-skinned tamarisks growing out of the sand, an acrobat among huge sandstone slabs. He makes his final pass, a dancer upside down, audacious, tiny with enormous attitude. He disappears in the boulders.

Show's over, coffee's done, *Orca*'s rigged, sun's over the canyon walls. The first few dozen paddle strokes work out the kinks. The kayak slices through the azure deep stillness of the lake with ease and purpose.

Occasional ravens cruise canyon walls, caw recognition, soar with an eye for opportunity.

Raven is the messenger between life and death. Raven stole the sun and gave it to mankind, stole fire so that it could be forever in the world, and originated death. Raven is a trickster.

For years I consider ravens a nuisance on expeditions. They come to steal if I walk a few yards away from camp, let alone leave camp and wander off. They teach me to keep my act together, tighten up. After awhile I leave scraps, crackers, and whatever I think they might enjoy. This is survival to them, not a vacation. They're excellent opportunists, beautiful creatures who survive in an unforgiving land. I feel we're kindred spirits, despite the fact I'm a blue-eyed white boy. I smile whenever I encounter ravens now, because it's like seeing iridescent black spirits of old friends.

Sun up, I reach into the *Orca* for my expedition hat. Serena got me to wear a wide-brimmed hat on expeditions. On a river trip down Labyrinth Canyon she convinces me to wear a white Resistol I bought in Durango years ago. I never could wear cowboy boots or hats. I'm an old beatnik, not a cowboy. I have the Resisitol on when the *Orca* flips in a cross current. The Resistol stays on and sags with river water, the exact same shape today.

I'm a couple miles down-lake, stroking steady, looking for a place to fish rigged with a Shad Rap deep-diver lure. Now it's a matter of finding structure, rocks, protrusions and constrictions.

This morning I hook into a couple largemouth, and take them along for a ride on a stringer. Close to noon, it's hot in the *Orca*. I stop for a skinny-dip after the long wall before Annie's Canyon. The cool swim stretches muscles. I duck into an alcove for a lunch of Stoned Wheat Thins, peanut butter and raspberry jam, a couple slices of cheese, and an apple.

Motor-heads are out in force, screaming around the lake. I have to be careful to keep the nose of the *Orca* into the wake-waves made by the bigger vessels. Most people are nice enough and wave, but there's always some jerk who wants to see how close he can come.

The wind picks up every afternoon. I put my head down, keep the paddle low and work into the bluster. When the attitude of the canyon changes around a bend, I take advantage of wind-shift and make time.

I'm ready to scream because of the wind and seemingly never-ending straight corridor I'm in. A minute canyon appears on the right, and I slip in. Immediately the wind is gone, there's blessed shade, an extraordinary camp, a soft sand beach, plenty of firewood, two fishy-looking pools and sandstone walls at least a hundred feet high streaked with desert varnish.

Exhausted, I'm asleep in seconds on the cool sand. When I wake, I wonder what it is I do in life that's so important to keep me from places like this. I'm hungry; it's time to de-rig, set up camp, fish before dinner.

Two more smallmouth are on the stringer in a matter of casts. I let them get acquainted with the two I caught earlier. Dispatched and filleted, they're shook in Uncle O's Yummy Fishfry Zango as heated extra-virgin olive oil smokes over camp-stove flames.

Fresh bass fillets with hand-squeezed lime perfect an evening begging for brandy after dinner. The small but lively fire entertains until time arrives to find Polaris amid the sparkles of Utah's desert sky.

Lake surface is mirror-slick, windless, chilly, with a raw smell to it. I slip out quietly before daybreak. Paddles slice into the water and drip droplets on the wrist-roll. Less than an hour out of camp, a rockfall below a sheer sandstone wall appears. I bounce the deep-diver lure off the wall into the cracks above the water.

Anxious, I react too quickly to the first strike. The bass shakes the hook and is gone in a flash of fins, tail, and a swirl of the lake's perfectly smooth face, disrupting reflections of sandstone walls streaked with black desert varnish. I cast a half dozen times more, but nothing doing. Away from the rockfall I let the deep-diver sink for thirty seconds and retrieve slowly, letting the lure drop every couple cranks on the reel.

A tug on the line, and I give it a second before I set the hook solid. At first I think I hooked a log or got caught between rocks, but when the line heads in the direction I came from there's no doubt. I ease up on the drag. The kayak moves without wind or paddling. Line comes off the reel steadily. I hang on until there's an opportunity to reel in.

I pump the rod and reel in. A dozen cranks on the handle, and the fish takes off again. The adrenaline rush has subsided, and it's all business now. The hook is set solid. This fish is mine.

He tows me to the middle of the channel. I keep the line from tangling on the kayak when he changes direction. I hang on, hooked into this fish towing me up and down the lake.

The walls of the canyon resound with my laughter, tears run down my cheeks, but I don't dare wipe them because I'm taking no chances with this fish. It's too early in the morning for anybody else to be out on the lake, so it doesn't matter there's a madman laughing hysterically, being towed to wherever this fish wants to take him.

The bass tires. I reel him in. He's beautiful - gleaming silver come up from darkness into light, I get him close to the kayak, slide my fingers into his gills, lift him out of the water and he's mine: best bass I ever caught in Lake Powell. I hook him onto the stringer, and we take off for the mouth of Escalante Canyon a mile south.

High on the slick rock there's a shade-blessed alcove under an overhang. I pull in the *Orca*, filet the striper and pack my kitchen up the scalding rock into shade, where I cook and eat fresh striper filets. There's no fresher way to eat fish. If I brought seaweed and *wasabe,* I could have fresh striper sushi.

Paddling up-canyon after lunch, I meet two women in whitewater kayaks who paddled down the Escalante. They have the touched look of people who speak with ravens. We share conversation, bobbing. I give them striper filets for their supper, and take my leave.

That night I share an alcove with a houseboat crew. They camp on one side of the alcove, and I make camp high up on a ledge fifty feet above the lake on the other side. If they make noise, I don't hear it. I find a moss-lined fern garden higher in the rocks. Water seeps silently out of the sandstone, feeding the spot. I sit for hours, not thinking, not hearing, just being.

At the first hint of turquoise and scarlet in the raw undefined desert sky, I'm on the water. The canyon narrows. I paddle as if in a dream, seeing a surreal quality to the morning light. The sharp crack of a beaver's tail on still waters wakes me out of my reverie. The color of the lake is murky; with silt, depth runs out. I turn back.

I hear ravens cawing and pull into an alcove. Three take to the sky. The alcove is shady under the arched overhang, with a narrow sand beach barely long enough to land, enough space for camp. I de-rig and revel in shade. In a narrow passageway behind a huge boulder I find a raven feather, a sun-faded red frisbee, a purple plastic sun-visor from Maui, and a cool and unopened battered old can of Coors.

The cool can of Coors I open immediately. I make a fire for company, a fresh pot of coffee with brandy, dig around, feel something sharp-edged, pull out a pottery shard with what I assume are Anasazi designs. The adrenaline rush chills out the alcohol. I dig on in earnest.

Anasazi pottery pieces are piling up when I feel something larger. My heart jumps. A blackened piece of moist wood surfaces, and I calm down. May as well bury all of this stuff and let it be the past. As I dig, I discover what looks like a spear point. Turns out to be a flawless awl, here for what I assume to be at least a thousand years.

Dusk settles on the desert. I run through possibilities of who lived here, how, why and when. Campfire smolders with the pungency of driftwood. The full moon rises and I still don't know if I dream this, or see it, or what. But I feel I'm chestnut-brown, with waist-length black hair, working on a flint weapon or tool in the moonlight, squatting over a fire smoldering and flickering on and off the walls of an alcove. There is no lake. I see myself looking up at the moon. My eyes are blue.

Next morning I bury that stuff where it belongs, pack my kayak and paddle my wild white-boy ass back where it belongs.

Spectacular in rain, without warning, the glow I experienced in Mexico reappears while I'm driving along the River Road to Moab, like I'm leaving my body. I'm convinced I can walk through the Colorado River, not walk on water but walk through water. The part of my brain that has a tentative but tenacious grip on reality guides me away from the river, along the highway to Serena's house. At Serena's I calm down.

Late fall I haul the trailer to Castleton, above Castle Valley in the shadow of the snow-dusted peaks of the La Sal Mountains, overlooking some of the most spectacular desert scenery in the world. A multitude of western films were shot here among the eroded pyramids, spires, turrets and vistas of the red rock desert above the shiny brown silt of the Colorado River. My river-rat buddy Bob Degles lets me park my trailer on his 90 acres if I keep an eye on the place when he's gone. I jump at the chance, hook up the trailer to electricity off the power pole, dig a shitter up the hill and haul water. Sam, a big old orange flat-headed alley cat, hangs around the trailer park. I take him along. Bob has Ojos, a blue-eyed white dog who comes with the place. We adopt each other. Sam takes no shit from the dog. Peace in the valley.

Mornings, Ojos the blue-eyed dog, Sam the orange alley cat, and I tread up the trail to the shitter and welcome the crack of dawn, anticipating light building under the stars since last sunset. I take my place on the throne and the three of us sit. Sam purrs in my lap and Ojos' tail thumps against the plywood.

Bob and I see each other when necessary, or when there's a fresh bottle of Jim Beam and obviously something to discuss. Silence soothes the situation, snow falls early this high. The first storms of winter cover the desert and insulate the silence. I go to town less often.

Serena has me make frames. I name her paintings. When I'm in town I stop to visit. I help her stage her shows. We travel the Southwest together developing markets for her work. We respect each other and don't get in each other's way, recognizing that people have to be who they are.

Serena and I comprehend that once sex subsides, the reality, quality and substance of relationship improves and grows, true with other strong women, friends with much more to offer than simply sexual encounters.

Inevitable

Their knock is inevitable, almost a relief. Three heavily armed men in dark blue jackets, with US MARSHAL emblazoned in yellow on the back, stand at my doorway. The one closest asks my name, then requests I step out. I'm under arrest. One plants the barrel of his big bore automatic firmly between my jaw and ear. The second has an automatic jammed in my ribs. The third cuffs and shackles me, wants me to relax, chains my wrists and ankles to another chain going around my waist: gleaming federal steel. He has a 12-gauge alley sweeper within reach. One marshal gets my wallet and medication, sticks them in my pocket. He leaves my passport and guns alone. I hop down the trail to their Bronco in my shiny federal hobbles. We're off for Salt Lake City and a blind broad with a set of scales in one hand and a sword in the other. I hope she isn't on the rag when I get there.

The Bronco pulls into prisoner processing, on the south side of the federal building on Market and Fourth in Salt Lake City. The building is squat, solid gray granite, with fancy bronze bars over the windows keeping some in, the remainder out. Carved granite eagles guard the entrances. Empires throughout history use the eagle as a symbol, including Romans and Nazis.

I do the jailhouse shuffle into the building along the marble basement corridor, answer questions the pretrial officer has for me. He asks how many times I've been arrested. Never. He asks about scars or tattoos. None. He scratches his head. The marshal runs my data through the international computer, expects me to be lying, returns amazed because I'm not.

The pre-trial officer asks me for the names of three people I want to use as references. Background check and verification complete, the driver marshal puts me through the chain-up routine on my way to the holding tank at the Salt Lake County Jail.

The processing clerk takes my wallet with $136 and my lithium. After a couple hours in the stench of the previous occupant's vomit in the holding cell, delousing and a shower are a privilege before the elevator ride down to the catacombs, where quarantine cells are located deep below the streets of Salt Lake City—where the sun doesn't shine, literally. Narrow corridors of quarantine cells with infinite bars confine wretched men. I find a bunk with my back to the wall and count 23 men in the cell, all of whom, according to their tales are innocent. I may be the only guilty party in the Salt Lake County Jail.

A few are in the ugly throes of heroin withdrawal, writhing around on the floor, vomiting, howling, pleading. The response they elicit from their fellow inmates is to shut the fuck up. Guards pay no attention, pass by without a glance. There's workout-mad bikers with elaborate tattoos, readers with dog eared libraries looking to trade, talkers with non-stop raps, listeners with ears full, blacks with ritual handshakes and territorial struts, Hispanics with macho bravado making like another stretch in the county can is a piece of cake, *Chuy*. Good stories happen here, whether they're fiction or fact. When your back's against the wall, you come up with some incredibly creative shit. There's an inherent sense of belonging once the bars slam shut, and most criminals—especially the innocent variety—try to make the best of it, more civilized than we're led to believe. Social strata exist, and you need to determine where you belong in this underworld scheme of things. If you fit, you survive. You have to watch out for the ones in uniforms for God & Truth & Right.

Art, Crime & Lithium

I don't want to have visions of bars and inmates turn to shimmering rainbows in the intestines of Salt Lake City. Stressing out to full capacity in quarantine cells won't do, and neither will a series of migraines. I request to see the doctor for the lithium confiscated on arrival. Three days go by. A guard takes me up the elevator to the sixth floor, where the criminally insane are kept. I'm locked in a room the size of a closet, with two Hispanics and a young man whose eyes dart around as if a cattle prod is goosing his cerebral cortex. His face and neck are covered in bleeding cuts, with toilet paper stuck to them. The Hispanics squat, I lean against a small counter. The cut man speeds into a story about how he shot it out with the cops but gave up when he ran out of ammunition. He's certain the doctor will let him out if he continues to pretend to be crazy. Soon as he's out, he's getting more ammunition and killing more cops. An hour of this, and I'm gauging the door to see if I can kick it out and get the fuck out of here. The door opens, my name is called, I'm led to the maximum-security section and told to make myself comfortable on the couch.

Immediately behind the couch is an internal two story holding facility, with a common area and cells. All the bull goose looney-tunes, the heavyweight psychopaths, sociopaths and criminally insane are kept in the playpen directly behind me, behind two-inch-thick hopefully-indestructible glass, a very tweaky zoo. There's an inmate with half his head shaved clawing on the glass, licking his contorted face. I'm fascinated at first, but relieved when my name is called. The doctor and I have a pleasant chat about the state of politics in Eastern Europe. I never have been quite as polite with anybody as I am with the doctor. He promises I'll get my medication.

I do the jailhouse shuffle into court. The magistrate reads the indictment, repeating 40,000 pounds of marijuana at least twenty times. It rings out in the dark wood paneled walls of federal righteousness, driving me further down in my seat at the defendant's table in chains, without a lawyer, alone.

The prosecutor gleefully reads the guidelines, ten years to life and an exorbitant fine. I'm almost parallel with the floor now, my nose barely above the level of the table. At the prosecutor's behest the magistrate wants to know if I will plead guilty right now and let the court determine my sentence. I politely decline.

One of the marshals who arrested me suggests the prosecutor is mistaken and the guidelines for my alleged transgression happened long enough ago to qualify under the old guidelines, zero to ten and a $250,000 fine. Silence in the courtroom, I turn to face my benefactor. He's smiling.

The magistrate releases me on my own recognizance. The front desk medic gives me my lithium. I sign the papers, check out of the halfway house with a date at the 10th US District Court in San Diego in three days.

My father sends $500 to Western Union in Moab. I call Robin Luketina. He provides the number of Federal Defenders in San Diego, a non-profit corporation representing indigent persons accused of federal criminal offenses, the best free federal defense outfit in the country. Luketina tells me to get there first just in case there's a line.

From a phone booth in Jacumba I call Federal Defenders and arrange a meeting with a lawyer, Knut Johnson, in the morning: a young man in a gray suit, slight build, medium height. We discuss the case. He excuses himself for a minute and leaves the office. The corner view from the eleventh floor encompasses the downtown. A framed quote on his wall intrigues me.

"You see, I knew how to fight early. I learned that. More important is to learn what to fight for. I was fighting for my family, for my future; I was fighting for, generally, the black race, for men who had given up their lives. You got to know what you're fighting for. Then the fight is much easier." Archie Moore, 1989.

Mr. Johnson wants to be my lawyer. I want him to be my lawyer.

We go to the first of many hearings over the next year and a half. The prosecution has no idea of who I am or why I'm here, caught with their pants down. They're better prepared at the next hearing. I live in my trailer in Utah, and drive to San Diego every few months. After a year and a half, the judge won't grant an evidentiary hearing to determine if the statute of limitation expired, claiming it would be tantamount to holding a trial. I'm all for going to trial if it means I get off cleanly via statute of limitation expiration or whatever. The lawyer cautions me it's an iffy proposition, you can never tell what's going to happen in trial. He tells me over thirty scammers I worked with have snitched me off, and the prosecution will parade all thirty before the jury. If I go with a jury trial there's a good chance I may spend 20 years behind bars.

The prosecutor offers a deal: I talk to the DEA and tell them everything I know and get zero to four, a felony conviction, probation and a probable two years.

I tell Mr. Johnson to tell the prosecutor to stick it up his ass. I lost my dog, home, mind and wife. The only thing I have worth anything is my self-respect, which is not negotiable. Knut Johnson relays my message.

Two weeks later the prosecutor proposes another deal. I admit to using a telephone in the commission of a felony, get a felony conviction, two years, eighteen months suspended, three years probation, a $50 fine and don't have to say anything to the DEA. The lawyer explains that it's my decision, but six months in a halfway house is one hell of a lot better than ten to twenty in the joint. He whittles a month and a half off my sentence.

My last appearance in court is for sentencing. I stand before the judge and tell him I called the U.S. Weather Bureau about conditions concerning a scam, a total fabrication. I shake hands with Knut Johnson and thank him in the elevator, on my way to probation six blocks away.

The prosecutor gets one more conviction, my lawyer negotiates a successful deal, and I pay the price and keep what's left. The probation office assigns me to the halfway house in Salt Lake City, but not until December. They warn me about having firearms and anything to do with known felons. I fill out the paperwork, act appropriately humble and leave.

December, I'm registered at Utah Valley State College, courtesy of the Utah rehabilitation service. I take Spanish, welding and sculpture fabrication. The federal government pays for my room and board at the halfway house. I drive my old Ford back and forth to school, and contribute urine to the government's peace of mind on a daily basis with an attendant watching. My stay at the halfway house is tolerable. Evenings, a white-collar felon and I match wits watching *Jeopardy*. During the day, I design and weld metal mobiles and stabiles. Mid-May, snows on the Wasatch Range are melting. School is out. My halfway experience is over and with it my criminal career.

I conclude feds aren't all bad, based on the reasonable attitude of probation officers, who work at easing an ex-con back into the mainstream doing what he wants to do as long as it's legal. I have regard for people in the system with understanding, respect, and a sense of humor.

You Got To Have Art

Driving daily to and from Utah Valley State College and the halfway house out by the airport, I meet Dave Erickson, owner of Gallery 56 in downtown Salt Lake, when I walk in off the street to check out the art. We get acquainted over a series of conversations. I tell him who I am and what I'm doing. Dave suggests I read Wallace Stegner's *Big Rock Candy Mountain*. Then he asks if I'll teach mobile-making to a Boy Scout troop he scoutmasters. His son is in the troop. I teach the class. The boys have a good time. A part owner of the architectural ornamentation plant who attends the class asks if I want a job.

Claudia Hoffman's interest and support initially gave me the faith I needed to take the next step and do shows. I did a show of mobiles in 1985 at the Winterland Gallery in Telluride, and at the Finn-Town Gallery in 1987, also in Telluride, at the Guliano Gallery in Santa Fe in 1991, at the Four Directions Gallery with Serena Supplee in Steamboat Springs in 1992, at the Dan O'Laurie Museum in Moab in 1993, at the Salt Lake Art Center in 1993, at Gallery 56 in Salt Lake City in 1993, at ArtSpace in Bay City, OR, in 1994, at the Hoffman Residence in Telluride in 1994, at the Eaglewood Gallery in Norwood, CO, in 1995, at the Riccardi Gallery in Astoria, OR, in 1995, at ArtSpace in Bay City, OR, in 2002, at the Triangle Square Gallery in Port Orford, OR in 2006, 2010 and 2012.

No matter what else I do, I always make mobiles: a source of identity and emotional security.

Word in the Moab artist community is that male artists won't teach classes because the kids frighten them. I teach a class to middle-school kids. We have a great time and build a mobile out of foam parts and wire I prepare. I tell the kids they can do nothing wrong, and cut them loose. I don't tell them what to do, but guide them when they have questions.

I teach workshops in mobiles in the Grand County School District in Moab, at the Ahhaa School of Art in Telluride, and Colorado Mountain College in Steamboat Springs.

The first mobile I made was in high school shop class, a sheet copper bird within a bird. At the Insley house in Portland, I made photo mobiles gluing two photographs together, cutting them into shapes and suspending them off wire swing arms. In Garmisch–Partenkirchen I made a free-form kinetic sculpture out of wire, strings and marbles attached to a wall like a US map. In Isla Mujeres, Yucatan, my mobiles were made out of limpet shells and seagull feathers sewn loosely together. In the Galapagos I made mobiles from broken beer bottle glass and wire clothes hangers. At the house we built from scrap on Whiskey Slide Road in Mountain Ranch, I hung a hefty piece of incense-cedar on chain off an oak limb. On the Sun Mountain platform in the sugar pines, I built circular glass mobiles. I built an elephant mobile that hung over Serena Allen's crib on Sun Mountain. At Useless Beach on Whidbey Island I built a driftwood mobile with the help of a guy I met in a bar in Seattle. I've built hundreds of mobiles, maybe more, all over the world.

Before I could commit to teaching a mobile class at Colorado Mountain College in Steamboat Springs, CO, I had to pitch my probation officer to get permission because I was going to cross state lines. She was an understanding woman. We didn't bullshit each other.

I load a large steel mobile in my pickup and drive to Steamboat, teach the class and present the college with

Art, Crime & Lithium

the mobile, which they graciously accept. It hangs in the entrance hall of their admissions building. 40 years designing and building mobiles, I earn respect as an artist with more to offer than mere desperation and bravado.

Towing the Silver Streak from Moab to a trailer park off Interstate 15 in Sandy, UT, we make the grade up Soldier Summit and keep the speed in check on the down side. In the morning I drive high up the west slope of the valley, to my new job at the architectural ornamentation plant. I learn to weld, grind, polish and apply patina to metals. The job is interesting and I'm involved. There is a bank on the way home where I open an account and apply for a credit card, my first mistake as a reborn citizen. I order telephone service.

Ray L'Hommedieu runs a fledgling stainless welding and fabrication shop in Tillamook, OR. He flies to Salt Lake from Portland, on a cheap weekend round trip fare. I pick him up. We rig a canoe and kayak to the pickup, and drive to Flaming Gorge National Recreation Area—a spectacular reservoir between southern Wyoming and the northeast corner of Utah—where we camp, cook, paddle and talk. Ray is involved and perplexed with a high-maintenance pixie looker, who sports an ass molded in heaven and mangles his psyche because she can. My advice is to dump her. I can see he isn't going to follow my advice.

Welding brass gizmos at the architectural ornamentation plant, the foreman takes the piece I'm welding and welds it in a fraction of the time. I offer, since he's so fast, why doesn't he finish the job and find something else for me to do. He fires me. I close out my locker, clean up, last check ready at the office. A meeting with my probation officer, and I drive to Tillamook.

Despite his predilection for misguided relationships based on cuteness, Ray is as close to a brother as I have in this life: truthful, smart, with a sense of humor, abilities in a variety of fields, polite and generous to a fault, hard-working and willing. A loveable character, obsessed by Christmas with trimmings, Ray frustrated occasionally launches tools as he screams "pig fucking whore," a good time to be out of his way. It gives Ray completeness beyond the smarmy, too cute veneer.

We go to work in the garage of a BP gas station, across Hwy 101 from the Tillamook cheese plant, fabricating for dairy farmers, repairing stainless at the creamery, working on milk tankers. Ray patiently teaches me stainless welding with argon gas basics. We share a rental trailer in an RV park in Beaver, a turn on Hwy 101 south of Tillamook.

Early one Friday, we quit work to get my trailer and drive it back before work Monday morning. Twenty hours later we pull in to the trailer park in Sandy, Utah, sleep a couple of hours, hook up the trailer and drive back with a stop for lunch in Ogden, at a Mexican joint across the tracks with bullet holes in the floor and portraits of Pancho Villa and JFK on the walls.

When flashing lights come on, I pull over for the state trooper on Interstate 84 coming into Portland, hand him my license and registration wondering why he pulls me over since I obviously wasn't speeding. He questions five-year-old expired Texas plates on the trailer. I explain the trailer has been safely parked, and I'm delivering it to Tillamook where I have a job. He asks if I intended to live in the Silver Streak. Yes. In that case, he says, be careful and good luck.

The Silver Streak finds a home at the Trask River Trailer Park, across Hwy 101 from the Air Museum, famous for a collection of WWII fighters housed in the biggest wood building in the world: a Quonset built for dirigibles defending the coast.

Tillamook is famous for cheese. Cheese requires copious amounts of milk, which requires substantial herds. The herds create by-product, which travels seven stomachs until ejected from bovine sphincters. That much cow-shit creates an odor that coastal fog and rain won't

Art, Crime & Lithium

allow to escape into the ethers. It stinks, thick, at 5 a.m. when I bolt from the Silver Streak to the newspaper kiosk and back to get my morning paper, covering my nose and mouth. My neighbor's light is on that time of morning. She invites me for coffee.

Marian Jones is an 85-year old straight-talking widow who drives a metallic blue Chevelle, bought new in 1966. Marian's passion is oil painting. She does it with enthusiasm and abandon. We discuss everything, no holds barred. She minces no words, tells it like it is and damn the consequences, my kind of girl. Occasionally Marian invites me to breakfast or lunch. Dressed up, hair done, Marian makes me buckle up, then puts the Chevelle's pedal to the metal; she likes to get where she's going fast. Time spent with Marian is always an adventure. When I admire her paintings, she gives me one—of fantasy dogs in a field. Marian died a few years ago. Her painting hangs in our kitchen.

Cape Meares south is rocks and driftwood, caves at low tide washed in surf, headlands, cliffs, and the navel of the universe—where a circular rock fragment fractured off the base cliff millennia ago—and good perch for fishing off the rocks. Head north to miles of clear beach, to the breakwater and the trail through the scrub pines, and the horse trail back to the parking lot. I walk the beach at Cape Meares, often leaving work on slow days.

Ray has a collection of scrap stainless steel behind the shop, which he sells for fuel money in Portland. I find the pieces fascinating and irresistible for mobiles. He isn't thrilled about my using his scrap but is supportive of my creativity.

Ray introduces me to Trisha and Craig Kauffman, artists and entrepreneurs who run ArtSpace, a restaurant and gallery in Bay City just north of Tillamook. Trisha had a vision, took $500—all the money she and Craig had at the time—and put a down payment on the building that became ArtSpace. She opened a restaurant and catering service. Craig did building and maintenance. They have three children who roam the building at will, doing what boisterous kids do.

John Aadland of Sun Mountain is in Waldport, OR, on the Pacific coast south of Tillamook, repairing and restoring Oregon's historic coastal bridges. I last see John in Tucson, when he visits on his way to a concrete construction job in New Mexico, in a $500 Larry Allen Ranchero find with Dawn Marie, his wife to be and inevitable bane of his existence. John offers me a job, but I'm selling cars at the time and politely decline.

John buys a house and ten acres outside Waldport, inherits Dani and Kyle from Dawn Marie's previous marriage. They have Boston Terriers, chickens, horses and a garden. John works to support it; classic.

A graduate of the California College of Arts and Crafts in Oakland, John is comfortable expressing his artistic vision doing cathodic repairs on the Yaquina Bay Bridge, in Newport, for a company his brother owns. I know John's a player, and approach him with a sculptural project based on a mother and two children looking out to sea, waiting for husband and father to come home. I do drawings. We meet early one Saturday under the south end of the Yaquina Bay Bridge, on a weekend when the crew is gone.

Three pieces of industrial 16" diameter, ½" thick pipe selected, one 12 feet long and two 6 feet, we go to work. I straddle the 12-foot long pipe and draw designs with chalk. John follows with an industrial oxy-acetylene torch. I smooth the cuts with a grinder while John brings a diesel stick-welder to our triangulated pipe sculpture. John is a crackerjack welder. He welds the three pieces, weighing approximately a ton. The mother's face is negative space, Modigliani-Picasso with negative-space breasts and vagina, children with incomplete features and minimal indications of sexuality. We rig and lift our handiwork with a forklift onto a trailer, and I'm on the road to Tillamook. The pipe sculpture stands outside ArtSpace for years. Now it's the Fisherman's Memorial in Bandon Harbor, where it has stood for more than ten years looking out on the North Pacific. A brass plaque commemorates John's fabrication and my design. Years after the fact, John informs his brother Ted of his donation to the Fishermen's Memorial.

Trisha and Craig let me use an abandoned—overgrown with blackberry brambles in true Oregon fashion—pig barn for a studio, which works well once I clear the brambles and hang clear plastic sheeting inside to keep rain from drowning the space. I spend day after day in the barn in a creative binge, cranking out piece after piece.

Shelly Bowe is partners with Trisha in the ArtSpace restaurant, a magician in the kitchen, an inquisitive, lusty enthusiast. Shelly has a fulltime boyfriend the afternoon she comes knocking on my trailer door. Polite conversation, a couple glasses of wine and no penetration, says Shelly, after all, she is in a relationship and there are things a girl might not do.

Trisha proposes I do a show. In February 1994 we do The Metaphysical Catfish Café show: mobiles. The concept of the Metaphysical Catfish Café is born on a river trip down Labyrinth Canyon in 1992 with Mike Boren. Recuperating from hip replacement surgery, I'm devoted to the idea that water heals. I get in touch with Mike in Abilene, and on April Fools Day we launch.

The concept of déjà vu in apparently unfamiliar places is born. We all experience the feeling of familiarity in situations we know to be the opposite, like walking into an obscure restaurant you know you're never been in, which looks familiar all the same.

Bolstered with fresh confidence from the metaphysical Catfish Café' show, I call Claudia Hoffman in Colorado. She suggests we do a show in October at the

Hoffman Residence on Wilson Mesa, a high-dollar neighborhood where Claudia holds sway as the art guru and leader of the pack for the more-money-than-sense crew, mostly her neighbors. Wilson Mesa by then is dotted with monuments to money.

    I go to work in the pig barn. The show is scheduled for October 9, 1994. First I have to get permission to travel to Colorado from my probation officer, which requires one more trip to the federal building in Portland. I take the change out of my pockets, take off my belt, and still the metal detector sounds alarm. The retired FBI types go over me with a detector wand, and settle on my hip, like I'd told them before we got started. My probation officer issues paperwork, and I'm free to cross specific state lines legally.

    Serena calls. Ray Perera is dead, killed on his motorcycle helping a woman in trouble, at Arches National Monument. Serena and Ray are an item at the time. On a Sunday ride on Ray's blue FLH, they encounter a distraught, battered woman scared to death her boyfriend is going to kill her. Ray leaves Serena with the woman and takes off for the headquarters building, looking for an armed ranger to take control of the situation. On his way back to Serena and the frightened woman, Ray is hit head-on by a pickup in the wrong lane, dead instantly, September 4, 1994.

    I book a flight. Serena picks me up at the Moab airport.

    Ray Perera's memorial is held at the Lion's Park on the north end of Moab, along the Colorado River. The Baron's Motorcycle Club from Salt Lake City rides down en masse, representing studded black leather, tattoos, chrome and Harley Davidson. Ray wore brown leathers, no tattoos, rode Harleys and Indians. The Barons are Ray's friends, as are Moab schoolteachers, river-runners, oil field workers, artists, mechanics, truck drivers, real estate brokers, bartenders, cooks and waitresses.

Art, Crime & Lithium

Caesar, the Baron's honcho and Ray's friend, rides Ray's red 1950 Indian Chief with Ray's ashes lashed to the handlebars to the Lion's Park. The day is sunny, warm, balmy. *Born To Be Wild* plays over and over the crowd of 200 people gathered to honor Ray Perera's memory. A bottle of Jack Daniels sits on the Indian's tan leather seat. One after another, anyone with a Ray story steps up, takes a hit of the Jack Daniels and has their say.

I tip the bottle, have a swig and this is what I have to say:

> a black cast iron motorcycle toy
> the tranny in my pickup
> the seat cover I traded him
> a silver skull with one ruby eye for
> the night he kept me from killing
> the dickhead doorman at the Rio
> days and nights we spent together
> medicated drunk recuperating after surgery
> old cicles we chased around the countryside
> and never found
> nights we'd walk into a bar and hear
> the murmur scoot out the back door
> the time he rode his Harley into Woody's
> right through the front door like a gent
> his helping hands
> his solid sweet and gentle heart
> his love of freedom
> his elegance and style
> his artist's touch around a bike
> the memory of his smile
> is what's remains
> of my friend Ray Perera

The bottle is empty, last story told. Wind picks up suddenly, swirling, dust and grit in the air. Raindrops pelt the red Indian. Sky darkens as a sudden storm clears memorial participants out of the park, scurrying for cars, motorcycles and cover. In a few minutes the park empties.

Minutes later the sun comes out and a rainbow appears over the park, over the red motorcycle with a tan plastic box lashed to the handlebars.

Serena gives me a ride to the airport.

Claudia Hoffman and Bonnie Erie, two looker artsy women, are in charge of arrangements for the show. Bonnie is Claudia's pal, and runs an interior design shop in Telluride. Between the two of them, they send out invitations to local art patrons in their social circle.

Monica Callard caters. Hers is the best delicatessen in Telluride, famous for its goodies. Many people attend for Monica's food.

October 9 is a clear, warm, spectacular, Indian Summer day. Both Claudia and David entreat me not to drink until the show is over. I enjoy a reputation for getting somewhat out of hand. It's the "Oleh Rule." As long as I'm not hammered I can talk with clients. Over the line, I'm useless because I tell them whatever comes into my head, which usually scares them. Honoring David and Claudia's request is no problem.

Claudia's is the best show I've ever had. I borrow her phone. Seated in a folding chair on the lawn at 11,000 feet in the Rockies, I call my mother in Philadelphia and explain to her in Ukrainian what is happening.

Thanks to Claudia's good graces, I make over $7,000 that afternoon. I'm convinced people don't necessarily buy my work because they think it's good. They buy my work because Claudia tells them it's good.

A Family

A tall woman in a dark blue dress, reminiscent of Ingrid Bergman, has my attention all afternoon. Tina arrives with my friend Thomas Zoline. He introduces us. Every time she and I are in proximity of each other, it's electric. She likes one of my mobiles, red and black enamel over stainless. We make a trade. She can't afford it, but can work it off over time. Something special is happening. She gives me her phone number on a matchbook cover, with a date for dinner.

The Ice House is a classy French restaurant in Telluride. With seven grand in my pocket, I can afford good food and better wine. I add poetry. We rock the truck in the Ice House parking lot, then drive the short distance to her apartment. By morning my knees are raw, and the world is changed. Something hot is going on.

On return to Oregon, I give my Silver Streak to John Aadland, pack everything I own and an iced cooler—filled with salmon, fresh and smoked, Dungeness crab and shrimp—in my pickup and drive back to Colorado. Tina goes to see her black trucker boyfriend for a goodbye screw. We're well-matched sluts in hot blossom stages of what appears to be love.

East of Bedrock a forked buck leaps from a berm above the road, shatters my windshield and shits all over the cab as he expires. I'm doing 80 mph, pull over, wrestle the carcass out of the truck and lay him in the grasses along the road. Then I kick out the windshield and drive the last leg to Telluride.

Cooler balanced on my shoulder, I climb three

flights to Tina's apartment and knock. Remy, her youngest, opens the door. I show him the contents of the cooler. The epicure of the family, despite being eleven years old, Remy helps me dump the seafood extravaganza in the bathtub. We arrange by species, Oregon coast bounty arranged on ice in a bathtub high in the Uncompaghres. The kid approves.

Bobby, Remy's older brother, joins in when we light cigars and crack open beers. I tell Tina family is what's missing in my life. She has three kids. Sasadi, the oldest, is away in college on the east coast. I have none. This makes sense. The boys wear ultra-wide pants fastened down past their asses so their boxers show, change the color of their hair on a whim, listen to rap music morning to night: middle-class white kids buying into ghetto black woes under the wings of the angel of art. The boys smoke Indica behind closed doors, volume up. Who knows what they're into in the streets of Telluride, where Halloween is a way of life and everything having to do with drugs is available.

Tina and I are in the throes of a budding relationship, when every touch is hot and a fresh future promising. We do it in the road, on the truck seat, on the bed under the canopy on our way home when we can't wait another second. I take exception to the stack of dirty pots, pans and dishes in her kitchen, some of which have green mold growing.

Christmas, Sasadi comes home from Wesleyan. I sense attitude, like I'm another slut-magnet her mother brought home to service orgasm producing plumbing and nerve bundles. I offer a mobile, thinking art might do the trick but am accused of bribery. She's convinced all men are scum. Her father molested her when she was eleven years old.

Remy doesn't take to minimized mother's affections well, parks himself on the other side of his mother's closed door listening when she and I engage in sex.

Art, Crime & Lithium

Annoying, never-ending rap music emanates from the boys' room. I can see this isn't going to work. I rent a house in Norwood, a community of 450 people surrounded by working ranches, 35 miles away but about as far from Telluride as a person can get on the planet. I move out three days before Christmas.

Tina isn't pleased, but at least I'm not listening to incessant rap and wondering about the mold on the dirty dishes, quiet in my redneck rental, dishes washed and stacked.

Peter Spencer, former Telluride mayor and cybermaster, revives *The Norwood Post*, doing well enough for advertising to pay bills and publish the paper. He does the reporting, writing, photography, editorials, commentaries, composition, pagination, editing and distributing, with the help of Gwen Davidson who checks spelling, does billing and answers the phone.

The opportunity is obvious to the right man at the right place at the right time again.

I report on county commissioners, county sheriff, town board, water board, do all the photography, write a commentary and a column and go any place after a story. We go after the Norwood mayor and town board, the exact same people who are on the water board. The mayor wants to turn the town into a doormat for urban expectations. She owns the local liquor store. There's a woman realtor on the board, representing realty interests and not local ranchers and townspeople. Public board meetings are often contentious. The mayor often declares meetings private in spite of the Colorado Sunshine statutes.

June Estep, Norwood's mayor, is out of hand with her own narrow vision of success measured in dollars in her pocket. Town and water boards are rubber stamp outrages of Estep's will. San Miguel's West End good 'ol boy way of doing things, like neighbor help neighbor, are an affront to the mayor's sense of mercenary propriety.

O.Z. Lysiak

I recognize a situation ripe for clarification, transparency, and go after the mayor with a vengeance, cultivating controversy. Circulation goes up, talk over the backyard fence and telephone increases. Normally apathetic Norwood is abuzz with news. Locals look forward to our next issue.

Peter and I work well together. He paginates the paper, edits the issue and writes a commentary. We win Colorado Press Association awards the first year, Peter for a column and me for a feature. If he changes even a comma of what I write, I raise hell. Peter talks me into going outside, and lets me rant until I run out of steam, when he assures me he'll put everything back the way it was, which he doesn't, but by then it's too late—and he usually is right.

Together we make a real newspaper dealing with real issues, crusading, firm in the belief that you can fight city hall. Whether you win or not is moot. When the recall election takes place in Norwood, the mayor and her board are ousted by a two to one vote.

A one-bedroom house on Cedar Street comes up for sale in Norwood. Peter juggles the numbers of my earnings so I can buy it. He wants me saddled with a mortgage so I'll stay. I buy the house.

We discuss acquiring other small newspapers in the area for our own chain, and a radio station. It all sounds too good to be true—and, like things that do, it is.

Tina moves herself and her two boys to Norwood, rents a second-storey place in the middle of town, gets a job as a waitress at Karen's—a Main Street eatery where the best thing is gossip, served hot, juicy, and as spicy as you can stand. The girls at Karen's know everything about everybody, all the dirt that's fit to serve.

Tina never has been dumped before, is outraged, bent on revenge, and wants to move into my one-bedroom house with her kids. I say no. She eggs my house and

Art, Crime & Lithium

tells me I'm not the best fuck of her life. She isn't the best fuck of my life, either. The best thing about fucks is that there's always another one, and the last one is probably the best because it's closest to the truth.

Remy and Bobby hitchhike to school in Telluride. They take showers at my house. I take Bobby fishing at Miramonte Reservoir. When the wind blows hard and fishing's impossible, we're off on a back-roads expedition blowing holes in road signs with my black-powder .44 Blackhawk.

Bobby is an out of bounds snowboarder, a shredder with intimations of greatness. The big boys take Bobby snowboarding to places nobody in their right mind goes. He thrives on it, comes home with blacked eyes from slamming his knees into his face on extreme landings. One of those landings—off a rock cliff at speed—gets him a ride to the hospital, a knee operation, a lengthy scar, and turns Bobby around. He gets interested in film and video. Dean Rolley of the Telluride Community TV gives Bobby opportunity to work in the medium. Bobby applies to Eastern Washington State University.

When Remy goes to ski-camp at Whistler Mountain, BC, I give him a hundred-dollar bill for incidentals. He sends me a really cool postcard with naked babe skiers waiting in the lift line. Progress. I keep that postcard.

The lights are on at the Norwood Post offices before daybreak when I open the door to find Peter, head-down on his folded arms in front of the editing monitor. Small screens reflect off his shiny baldness. When he groans I figure he's alive. He requests coffee with three sugars. I get it for him. He invokes a blessing of his Jewish forefathers on me for this small favor. After some sips of fresh over-sugared coffee, he relates his adventures in Telluride the night before.

After finishing an interminably long county commissioners meeting off with a drink at the Sheridan bar, Peter encounters a feisty 23-year-old blonde on the stool next to his. She immediately perks up when Peter mentions he has blow, and is she interested? She is. Peter gets a room and a bottle of Perrier-Jouet. She is a good-looking little coke whore, cute and pliable. They do bumps in the elevator.

She sucks him off. He sucks her off, repeated penetration inevitable. Sweaty, they fall asleep. She wakes up hot for a cruise up the Hershey Highway with the champagne bottle. Peter, being a gentleman, obliges her. Back to sleep. She wakes up thirsty, takes a hit on the Perrier-Jouet and exclaims—"THIS TASTES LIKE SHIT!!"

Peter can't stop laughing. She takes offense, and leaves in a huff. He gets dressed and comes to work, but passes out in front of the monitor. This is why I love Peter. We understand each other.

Meanwhile, the paper is going broke. Peter owes big bucks to creditors in Telluride. He puts an ad in the *New York Times* offering the paper for sale.

Robert Chickering, a symphony bass player from Maine, sees the ad and buys the *Norwood Post* despite being unable to write a lead, load film in a camera, or have an inkling of what a real community paper is about—a fat boy without a clue.

Peter's answer, when I'm in his face about why he didn't tell me, is he figured I'd quit. A few weeks with Chickering and I'm in his face. Chickering calls Bill Masters, our sheriff, to complain I'm threatening him. Masters laughs and tells him to relax. I quit to write an adventure novel. I don't know how I'm going to pay the bills, or mortgage, or buy groceries, but I'm finally writing a book.

I lock the doors and write 8 to 10 hours a day, dream descriptions and dialogue, live on potato pancakes. Tina pounds on my locked door, but I won't let her in.

Claudia shows up. I let her in and explain what I'm doing. She gives me $1,000 a month until I finish the book. We dance around each other, get close, but never do the horizontal rumba. Claudia is proud we skip the dirty deed, friends.

Done writing and editing a thinly disguised novel based on my smuggling experiences, I think about finding an agent and publisher. Cliff Ward, a fishing pal, adventurer, and worldwide oil explorer, mentions he can get me an industrial job doing oil research off the coast of Nigeria, makes the call to a supervisor pal of his with LCT (Lafehr, Chan Technologies) in Houston who wants to know if I have a valid passport. Next day I fly out of Grand Junction to Denver, to Minneapolis, to Amsterdam, and a ten-hour layover where I meet my Canadian partner before boarding for Accra, Ghana.

A sixteen-year-old girl, coming home from visiting her grandmother in Sweden, sits next to me. She lives in Accra. I ask her how she likes living in Ghana. No other place on earth she'd rather be. The kid loves Africa enough to hate leaving, even for a visit with her grandma.

The flight is filled with Russian crewmen on their way to a changeover on the R/V *Mezen*, the ship I'm destined for. We land in Accra. The ship's agent hustles us though customs. Humidity, darkness, a near-full moon, and beggars greet us emerging, jet–lagged, from the terminal. Greeted by the ship's agent, we're hustled into vans and driven to the port and resort town of Tema on the Atlantic coast. The port looks like a black-and-white '30s movie, lights and shadows softened by intense humidity, with a rusting tramp steamer as one of the primary players. We each have a cabin to ourselves. The first thing I notice about the *Mezen* is the smell. She was a fisher in Russia before being turned into a research vessel. My Canadian partner and I toss our gear in our cabins and venture into the night.

A taxi owned and operated by local Joe, who looks enough like Joe Frazier to be his double, takes us to an outdoor disco the Russian sailors of the *Mezen* frequent. The Canadian kid and I enter the roofless enclosure through a doorway with no door, into bright colored light strings, disco music, couples dancing. I'm tired, jet-lagged, but game. A tall, skinny, young, pretty, African girl latches on to me. A Nigerian, she later displays buns of glistening ebony, incredible. I'm too tired to play. She's patient enough to wait until morning.

The cabins each come with an allotment of roaches. Killing roaches is useless, more immediately take their place. Trips to upper deck toilets are an olfactory experience beyond belief. Showers require sneakers or flops at the very least, with a nose-clip of some fashion to endure the stench.

Mezen expedition funds are distributed for fuel, food supplies, docking fees, etc. The captain takes his share. The party chief, who outranks the captain, takes his cut, and so on down the line. After the kitchen crew—who are, it is rumored, Moscow mafia—there is precious little left for food supplies, so what we get is a thin white borscht, Russian style, and hardened pucks that pass for burgers. We live on tea, toast and marmalade.

Warned about conditions on the *Mezen*, I fill a satchel with pogey bait – Snickers, Milky Ways, Three Musketeers. Another satchel I fill with books. The *Mezen* cruise is one of the best reading journeys of my life—in my bunk, porthole open, getting what little breeze there is, a Snickers on the bed next to me, the bunk light on and my pet roaches balancing back and forth on the clothesline.

The work isn't hard, but is tedious. I babysit a computer 12 hours a day, and extract data. The Canadian kid and I rig a gravity meter in the bottom of the boat, as close to the ocean as we can get it, a magnetometer behind the boat. A hefty cable on a wooden spool bolted to the ship's stern keeps the magnetometer from running off. We measure gravity density and magnetic intensity to enhance seismic data.

Only the navigation shack has air conditioning so the ship's computer system won't cook. Russian

Art, Crime & Lithium

technicians on board are capable, but underpaid by our standards. I make $150 a day for babysitting a computer I can barely work. The Canadian kid, the first operator, knows how to work the gravity computer like a first violin in a symphony orchestra knows his Stradivarius. What the Russians lack is the ability to speak English.

I set up English lessons in the navigation shack and compose English-friendly resumes for the party chief, a Ukrainian from Kiev, and the chief navigator, a Russian from Murmansk. Viktor Mironenko, the party chief, treats the Russians aboard with derision and disdain. He and I have several conversations about what we don't know about the other's situations. It is interesting talking with a Ukrainian raised in Soviet Ukraine, now loose in the "free world."

Sergei Kharitonov speaks the best English. His mother is an English teacher in Gelandzek, Russia. I give him *All The Pretty Little Horses,* by Cormac McCarthy.

All my students are curious about cursing in vernacular English, surprised when I explain "motherfucker" is pronounced as one word with no pause, despite reverence for motherhood.

An engineer from Rostov-on-Don discovers I'm Ukrainian from America, decides to repatriate me by getting me drunk. Alcohol is forbidden on board, but for people from Russia, rules are meaningless. The third-rate vodka, which the engineer mixes with Coke, fails to lure me and he sadly decides I'm Polish.

When the *Mezen* stops for refueling or repairs, the fishermen on board immediately break out the fishing gear. I'm invited. We catch mostly mackerel.

The conditions on board are grim. The people aren't. They have a sense of humor, happy to be alive, with a job, a place to come home to, someone to love; they make do with almost nothing, veterans of communism.

Two Nigerian naval officers come on board ostensibly to assure no Nigerian regulations are broken.

They accumulate as much as possible before debarking: chocolate, marmalade, canned hams, and finally their "envelope" to ensure smooth sailing for the *Mezen* in Nigerian waters, business as usual in Africa.

Six weeks gathering data, and we dock in Tema. The Canadian kid and I prep the gravitometer for shipping. The magnetometer cable is a sweaty all-night wresting match. A crane lifts our equipment and deposits it on the dock. The ship's agent is scheduled to arrive later in the day, pick up our equipment and ship part to Johannesburg, South Africa, and the remainder to London. He arrives two days later, , and says "That's Africa." I keep a 24-hour vigil over our equipment, to keep it from being stolen off the dock. That's Africa.

Joe the taxi driver is my guide, takes to me the main market: a huge, sprawling affair with a few booths, but mostly sellers with goods on blankets on the ground. Smiling faces greet us wherever we go. Nobody cops an attitude because I'm white. Joe takes me to the Muslim to change dollars for *cedis*. The black market exchange rate with the Muslim is ten times the official government rate at the bank, and no standing in line. The Muslim stands alone under a stairwell, in the shade, in tribal robes with tribal scars on his face. Joe tells him I want to exchange $300. I hand over the money. The Muslim pulls out a wad to choke a bull elephant, counts out what's right and smiles, no vaults, no locks, no guards. Nobody fucks with the Muslim. I like Ghana.

Joe takes me to a lengthy alley of booths with colorful, imaginative, batik fabrics. I buy several for women back home, handmade buffalo-horn jewelry, and I'm tapped out. On the way back to the ship around a traffic circle, I see a tall, large black woman walk off the roadway balancing a tray of cut fruit on her head. In bright yellow batik fabric she sways for the market, barefoot in African rhythms.

Art, Crime & Lithium

The agent takes me to the airport in Accra. When my flight is announced, Africans stampede for the boarding gate. I don't know how or care to play this game. The agent arranges for a ticket on British Airways leaving at midnight. I sit in their lounge drinking beer until the flight is announced, and in true British fashion we board at a leisurely, orderly, civilized pace. One more layover at Heathrow, and I'm home.

O.Z. Lysiak

Home From Africa

On arrival in Denver, I call my folks and let them know I'm OK and home from Africa. My mother immediately whips up the emotional extortion over the phone, two thousand miles away, subtle as a truck. Apparently my father isn't doing well and when I can be home?

Flight to Philly booked: it's snowing hard over the Rockies, blizzard conditions. I call Philadelphia, and my father answers with a fresh dose of emotional extortion. Does this mean I'm not coming? No. It means I may be delayed. I have a four-wheel drive three-quarter-ton GMC pickup, chains and shovel. I've done the tough and stupid all my life, so why not now?

It's slow going following the plows up to Eisenhower Tunnel, slower yet on the east side going down. I stay with a friend in Denver. 5 a.m. in streetlights, I broom three feet of snow off the truck cab, hood, and lights, wipers frozen to the windshield. Truck starts, warms up, defroster clears the windshield, snow up past the running boards. I dig out, lock the hubs, put the transmission in compound low and rock my way out of the parking space on my way to the airport.

In a mid-October whiteout I merge onto Interstate 70. Traffic in all lanes crawls. Two exits before the airport traffic stalls. I put the GMC in reverse, turn around and work my way through oncoming traffic to the first exit with a gas station available, fill up and discover on the station's TV the airport is closed until further notice.

A motel room and a call to my folks: I tell them I'll be there once the airport opens. Chained up, I pull cars out of trouble with my 4X4 for the next three days to keep from being bored. Finally the skies clear, the airport opens, I get a flight.

My folks are glad to see me. No use telling them what it took to get here: they don't care. I may as well tell them I got caught in a TV show about a blizzard. They care about their aches, pains, and friends dying.

A few weeks off, and LCT calls with a job on the Gulf of Mexico, be in New Orleans Friday. The ship is Cajun crewed and owned, my first operator Dmitry Kuriyakin, Dima, a Russian. Dima is a super smart sweetheart of a Muskovite, tries to teach me binary numbers so I'll have a basis for understanding the workings of computers. Either too dumb or too lazy, I settle on learning the machinations of a gravitometer.

Weather goes sour, hurricane coming, Gulf seas rise to 26 feet, wind over 100 m.p.h. slices the tops of the waves off creating thin sheets of water in rainbows as far as I can see. The first mate, steering the ship from his perch in the captain's upholstered leather chair, cackles while he rides the ship like a bull-rider in an ocean rodeo beyond insane. We make for Galveston and beat the heart of the storm in. Dima and I pack the equipment all night, into morning. I'd like for my father to meet Dmitry Kyriakin, a Russian I like and trust.

The 1998 World Cup is the topic of conversation on the Norwegian seismic ship I work on next in the Gulf of Mexico. A Brazilian mechanic who lives in the Canary Islands is beside himself when Brazil loses, and France wins the World Cup. He mopes around the ship disconsolate for days, in tears. We fear for his life.

My mother's on the phone, my father's dying. She offers to have the nurse verify the fact. A brief call to LCT headquarters in Houston gets me nowhere. They won't send a helicopter for me because of the distance and cost involved. I'm on my own. The party chief arranges a ship-to-ship connect across the Gulf to Galveston.

The athletic man who dominated my youth is diminished, shriveled in a diaper, in a hospital bed in the living room. Who is this man, he asks my mother. Fifty years of war and misunderstanding, and the son of a bitch doesn't remember who I am. He has to have the last word, the last laugh.

My father hangs on for days. I tell my mother I have to go home, take care of business and pay bills. A few days after I arrive in Norwood she calls. He's dead. I have a suit for funerals and weddings. The tie for this one is black, like I promised him. My father dies August 17, 1998. We bury him in the traditions of his tribe. Remnants of the First Ukrainian Division carry his coffin into St. Michael the Archangel, stand guard over him at high mass. The undertaker puts cardboard into his pants-legs to keep them from flopping flat.

My mother, in black with a black hat with black veil, and I stand together in the front row, facing the icons of saints and other semi-historical characters. We put him in the ground at the Ukrainian cemetery, in a plot of black granite tombstones reserved for members of the First Ukrainian Division. I sent my parents a photo of the house I bought in Norwood. My father sent me one of black granite marking his and my mother's grave, with a note saying this is his new house—cynical, grim son of bitch.

After the funeral I buy a bottle of Herradura Anejo and introduce my mother to the joys of tequila. She makes awful faces downing the liquor, shakes her head and puts her glass out for another. We reminisce in the afternoon to evening shadows, in the dining-room where we shared so many good and bad times.

When I was a kid, my parents took me to Wildwood on the Jersey shore. We'd walk the beach, my mother and I. When I was little she held my hand. The day after the funeral and tequila is a Sunday, but instead of church I propose we go to Wildwood and the beach. Mom is game. Now I hold her hand. We walk the beach.

Next day I clean out more than forty empty bottles hidden around my father's room and closet, reminded of when he entreated me to buy him some alcohol. It could have been anything. The last years of his life are spent pickled in alcohol, disappointed, depressed, wondering what happened to his beloved Lviv, Ukraine, the war, his friends, his marriage, his wife, his son—living in a Philadelphia he tolerated, along with other Ukrainian immigrants similarly trapped. In his way he was brilliant, but alone, allowing no one in. That brilliance is small solace in the years of his torment. He dies knowing he fulfilled his purpose in life, explaining the role of the First Ukrainian Division in protecting Ukraine in WWII.

LCT wants me to go to work immediately. I tell them it's too soon, and I need time. They need an operator. I ask them to reimburse me for the flight to Philadelphia. They refuse but would have had to pay for my flight home if I hadn't had an emergency. They refuse to send a chopper, and don't arrange for transportation in my family emergency. They can go find another operator. We part ways. I find employment with a different seismic outfit out of Houston, a couple weeks later. They send me to Lome in Togo, and a Togolese government chopper to the Ramform doing a seismic survey on the Gulf of Benin, the most modern seismic ship ever built.

The *Valiant* is wedge-shaped, nearly 90 meters long, half again as wide at the stern, spanking clean, organized. The instrument room, where I'll spend 12-hour shifts for the next ten weeks, is a cross between the bridge of the Starship *Enterprise* and a five-star Hilton lobby. The food is terrific, prepared by enthusiastic young Polish chefs.

Navigators and seismic observers are 20 to 30 years old. Able-bodied seamen are older, as are the bridge crew and captain. The attitude on board is more relaxed than any ship I've been on. Perhaps Norwegians figure out seafaring psychology improves when you give good people a good situation and treat them as adults, with pride in their responsibilities.

The *Valiant*, her sister ship the *Viking*, and two more Ramforms, which are due out of the shipyard soon, are a view of the future: multinational cooperation to accomplish worldwide goals.

During 12-hour shifts I research agents for my book and find one in mid-Ohio. Too good to be true to find a competent agent in Ohio, via the net, from a Norwegian ship off the coast of West Africa.

We're on the ship just a couple of weeks when the party chief informs us we have until morning to get our gear packed and off the boat. The *Valiant* is going to Nigeria. We're not. We work all night. In the morning we're on a tug for Lome. The *Valiant* makes a course adjustment and is lost in the fog.

The tug arrives in Lome in brilliant sunshine. The view from the bridge reveals rock jetties and an open market beneath a palm frond roof, and hand-hewn canoes 40 feet long painted in primary colors, decorated with primitive animals and fish, flying long, bright flags. A children's chorus applauds each canoe flying a white flag, meaning fish on board, like a school of tiny silver fish in unison across the morning. The harbor is a raucous combination of color, movement and sound, thick with fishermen, boats, sellers, buyers and gawkers. The children continue to applaud late arrivals.

Our agent, a Scot, arranges for a taxi to take us to the Barracuda Club for lunch, with a warning not to stray for fear of being robbed or killed or both., He arranges visas, paperwork, and flights while we dine.

Open air with thick whitewashed walls, palm-frond roof, orange tile floor, the Barracuda Club features a blackboard with lunch specials in French. Four beautiful

Togolese women speaking French exclusively bring cold white wine, lobster bisque, shrimp and sautéed fish.

Red tape resolves at customs, and I'm on the tarmac, boarding. An elegantly dressed woman, a Moroccan on her way home from vacationing in Lome, says a throaty "Pardon'" and slips into her seat next to me. Her perfume launches my imagination. She disembarks in Abidjan, Ivory Coast.

In Paris, I buy Chanel No. 5 at the duty-free shop at Degaulle for Tina. Tina tells me, if we're going to stay together, I need to get another job where I can stay home instead of being gone months at a time.

The *Aspen Times* advertises for a reporter. I interview and get the job.

Tina gets a job as manager of Cashmere Aspen, a high-dollar cashmere shop catering to the stars and bodies less celestial with big bucks to spend. We rent a place outside Basalt, and set up house. Remy enrolls at Aspen High School, makes the soccer team, happy in the Roaring Fork Valley, dollar signs in his eyes.

Bobby comes for Christmas vacation from college. I have a couple Nikon F-bodies, with a full complement of lenses, that I used in the Army and at the *Norwood Post*. We load the Nikons and go shooting every day. We shoot rocks, snow, water, mountains, any and everything we encounter. At the end of the day's shooting I open a bottle of wine, and we drink and talk until Remy and Tina come home.

Everything is going along swell. Bobby goes back to school on scholarship in Washington, Sasadi graduates from Wesleyan and is in France teaching, Remy is in high school in Aspen, Tina and I both have jobs.

We buy Tina a van to get back and forth to work. Since our previous vehicles had been registered in Telluride, San Miguel County, we decide to register her van there also. We know everybody in the County

Courthouse. I suggest Tina and I get registered. She likes the idea. Colorado doesn't require an intermediary with an assumed connection to what may or may not be a supreme being. Colorado passed legislation allowing two parties to marry each other, with no interference from any deity.

Christina Anne Peterson and I are married—or rather, marry each other—January 15, 1999, at the San Miguel County Courthouse in Telluride, CO. Doris Ruffe, the county clerk, buys the license. Doris maneuvers so many of my questionable vehicle trades and purchases, she tells me I change cars the way most guys change pants. Doris is in tears as Tina and I sign the Marriage License.

Claudia Hoffman brings a bouquet. Cliff Ward photographs. Tina's former lesbian girlfriend Stephanie brings her son. Janice Zink, Tina's best friend, wears another outrageous hat from her infinite collection. Tina and I wear black. At the time, we don't quite comprehend the significance. As a slut, Tina is at minimum a match, if not my better. We kiss and seal a deal made anywhere but heaven.

Our self-styled ceremony over, we go to Monica's, the best joint in town. Janice buys a cherry chocolate cake. Claudia buys champagne. The party is short but heartfelt. We take our leave and drive to Moab. Our wedding night, superfluous but fun, is spent at the Apache Motel in Moab.

Pink vomit covers apartment stairs. Tina called to warn Remy we're coming home. Past the pink vomit is a room with pre-teen and teenage kids drunk, stoned, incapacitated. A half-gallon of Jim Beam with maybe an inch left on the bottom is on the dining room table. The apartment reeks of pot. Remy, Tina's little prince, objects to our getting married and throws a party the implications of which I don't want to consider. I tell the kids to get the fuck out of the house or I'll call each of their parents. The room clears in a flash. I hose the vomit off the stairs. The game changes.

Remy's counselor at school calls concerned Remy is cutting classes. Remy denies it. The kid smokes pot. I can't assume a morally superior position. He tells me I'm not his father. What he does is his own business, but I'm not having any in our home since I'm at jeopardy. He hangs out with an unsavory rich kids gang at school, who are later convicted of armed robbery and sentenced to hard time.

I quit smoking dope in 1985 after being continually stoned 25 years, give or take what I remember. My reasons for quitting are simple. I was working on a project stoned, as usual. I did everything stoned and was proud of it. Then I forgot where I put the screwdriver I was working with. While looking for the screwdriver I forgot why I needed one, sufficient reason to quit getting stupid and give my self a break.

At approximately the same time I quit cocaine. What started as a pleasant pick-me-up now was induced paranoia, an expensive habit with nothing going for it but peer pressure and fear.

Another reason why I quit was the "Break one law at a time" rule. I was involved in a serious, complex criminal enterprise in 1985, which required all my faculties.

What I immediately notice is my dope-smoking pals now view me with suspicion, still looking for their screwdriver but forgot why they were looking for it in the first place.

Remy isn't ready to listen, a teenager with raging hormones, living in a home where his mother is screwing another in a long line of losers: war.

The next few months with Remy are the worst of my life, culminating in a screaming match where he tells me to get fucked and slams the door to his room. Unaccustomed to being spoken to in that manner, I kick his door in, hit him once in the chest, straddle him, grip his throat and politely request he repeat what he said to me.

I let him up and apologize. I don't take that sort of abuse from anybody. I had never taken that much abuse from anybody in my life as I did from Remy in the months we lived together.

Tina ships Remy off to his pedophile daddy in California, afraid I'd kill the kid. Remy's argument when things aren't going his way is he's going live with his father. He gets his wish.

Sasadi stays with us after her teaching gig in Lyon. Her walkup flat is cold. The French are cheap. Sasadi comes home. Tina gets her a job at Aspen Cashmere, which Sasadi parlays into a job at London Cashmere. In London she meets Ade Odunsi, a dashing young Brit-Nigerian Cambridge economics graduate.

Sasadi and I have a discussion when she isn't certain about working at Cashmere Aspen for her mother. My advice is to explore the opportunity and not sweat the small shit. She is no longer an arrogant little save-the-world college punkette.

I last three months at the *Aspen Times*, tell the managing editor, John somebody or other, who is dressing me down for some imagined affront to his sense of political correctness, to back off and be polite or I'll leave him on the floor. He believes me. I go to work a couple blocks away for the *Aspen Daily News*.

Three months is my usual length of employment. About the time the insurance kicks in, I find a reason to quit, or create one to get fired. Getting a job is never a problem. Keeping a job is. Could be I'm easily bored or I have a problem dealing with authority, especially when it involves political correctness. Political correctness and I can't be in the same room. Gina Dearth, Port Director of the Port of Bandon in Bandon, OR, a friend, once explained it. She said most people have a self-sealing valve at base of their skull that closes when they need to shut the fuck up in the cause of self-preservation. Gina said I have no such valve.

My father is right; I'm not normal. Whatever normal is, I'm not. The possibility exists, since I'm bipolar, this is what happens.

I last at the *Aspen Daily News* for a few months, but tequila gets the best of me. I write offensive emails to Rick Carroll, the editor and a good guy. I could be writing for the *Aspen Daily News* still but I don't like Aspen; something about the Gucci attitude, and emaciated old broads with ash-blonde hair and severe skull-hugging facelifts, or what should have been reasonably-priced homes selling for two and three million, doesn't agree with me.

We are making in the neighborhood of a hundred grand a year, and barely getting by.

I get a job at Big O in Basalt, selling tires. They regularly give me raises. We rent a house with an orchard and a great view of the mountains and valley, directly above Basalt. I walk to work, and see Art Rowell daily. We fish the Frying Pan, the Roaring Fork, auger holes in Ruedi Reservoir in winter, and have War Wonton for lunch at the Green Jade.

Mariyka, my mother, comes for a visit. We take her to the Pitkin County Fair and buy her turquoise earrings. I have a 1985 Mercedes Benz Turbodiesel. She gives me endless grief that I should be a millionaire, loves riding in the Benz like the empress of emotional extortion she is, but gives me grief about it anyway.

I call her every day since my father died. She's in her Ukrainian immigrant world where she sings solo in the church choir at high mass Sundays, gossips with her friends, goes shopping, wonders who is going to drive her, tends her flowers, gardens and befriends local squirrels in the back yard.

My Big O job comes to an abrupt end when an obnoxious, loud, demanding, drunk Aspen woman comes into the store. My assessment of her state of inebriation and lack of decorum is succinct: "what a cunt." She hears me. Despite a call from her to my superiors, apologizing the next day, I'm let go.

Wood Biz to the Coast

Cliff Ward is home from his most recent globe-trotting adventure, looks me up with a proposition. A pal of his from the seismic adventure series is in control of a demolition job of wharves and warehouses in Vancouver, BC. Apparently millions of board feet of reclaimed old-growth Douglas fir are available. Cliff feels confident organizing, but wants me to do sales.

The Roaring Fork Valley is building rustic monuments to money, requiring large amounts of Doug-fir beams. I write classified ads with reclaimed hooks, get bites and orders, make contacts with builders in the valley, and establish a reputation. Cliff buys a Woodmizer mill and a trailer, and rents space in Norwood. We add the ability to mill our own orders. Every connection I make increases our customer base, which leads to increased networking. We get past just working with the demolition project in Vancouver on the supply-side. I find reclaimed-yard owners and demolition operators in Oregon, Washington, California and Montana.

Here's a job where I can't be fired because I'm not normal. The only way I can fuck up is to misrepresent the product, not deliver on time, or get too lazy and not work. My father's "Be on time, keep your word, there is no justice," is precisely the ticket. The people I work with are a rough-and-tumble crew who didn't mind if I call somebody a cunt. They know precisely what a cunt is, and don't get bent out of their underwear with politically correct pretension.

Skills developed as a reporter come in handy: research, precision with language, ability to ask questions, specificity, fact checking, photographic skills and ability to spot bullshit. I create a solid customer base with architects, builders and contractors. What I need are supply contacts. A mid-winter trip through Oregon provides me a new circle of connections.

Cliff, in the meantime, is playing hide-the-salami with Rachel, his girlfriend, in a motel with a hot springs. He and Rachel bonded while she was a student at Telluride High School. Dressed in a cowboy hat, fur coat, cowboy boots and nothing else, she'd meet him at the airport when he came in from exotic locales, flashing him in full view of passengers.

All for him exercising his libido with the slut of his choice, I have to pay the bills and can't do that without getting in touch with him. The contractor offers to pay my commission and add it to the bill. Cliff later takes exception. He leaves a message on my answering machine saying he'll never talk to me again, a man of his word. I never hear from him again. He dies of some exotically lethal malady acquired in his travels—a good man, full of life, enthusiastic, with a great sense of humor. What he lived by killed him. I miss him.

Beating pianos with chains for interior design effect is merely one of the unusual processes Kary the obtuse builder employs. On the tap dancing side of manic, he's a self-styled genius with disdain for anybody who doesn't immediately and wholeheartedly agree with him. He successfully builds for clients from Florida to Colorado: one born every minute. He finds me through the reclaimer grapevine, and arrives in Basalt to inspect inexpensive timber jacket-siding for his personal domicile in Old Snowmass, right on the creek.

Done examining samples, he declares he'll pay no more than a dollar and a half a board foot. In fact that's what he'll pay, exactly. I keep my mouth shut until he's done ranting and raving, sell the timber jackets to him for precisely what he wants. The customer is always right.

Richard McFarland, a reclaimed-wood supplier in McCloud, in the northern California Siskiyous, shows me more than 100,000 board feet in stacks of timber jackets just a few weeks before, on my West Coast reclaimed-wood research tour. I call Richard. We negotiate a price just a fraction of what Kary is willing to pay, and arrange freight. I rent a forklift at a yard in Aspen and drive down Hwy 82 to Snowmass, and unload the truck. Kary rants and raves, making me realize I'm not the only mentally ill scammer in the wood biz. I keep my mouth shut. He hands me a check for $22,000. I drive the forklift back to the yard, pay Richard $4,000, pay $1,200 for freight, and keep the rest less the forklift rental.

For months I research Internet property on the Oregon Coast. Time to walk on the beach.

Charlie Bishop has Maxine in Crawford, CO, my 1952 International Harvester RV schoolbus I left in Laguna Manuela. Charlie retrieves Maxine 12 years before, uses her for Lake Powell family outings and vacations in Baja. His girlfriend's teenage daughter resolves raging hormones in Maxine.

Charlie sells Maxine back to me for $1,500, the cost of rebuilding and installing a 345 cubic inch International Harvester V8. Maxine weighs 20,000 lbs and the original six-cylinder 221 cubic inch motor didn't have the power to make Maxine competitive on the open road. With the 345ci engine Maxine does a steady 80-85 mph on the Interstate, a road queen with hotrod muscle.

We drive to the coast in Maxine to look at a barn on an acre for $35,000. We have $30,000 in the bank, thanks to Mariyka's generosity and my ineptitude as an investor. I advised her to invest $30,000 in a mutual fund when my father died. After three years, there was less money in the fund than originally invested. We pulled out of the fund. I'm investing it in real estate.

What I can't tell from the web photo of the property is that it sits on a hill overlooking a large pond from the east, with a modest view of a bay and the Pacific from the west.

My first instinct is "This is it!" Tina wants to shop. I know we won't find another situation as functional or beautiful for the money we have. We can take this, or use the thirty grand for a down payment on something we'll have to make payments on for the next thirty years. We make an offer. A couple days later the realtor calls, offer accepted.

The barn is two levels, 82 feet long, 44 feet wide and 32 feet high, with a 14-foot overhang on the upper level. Upper level flooring is a shambles, will take a lot of work. Fortunately, the barn has electric service for four decades, and a makeshift backcountry septic rigged for a trailer. Enclosed in galvanized sheeting on three sides, the barn has a metal roof. The upper west side is left open to facilitate feeding hogs, which the barn had originally been built for. It will have to be closed in.

Three trips from Basalt to the coast complete the move. First I drive Maxine, loaded to the limit. We stop overnight in Nevada. By morning Maxine's clutch is history. I slip her into first and turn the key. She rumbles and fires up in motion. I shift to second, to third, to fourth, and we're rolling down the Interstate, passing semis with blasts on Maxine's twin black air horns. I drive straight through, with stops for fuel and a short visit to see Richard McFarland, to share the story of the timber-jacket sale in Snowmass.

At the base of the coastal range, I'm 15 hours on the road with nothing to eat or drink when I pull up to a small country store. The owner is putting away her CLOSED sign. I beg her to sell a cold six-pack of Rogue ale, open all six bottles on an antique Coca Cola opener screwed to the wall in the bus, and put the cold ale beside me.

Three empty bottles later, I crest the coastal range and drink the remaining three on the downside, call Tina on my cell phone before the signal evaporates and tell her I'm driving a Maserati bus home. Maxine is hell on wheels coming down the curves to the coast. Up the incline to the barn, I decide to park Maxine downstairs and drive her right in, misjudge by a couple inches and clip her air horns off before coming to a stop, crack a few joists and separate the south wall by a bit, but I don't find that out until I sober up the next day. Maxine is squeezed in tight with nowhere to go: home. I find a comfy spot on the floor and go to sleep.

Repetitive, boring, loud, Rap-rhythms wake me from pained slumber. I sort of have my bearings recognizing Maxine's cockpit, and make my way up to the boom-box the rap comes from, and turn it off. Before the woman who operates the boom-box can object, I tell her I own the barn, the property, and if she doesn't stop the Rap I'll blow holes in it and have her arrested for trespassing.

I gave permission to John Amos, my neighbor, to hold his annual yard sale at the barn. We made no agreement as to Rap. Rap is out. John is a good guy with a couple dogs, lives in a trailer a few hundred yards away. Pat Amos, John's father, built the barn and the pond. Pat Amos was a diminutive D9 Cat jockey who helped build Hwy 101, a drunk, bar-brawler, womanizer, and a generally all-around good guy. Pat would help people out if he liked them, which usually meant women.

A Pacific storm blew over a barge full of lumber destined for Seattle. Pat and his pals put a boom around the lumber. Pat hooked it to this D9 and pulled it in to the beach. Our barn is built out of this reclaimed lumber. I bought the barn because it's overbuilt. Drunken redneck construction is responsible for it being intact today, more than 50 years later. I ask John Amos, Pat's son, why the 82-foot long concrete retaining wall sports quirks and bows.

"Depends on which hand he held the bottle in that day," says John.

Whatever hand Pat held his bottle in is of no consequence, since the 82-foot long, 44-feet wide, three-storey barn is solidly crafted, overbuilt, and will probably outlast our grandchildren's children. I can attest to the fact that the barn survives storms with winds exceeding 120 miles per hour.

John sells the barn and acre to pay back taxes Pat owed. Pat died the year previous. John took care of him for six years. We have cash, and make the deal. John turns out to be the best neighbor I've ever had, minds his own business, and appears without being asked when we need help. When John sells the adjoining property he lives on, I tell him he's a no-good son of a bitch for depriving me of the best neighbor a guy ever had.

Pat planned to raise hogs out of the barn, and ran 3,000 of them. When the financial end of his plan failed, Pat sold the hogs, fired up his D9 and built a dam below the barn. The dam filled the hollow, and the pond was born. Pat asked permission from nobody, filled out no forms, didn't care about county, state, or federal government. He built what he wanted, where he wanted, and they could all go kiss his old-time Oregonian ass.

Pat's Pond is sanctuary to varieties of Pacific Flyway waterfowl. Jackson Creek fills the hollow below the barn and forms the pond, which imparts a magic quality to our property today. Wildfowl of the western flyway take advantage: Canadian geese, red-winged blackbirds, barn swallows, buffleheads, cormorants, wood ducks, teal, mallards, blue herons, egrets, red-tailed hawks, kites, kestrels, osprey, ravens and bald eagles. The pond harbors and reflects light, changing with seasonal winds shifting and vegetation undulating.

Art, Crime & Lithium

At the end of hot, dirty, sweaty, working days at the barn, I jump in the pond with Dr. Bronners for a chill, a wash, and a swim to stretch out tired muscles.

One last train trip to Colorado, and I buy a Chevy 2-ton flatbed cowboy truck from a welding outfit outside Basalt up the Frying Pan, with horseshoes welded to the bed for tie downs, horseshoe step-ups to the cab, an Edelbrock manifold and four-barrel to deliver 350 cubic-inch power with a touch of a booted toe. I don't wear cowboy boots because I have a Ukrainian wide shovel-foot, so a touch of my sneakers will do. A rental truck costs $1,600. The cowboy truck cost the same, and I have something other than a receipt to show after the move. I sell the truck to a cranberry grower a couple years later, for what I paid for it originally.

Three-foot tall sideboards for the truck prove inadequate, as we pile and shift and pile on more stuff. Women don't move easily or lightly. I build four-foot sideboards, and buy a heavy-duty canvas tarp. Rigged to move, the load is solid, covered with the olive-drab tarp.

First light comes up behind us on Interstate 84 in Idaho. I drive the cowboy truck. Tina follows in her blue van. We're nearly to Mountain Home when an explosion, like a shotgun going off directly behind me, goes off. I grip the steering wheel for dear life. A tire-casing shoots across all four lanes, rolls harmlessly into tumbleweeds. The outside driver's-side tire delaminates. I slow along the edge of the road for the Mountain Home exit, and ease into a Les Schwab Tire facility. This is farm country, and despite being daybreak, Les Schwab's has hot coffee and tire guys ready to go. Fifteen minutes and a few bucks later, we have a brand new tire on for the last leg home.

Tina returns to Colorado to finish managing Cashmere Aspen. I clean out the barn so I can get started demolishing upper level plywood flooring, a portion of which looks salvageable.

The trash-pile grows daily off the east end of the barn. In barely discernible dawn light, I pour gallons of gasoline on the pile, step back a few paces, light a match and throw it on the trash-pile. The explosion knocks me back, flat on my ass up against the barn. Gasoline-inspired flames leap to the sky. I'm stunned, holding an empty gasoline container full of fumes.

John Amos takes the gas-can out of my hand and tosses it away. He hears the explosion, sees the flames and races over in his jeep to see if I killed myself, wants to know if I'm all right.

The plywood flooring in the barn is a shambles. John and I tear it out, saving whatever's worthwhile. I piece together flooring in the south part of the upstairs with reclaimed plywood, using the jigsaw method of plywood construction that Ray L'Hommedieu developed at the shack in Mountain Ranch. I glue, screw, and piece the floor together on 2-foot centers and ask Tina if she wants a plywood sub-floor with covering, or one built of 100-year-old reclaimed 3"x13"x22-foot Douglas fir planks. I'm a reclaimed wood broker, and have access to prime material cheap. Tina wants the plank floor.

A forklift stacks three units of 22-foot planks, weighing about 15,000 lbs, on my Chevy flatbed at a reclaimed-wood yard in Sutherlin, Oregon. I drive home with the front wheels touching the road every so often.

Ray L'Hommedieu shows up from Tillamook to help install the first few rows of planks. Once construction adhesive is applied to 2x12 joists, we wrestle a 150-lb plank into place, toe-nail it, drill and countersink it, sink a 4" Teflon-coated screw through the plank into the joists, and drive a wood plug home into the countersunk hole. I finish the floor on my own, often tweaking recalcitrant planks into place with clamps. Tina works down crowns in the planks with a power hand-planer.

Art, Crime & Lithium

Maxine is parked under the overhang, next to the finished jigsaw plywood floor. We sleep and cook in Maxine. Don Barrington, an old-timer local, drills a well with his son Ron. Another local, Tom Brown, won't install a septic system until I have a survey done. John Amos recommends John Prahar, infamous local drunk and excellent surveyor.

Prahar asks if I want the good or bad news first, once he's done surveying our property. Steve Stalcup, the realtor, advertised a barn on an acre. Apparently, half the barn is on the acre, and the other half isn't. John Amos arranges a meeting with his brother-in-law, a bigwig businessman in charge of family real estate. He wants to know what I want. I want what we paid for, as advertised. If not, we'll sue him for everything he's worth. We get a lot-line adjustment putting the barn on the property, now an acre and a half. Tom Brown goes to work. The county inspector looks in the hole and charges me $750.

With water to the barn, I hire a plumber and buy a second-hand washer and dryer for fifty bucks. Tina's thrilled.

Bobby, Tina's older son, stays with us preparing for a round-the-world journey. Bobby completed two years of college at Western Washington State, where he majored in snowboarding and sluts, a straight-A student in both. He got a job, and made enough money to buy a round-the-world airline ticket.

Bobby sands the plank floor a half-dozen times with an industrial floor sander. He also helps me complete the 82-foot long, 14-foot high, cedar and Doug-fir board and batten wall, closing the barn in.

He leaves on his trip. Camping in the Atlas Mountains in Morocco he decides he wants to be a cinematographer, applies to NYU Film School, is accepted, graduates and now works in the film industry in New York.

Remy is in his senior year of high school. He has a job at the GAP. His father "borrows" the money Remy makes.

Remy writes me a letter explaining he understands I love his mother and he's fine with it. The kid has courage and a forgiving heart. Also smart.

Just before he graduates we buy him a used car, provide him with opportunity to leave on his own terms if he wants to. Tina delivers the car. Remy goes to work with his uncle Jay in San Diego, doing specialty concrete.

The World

Areporting job opens at *The World* in Coos Bay, 25 miles away. I know what will happen, but apply and interview anyway. I'm doing well brokering reclaimed wood, but I have to do it. I get the job. None of the young reporters are willing to take on the business and religion beats. The religion beat is amusing, with preacher's personalities spicing up dogma. Business, on the other hand, is essential and exciting. I meet inventors, farmers, and other entrepreneurs.

Cranberry growers are the big story. Ocean Spray screws poor bog farmers, and nobody is willing to publicly talk about it. Ocean Spray is a huge, worldwide corporation that controls cranberry stock and prices. Local growers are getting less for a barrel of cranberries than it costs to grow them. I research six weeks before writing a three-part series.

Kathy Erickson, a stubby editor with a bouffant hairdo reminiscent of a '50s movie Martian helmet, is more concerned about eradicating vernacular epithets in the newsroom than she is with the quality of the newspaper. She insists reporters put a quarter in a can if they should let slip a shit, fuck, cocksucker or motherfucker. I feel a confrontation coming.

Friday staff meetings we discuss story ideas, progress, what to do, when and how to do it. When Kathy Erickson calls on me I pull a ten-dollar bill out of my pocket, slap it on the desk and insist on talking without interruption. If the fucking ten spot runs out, please let me know.

Kathy is mortified. Nobody has ever talked to her this way. When my three-part series runs, it runs as a single front-page story—mostly photos, and a fraction of what I had researched and written. Kathy said I should be happy with a front page in the weekend edition, claims company lawyers recommended editing the story. Faced with a Pulitzer opportunity, she folds to minor league corporate pressure.

On 9/11/01, before 6 a.m. PST, Sasadi—who lives blocks away from the World Trade Center—calls, saying airplanes have crashed into the Twin Towers and there's reports of a similar attack on the Pentagon. I thought she was joking. Her husband, Ade, was at work next door to the World Trade Center. I thought she was kidding. When I got to work the newsroom TVs replayed the horror over and over and over. Ade got home in one piece.

After 911, Kathy wants me to research what a heightened state of awareness means. I call the Coos County Sheriff. A deputy sheriff doesn't know, won't tell me his name. I tell him my name and my professional capacity, but paranoia infiltrates local cops to the point of idiocy.

I call the FBI in Portland. Their media representative says I should watch for unusual or suspicious behavior. OK, I say, if my neighbor comes out of her trailer after taking a shower with a towel on her head, I should call the FBI? Any suspicious behavior, she says.

I'm laughing when a stormy Kathy Erickson demands I come the conference room immediately, where she angrily explains I can't engage in racial slurs and work at *The World*. She just won't have it because her readership holds her to a higher standard and she's responsible to them.

"You're not serious," I say.

"The buck stops here," she proclaims, preparing another run of socially responsible third-grade ethics.

"Kathy, you don't look a fucking thing like Harry Truman," I say, and walk out, leave my key on my desk and don't look back. 2001 is the last time I try my hand at a regular job.

The Empress

With a reliable supply of reclaimed Doug-fir, I pursue clientele in the Rockies, where I feel comfortable and understand construction specifics, ski-town mentalities and abilities. They need what I have, and can have it the way they want it, on time, for ten percent over cost. I make sure everything, especially the money, is right. I work phone and computer, with an occasional drive to make sure that what's advertised is so. After a while I know who to trust, make connections with freight brokers who do a creditable job, and get the load to where it needs to go on time.

I build a 30-foot long, 9'6" high wall dividing the barn in half. The barn enjoys a 14-foot exterior overhang. Our three-cord winter's wood supply stays dry under the overhang, as well as occasional projects in progress. The remaining walls are galvanized metal. The roof is pale blue metal. The flooring in Tina's 1,200 square-foot studio is two layers of reclaimed ¾" plywood glued and screwed together. In the combined living room/dining-room/kitchen, as well as in the bedroom and bathroom, the floor is 3"x13"x22-foot planks finished with three coats of clear Behr floor coating. Tina insists on windows. I am opposed to cutting holes in a perfectly good building not designed for windows. We now have windows to the east, north and west. Tight cuts in the galvanized sheathing, precision framing and copious amounts of caulk, keep our barn nearly dry.

Before I build window frames, I close in former downstairs pig housing with leftover rusted galvanized siding and two 12-foot-wide John Woodjack-style modular-frame plywood-and-gusset barn doors. The original sliders were requisitioned by an unknown party. The doors are light and solid, survive twelve years of Northwest Pacific winters. Sturdy feeding troughs, redneck designed to withstand the onslaught of hog attitudes with power, built of 20-foot-long old-growth Doug-fir 3x12s, braced with angled 4x6s, floor to ceiling, take a week to dismantle. I estimate I'll dismantle the troughs in an afternoon, two at best. Wrong. I buy a reciprocating saw, and cut through the spikes and nails rather than struggle to remove them with a cat's-paw and gorilla-bar. Drunken redneck construction may not be pretty, but it's sturdy, and lasts. I build shop-shelving and a bench with reclaimed planks and bracing. Now I have a place to work.

Split bracing, planed and sanded, is used to frame the kitchen, dining, living-room, bedroom and bathroom ceilings. I buy a planer. The living and kitchen area ceiling is built of farmer-grade Port Orford cedar, acquired from a mill a quarter-mile from the barn, milled, planed and installed piece by piece over six weeks: tedious, but worthwhile. Tina insulates the ceiling and walls with fiberglass. Ray L'Hommedieu donates a woodstove.

Once the windows are in, I build the kitchen/dining-room table, coffee table, end tables, window and door trim and lamp tables out of reclaimed South American pallet-hardwood and salvaged figured myrtle-wood. A local plywood mill in Coquille, Oregon, uses hardwood veneers imported from South America. The veneers arrive on hardwood pallets. The mill sells the pallets for $2 each.

Walter Radke, a pal and local drum-builder, and I arrive at the mill at 6 a.m. on hellacious rainy winter days to avoid other hardwood-hunters not as foolhardy or as determined. We pick, pull apart, and sort through the pallet piles, pay $2 each for the best. When the pallets sufficiently air-dry I dismantle, sort, plane and stack them. Walter builds African drums. I build and trim the interior of our house out of this beautiful wood.

Tina is resourceful when it comes to collecting funky, classic accoutrements for the house. She conjures industrial-galvanized front and studio doors, an 8-foot tall framed exterior door, all for less than $100. She's a bargain-hunting demon. John Amos gives us a Kohler pale, Virgin-Mary-blue toilet. Tina scrounges a double white-enameled kitchen sink and a venerable bathroom sink with classic fixtures. The left faucet drips for years, leaving an aqua stain on the sink, benefit of the scrounger's art. Tina has to have a claw-foot bathtub. Girls need to soak. Claw-foot bathtubs are $600 at the salvage stores in Portland. I find one for $100 in Eugene classifieds. We haul it home, muscle it into the bathroom, and Tina paints the outside navy-blue with gold legs. Ray L'Hommedieu builds a stainless-steel shower out of reclaimed tanker-truck skins. I frame the shower. Ray and I install it. Our bedroom ceiling is rusted galvanized roofing I score on a grain-elevator demolition job in Amity, Oregon. The copper headboard on the bed I hammer and fasten to a ¾" plywood frame. The copper is from behind the woodstove in Roy Palm's house on the Frying Pan River above Basalt, Colorado. The bed-frame is made of reclaimed Douglas fir, with mahogany trim inherited from Tina's children's great aunt's stash we picked through at a storage yard in Irvine, California.

For years Tina wants a deck. I install Tina's framed 8-foot-tall exterior door in the dining area to get it out of the way. For eight years I fully intend to build a deck, so the door will open onto something and have a reason. Tina pins a white canvas sheet over it. Bobby makes a surprise visit for her birthday a couple years ago. I buy treated posts. When Bobby arrives I ask if he'll give me a hand building a deck. We engineer and lay it out. He digs holes, cements the posts in. Two days later Tina has her birthday present: a brand new Port Orford cedar deck.

Tina creates an extravagant flower garden over ten years, a color explosion, spring, summer and fall. She plants local and exotic tree varieties. Spruce, cedar and seedlings, liberated from the national forest ten years ago, have grown tall. I climb a fir ladder now to string lights on the tree we choose to represent holiday spirit every December.

For ten years Tina intends to tile our kitchen counters. I paint them with gray marine enamel and install stainless sheeting, left over from the shower project. Our house is unfinished, like we are. I work on the barn for nearly ten years. It takes most of my life to acquire the skills to make it work.

For Tina's fiftieth birthday party, we ice and fill the same 80-quart cooler I brought to our first Thanksgiving with ling cod, smoked salmon and Dungeness crab, put it in the trunk of the Mercedes and drive to her folks' house in LA. Geneva, Tina's mother, trusts me to cook lingcod in her kitchen, although she reserves the right to clean the kitchen to her own standards.

We visit Remy in San Diego. The tough times we endured in Basalt are history, forgiven, forgotten. Remy and I talk on the phone when he calls to ask about something I might help him solve. He calls wanting advice about buying a boat, an old wood motorboat with a hole in the hull and twin V8's. My advice is to keep looking for one with a fiberglass hull with a diesel engine. Remy shows up for family Thanksgiving celebrations at the barn.

Six years of daily conversations with Mariyka culminate when she says she can't deal with living alone in Philadelphia, wants to come live with us in Oregon. I fly to Philadelphia. My mother's house goes on the market. I attempt to clean out 30 years of stuff collected by a woman who lost everything in the war. The only time I can move stuff out of the house without argument is when my mother holds court, like a Ukrainian empress, when visitors call. I go through my father's papers making decisions only he should have made.

I assure my 86-year-old mother we have everything she needs in Oregon, but she insists on having her own stuff. I order a moving van. Finally the house is clean, trash removed and grass mowed. The realtor comes through with a qualified buyer, an African-American teacher. My mother signs the papers. We say goodbye to our Santo Domingan neighbors: Jose, a Philly cop who drank beer with my father, his mother and sister.

The TSA guard at the Philadelphia airport checkpoint takes my mother's favorite European nail clippers, ones I'd warned her about taking on the plane. Not hard of hearing, she's hard of understanding. And, she has spare pairs in her luggage.

Maxine, with fresh paint, is parked under the overhang, prepped for Mariyka's arrival with a non-skid ramp and handrail. I lower the bed and build drawers, insulate cold spaces, run a TV cable complete with the soaps channel. She has to have her soaps. We know she'll miss Sunday mass at St. Michael the Archangel. Mariyka's friends arrange for a high mass tape. Every Sunday she turns her tape of high mass on and sings along like she was there.

She complains Maxine is drafty. We buy a 28-foot Airstream trailer. I repair the toilet, reinstall her TV cable and make certain everything works. She likes the Airstream better. She likes the upscale Chinese food restaurant better than the one I frequent. Mom gets settled in. She sends the stuff she had hauled out to Oregon back to friends in Philadelphia. It gives her something to do that she's familiar with. I arrange for a cell-phone so she can stay in touch with her Ukrainian cronies. Both the phone and TV remote prove to be troublesome when she pushes buttons that interrupt service, then pushes more hoping to make the infernal machines work. When frustration overcomes her she summons me in wounded tones. I figure out what she did, fix it so she can continue with what she wants.

Mariyka has a pacemaker, needs blood work continually. I discover a Ukrainian doctor, a woman, at the Bay Area clinic. It makes my mother feel more at ease, gives her an advantage for her inimitable, charming, extortive style. She spends time on makeup before leaving for the clinic, carefully picks her outfit, and puts on too much perfume. I open the door to the Mercedes and close it behind the empress on her way to reign at the clinic. She appreciates the Mercedes, and pats the dash with approving strokes, a stylish matron in her chauffer-driven Euro ride. The car has electric windows. I crack her side a bit to ease the olfactory impact.

After the clinic, breakfast with Mariyka is extravagant: a diva entrance at our usual restaurant, hugging and kissing owner and waitresses on entry. Hugging and kissing done, we're seated and place orders. At Billy Smoothboar's restaurant south of town, where we occasionally go for lunch, the owner puts Mariyka's photograph up in the kitchen.

She contrives pressing needs to shop, which require my following her around the store as she leans on her shopping cart and peruses every single can and container on every single shelf. Any attempt to hurry her is met with dark, angry looks. She goes to extraordinary lengths to keep momentum going, keep the shopping, the need, alive. Her forays aren't malicious or malevolent; she just loves shopping.

At Walmart or Fred Meyers she's in her glory. If I look at something of interest, she immediately offers to buy it, insists she pay for everything, not negotiable. Our dryer dies. She buys us a new one, proudly flashing her charge card. She is a woman who will do anything for you but won't let you return the favor, the empress of emotional extortion. She speaks her own language, not quite

English, not quite Ukrainian, but all communication. She gets her point across and the deal done.

We try walking the beach once, but soft sand makes walking difficult and harsh winds add to the difficulty. So we stroll our local boardwalk at the harbor, mornings, before Pacific winds blow strong. The port provides handmade benches to sit on, a more civilized situation than the beach. And we can get fish and chips for lunch.

Mariyka's favorite walk is around the barn. In summer, when blackberry bushes are heavy with fruit, she picks to her heart's content, bowl in hand, in afternoon sun, barn blocking the wind.

I hear repeated cries, check the front of the barn: nothing. Around the barn I find my mother tangled in blackberry bushes, head down hill, screaming. Cutting her loose is no small chore. I lift her up an embankment and clean wounds inflicted by blackberry thorns. She parries my obvious question with reasoning that the blackberry she wanted, the really good big one, was just out of reach. When I laugh she stomps off, pride wounded more than her wrinkled, thin, old lady skin.

She opens the living room door just a bit, steps in and sniffs the aroma of whatever I'm cooking for lunch or dinner. Shrimp is her favorite, which she calls "shripmsy", plural in Mariyka speak. If the aroma meets with her approval, she steps in childlike and claps her hands. I cook for her the nearly two years she is with us. I'm her chauffer, translator, technical advisor, confidant and protector.

I drive her to Seattle in the Mercedes when she wants to fly to Philadelphia to visit her friends. No direct flights out of Portland then. I put her in a wheelchair despite her protests, her vanity palpable. TSA goons separate us at the checkpoint. Mariyka has to go into a separate line because of her pacemaker. I see fear in her eyes. I beep through the detector after depositing all my metal in a tray. An explanation does no good. A TSA goon

Art, Crime & Lithium

directs me to the space reserved for suspicion. They have me lift my arms and run the wand over me. The wand reveals I told the truth.

Meanwhile, a large black woman in a TSA uniform is feeling up my 88-year-old mother in a wheelchair, looking for explosives. I can't move to help her without being tasered and cuffed. We prove to be good law-abiding sheep, allowed to proceed. My mother makes her flight to Philly.

We lost when the planes crashed into the Twin Towers and made us afraid, cost us billions, trillions, eroded our economy and continue to do so daily. The damage is done with the shock of that act. We'll never be the same. We're afraid of something similar happening, whether it does or not. The terrorists don't have attack us again. We're already afraid, no matter how many young people we sacrifice as heroes in distant places none of us will ever comprehend. If we're going to support our troops, let's bring them home alive and take care of them. I'll certainly never be the same, but refuse to be treated like a terrorist, which I'm not, by third-rate government cop-wannabes in order to board an airplane.

Mariyka is home from her visit to Philadelphia when Mike Carter and his oldest son show up unannounced. I like Mike. His son is an engaging young man, a chef. They prepare a delicious fish dinner. Leery when Mike spins talking circles that fade in and out of sense, intimating something is going on without quite saying anything, I recognize the same old bullshit he wove when we were smuggling. 25 years later, he suggests we go to work in the dark again. In no uncertain terms, I tell Mike I'm unavailable and he needs to get the fuck out of my house and not return. My criminal run ended decades ago.

Weeks later Mike calls and says he has nothing to do with the bust that had happened on the Columbia near Astoria. Mike, for all his charisma, is a three-time loser, looking for a fourth, which will insure he'll die in the joint. He didn't do such a swell job when we smuggled.

I go to the mental health clinic at the Roseburg VA hospital. Over six visits I see six different shrinks. One is an African-American poetess from Washington, DC, who wants me to listen to her poetry. Another asks me if I'm homicidal or suicidal, and if not, what the fuck then am I doing here? He was a prison shrink. I tell him all I want from him is lithium carbonate, and I'll take it from there. Shrinks at the VA are crazier than me, doing the best they can. I go it alone. They're part-timers and can care less. I sign up for the general care program.

The VA doctor agrees to put me on the list for knee replacement surgery. For months I drive to Portland to the VA hospital for tests on my right knee, which is collapsing to the inside steadily over the last decade. Running out of time, I have to do something before the knee totally collapses. The Portland VA surgeons agree. I'm scheduled for a knee replacement.

Before the knee replacement with the VA, I have an appointment with a dental surgeon in Coos Bay to pull six abscessed teeth.

My left hip was replaced at the excellent VA hospital in Grand Junction. I'm not sure about VA quality in Portland. Scalpel wielders at the VA aren't always the sharpest, but they are adequate.

The operating room is cold, extremely bright, with crisp green linen. I'm given an epidural. Surgeons remove my knee, replace it with prosthesis and staple the incision.

A nurse in recovery notices I flatlined, shoots me up with adrenaline. Some part of my consciousness floats in the vicinity of the ceiling, not on the table with the rest of me. Tech's voices in the room guide me back to my body. I have low blood pressure and the epidural compounds it. I was on my way out through the ceiling.

Art, Crime & Lithium

My father referred to death, in Ukrainian, as "laughing to the ceiling".

Tina sleeps on a cot in my room for the duration of my stay in the hospital. Surgeon and entourage arrive. He asks how I'm doing.

"Get me the fuck out of here," is my reply.

An armada of painkillers course through my veins, blowing holes in my psyche, sending shrapnel through reality. My perception of the room literally breaks up from painkillers. I can't tell the time because the wall clock disintegrates, like a post-surgery acid trip gone bad. I want out! The surgeon looks in on me and says he'll sign off and let me go home if I can present evidence of having shit. I request the nurse stick an enema up my ass. I manage to work my leg over the side of the bed and hobble to the toilet. It works. I'm released. Tina wheels me to the elevator, down to parking garage level and brings her van around, helps me load in the back of the van. I'm on my way home!

My mother cooks good Ukrainian things to eat in anticipation of my arrival. I can't stand to smell anything, much less anything that good. She's momentarily devastated.

Months of rehabilitation are effective, but painful. Movement exacts a price. I bring the cane I made out of our pond's pearwood, a cane to crack skulls and shins with, to one of the last rehab sessions. I place it by my side and advise the rehab tech that I'll crack his skull if he hurts me today. Rehab over, I join the local gym for a strengthening program with a vengeance. Sessions at the gym swell my knee. I relent. Enthusiasm isn't going to do it this time. Getting in and out of an automobile without pain is grim, but worth the effort once the car is in motion. The prosthesis functions with distinct rhythms, like muffled wrenches bouncing off the sides of a galvanized garbage can. In time I become used to the quirks and sounds, and motivate relatively painlessly.

Tina leaves early. We meet in New York a few days later. Sasadi and Ade are getting married August 16, 2003. Bobby lives in Brooklyn after graduating from NYU Film School. Remy lives in San Diego, working for his uncle doing high-dollar concrete. We're meeting in Manhattan for Sasadi's wedding.

My plane lands in Newark approximately 4 p.m. Passengers advised we may encounter some inconvenience due to a power outage. The terminal is overrun with people unhinged. Cell-phones don't work, local tower overloaded. Passengers park themselves on a carousel, until a luggage carrier arrives and bags are brought in by hand. My cell-phone miraculously connects to Sasadi's loft. Ade advises to get a taxi to Jersey City, and then ferry across the Hudson River to lower Manhattan. The line for taxis looks to be hours long. An hour and a half later, I'm assigned a taxi with a Haitian driver who wants to pick up more fares to maximize his efforts. I give him $50 besides the fare to get me out of there. He drops me off at the ferry terminal in Jersey City. On the ferry I call Tina and tell her I'm on my way. All I need are directions. The sun is going down, a big chunk of the east coast without power.

Lower Manhattan residents sit on stoops drinking what remains of their cold beer. No lights illuminate the streets. Crossing main arteries is more dangerous than usual because traffic signals don't work. Cars fly up and down the streets seemingly faster than usual, headlights the only illumination available. Timing crossing streets is crucial. I find Church Street, make a left and walk north, bag slung across my back, clueless.

Tina spots me by looking for the tallest person in her view. At Sasadi's I'm told to keep it down because babies are sleeping. The Nigerian and London side of the family endure considerably more getting to Sasadi and Ade's loft. The Tribeca Grand is a few blocks away, where we have a room. We check in to flashlights. The electric

Art, Crime & Lithium

door cards are useless, but we can close the door with a mechanical latch. No hot water or air conditioning, but the toilet works, a plus.

Remy flies in from San Diego with one of his fancy framed mirrors for a wedding present, brings it in on a dolly on the subway. I volunteer to drive a 15-passenger van and be the designated driver.

The wedding is held at the Bronx Botanical Gardens. It's five decades since I drove in Manhattan, but with a current map I negotiate the complexities assigned to deliver the VIP contingent of the Nigerian family.

Ade and Sasadi's wedding is elegant, classy and stylish. They pull it off in extremely difficult circumstances with no drama.

I deliver wedding guests to respective Manhattan hotels, drop the van off and take a taxi to The South, our adopted bar across the street form the Tribeca Grand, open at 5 a.m. Several Patron Anjeo doubles later I cross the street, find the room, and collapse on the bed next to Tina.

New York was a wonder when I was a kid. I and Olenka, my cousin, who lived in a fifth floor walkup on 7th Street and Second Avenue, skated in Central Park in winter and went to radio City Music Hall for the Easter pageant. Weeknds in Washington Square and Greenwich Village I spent with beatniks, bohemians, poets and musicians. I frequented the Museum of Modern Art, the Guggenheim, the Whitney and the Museum of Natural History. My favorite thing to do was ride back and forth on the Staten Island ferry, which cost a nickel then. Later I rode a motorcycle to Manhattan to see my girlfriend, a spectacular Ukrainian blonde who lived on the east side.

Now it's expensive, dirty, smelly, crowded and dangerous. I single out New York because our kids and their kids live there. I feel the same about Los Angeles, Philadelphia, Chicago, Atlanta, New Orleans, or any big city. The negatives of living in a big city in America outweigh the positives by a long shot from my present point of view.

Mariyka takes care of the dogs and cats, watches soaps, walks around the barn, picks blackberries, talks with her friends in Philadelphia on her cell-phone, in charge of everything, the way she likes.

A year passes in relative tranquility. I cook for my mother, chauffeur her to her medical appointments, subsequent breakfasts and lunches. She carries on in inimitable diva style. I book another flight for her to Philadelphia, drive her to the airport and pick her up after. On her 88th birthday we celebrate with a specially made cake. Mariyka is the star of the moment and, of our little family by the sea, a happy girl.

Tina has a retail job, managing the gift shop at a local links golf club with a national and international reputation, a couple miles from our home. I broker reclaimed wood deals on monument to money projects, mostly in Colorado ski-towns.

Three cords of myrtlewood and madrone firewood are delivered and dumped in our yard early in September, as usual. Tina stacks the firewood when Mariyka emerges in sneakers, white pants, jacket, scarf and yellow rubber gloves. She insists on helping stack. I request she not do it for fear her heart might give out. With an emphatic 'NO," she picks up another piece of firewood and adds it to the stack.

A few weeks later, Tina is in LA visiting her mother. The dogs and I come from our daybreak walk on the beach, emerge from the underpass to our property. My mother stands on the hill. I can feel the anger coming off her from several hundred yards away. The dogs leap free and she comes for me directly, screaming. I can't make out what she's angry about. I listen, trying to make sense of her angry rambling. She keeps screaming.

"Momma, please, shut the fuck up," I plead.

That doesn't do it. She goes off on another tirade and slams her door. I follow to calm her down. She keeps screaming. I tell her this scenario reminds me of all the times she and my father went at it, screaming, slamming doors, and breaking glass when I was a child.

"You're not my son!" she screams.

I have enough, and leave. I hear her screaming as I go in the house. What usually happens when my mother and I argue is, we act like nothing happened the next day, and our play continues.

Tina isn't home to help. I call her at her mother's house in LA, and ask her to call my mother and calm her down. They're friends. My mother will complain about what a no-good I am, but Tina doesn't call.

With an appointment at an orthopedic surgeon's the following morning, a three-and-a-half-hour drive away, I leave before daylight and get home after dark. No lights on in the Airstream. I'll talk with her in the morning.

No answer to my knock. I open the Airstream door —and know immediately she's dead, a thin trickle of browned blood down her chin from her partially opened mouth. I check her pulse. None. Cold. Waves of an unfamiliar gray, heavy, dull emotion wash over me. We won't make up this time. It's September 24, 2004.

At the end of Nikos Kazantzakis' *Zorba the Greek*, Zorba gets up from his deathbed, grasps the windowsill, looks out on the world and laughs before he dies. If a person dies in good humor with a positive outlook, that makes everything positive or negative endured in life moot. Neither of my parents go out that way. My father doesn't know me. My mother tells me I'm not her son after a lifetime of emotional extortion insisting I am. Maybe I'll succeed where my parents failed. Or maybe Kazantzakis is full of shit and the Zorba death scene merely literary contrivance. Maybe we get to figure it out when the time comes. It matters only to the living.

A Coos County Sheriff arrives, checks Mariyka over, takes her prescription drugs and calls the mortuary. They put her in a zippered black body-bag and haul what remains of my mother to a slab where they strip her, drain her blood, and pump her full of embalming fluid.

Mariyka insisted on being buried in the Ukrainian Cemetery in Fox Chase, outside Philadelphia, in the crypt where my father's body waits. She prepared the dress she wanted to be buried in, the shoes, and the bag of Ukrainian soil from her parents' grave in Monastyryska, Ukraine. The local mortuary ships her to the Nasevich Funeral Home in Philadelphia. Michael Nasevich, who I know since childhood, picks her remains up at Philadelphia International Airport. She has to fly to Atlanta before making connections for Philly, cold in that body-bag in the belly of the plane.

Tina and I rent an airport car, get a room close to the cemetery, and drive to Nasevich Funeral Home on Second Street to see Maria Magdalena's remains one last time. The journey in the body bag isn't kind to my mother the looker. She wouldn't want to be seen in that state in public. I instruct Michael to close the coffin. We visit Jose and his mother, Maria, next-door neighbors from Santo Domingo. In the morning, at the church, we make final arrangements for the funeral and wake. A taxi pulls up with Ray L'Hommedieu, here from Oregon to help maintain my façade.

Mariyka's dark wood coffin stands in the center of the church before the altar. We take up the entire front pew in the church, a family representing nearly every race on earth. Bobby and Amy, his Chinese-Polish girlfriend, stand next to Tina and me. Next is Ade, Sasadi's Nigerian-British husband, and Sasadi, a Basque and California hybrid. Then comes Remy, out of the same mix as Sasadi. Ray stands behind me and pokes me when it's time to stand or kneel, next to Jose and Maria, from

Santo Domingo where black is beautiful. I wonder why the socks on the saints and angels in the icons shielding the altar are different colors, and if they denote distinction in the hierarchy.

Michael Nasevich approaches me before the funeral, and says he doesn't have enough pallbearers and will have to hire some for eighty dollars apiece. Ade, Bobby, Remy and Ray help me carry my mother out of the church to the hearse, and from the hearse to her grave.

The choir sings high mass in Mariyka Lysiak's honor. She was soloist here for decades. Mass complete, the young priest from Ukraine stands by her coffin offering a large gold cross for participants to kiss on their way out of the church. When he sees Jose and his mother approach, the priest draws back in horror at the possibility of black lips touching his cross. I want to slap this racist piece of shit priest, ashamed for the Ukrainians in the church.

Following the hearse in procession to the cemetery, I look in the rearview mirror and see what looks to be a quarter-mile string of headlights making the turn for the cemetery.

The punk priest revels in his ride to the cemetery in a limo, and does his bit, spreads the soil from my grandparent's graves on my mother's coffin. My mother's coffin is lowered on top of my father's in the crypt. The show is over. A polished black granite headstone stands with her name and my father's in Ukrainian. What remains of her spirit I carry with me.

She often joked she'd be on top of him for eternity. Could be she had her joke ahead of time, and laughed at life at the end. So many times she rhetorically asked why life is so hard.

Ray, Tina and I talk the waitress into bringing us tequila and beer chasers at the tearoom on the top floor of the Benjamin Franklin Hotel. Ray has a flight out the next day, and I want to make sure he makes it hungover.

We bar-hop in downtown Philly, and get a room in a hotel along the Delaware River waterfront. Ray makes his flight on time. Tina and I drive to Brooklyn for a barbeque with the kids, make our flight to Seattle, Portland and North Bend, and pick up the dogs at the kennel.

Two months following my mother's death—she didn't pass away, but died screaming—the Orange Revolution in Ukraine helped overturn an election rigged for Viktor Yanukovych, acknowledged thug and pro-Russian candidate from Russian-speaking eastern Ukraine. Massive protests started in cities all over Ukraine. Kiev's Independence Square attracted 500,000 participants who peacefully marched on the Ukrainian parliament, many dressed in orange or carrying orange flags, the color of Viktor Yushchenko's campaign coalition. The scale of the demonstrations was unprecedented in Kiev. Up to a million protesters braved the freezing weather. My parents would have loved to see this.

The victory of the Orange Revolution pointed Ukraine solidly toward Europe. Ukraine finally was a free nation, with free people, according to Yushchenko. Unfortunately, Yushcheno's victory didn't last. Bickering with Yulia Tymoshenko, his prime minister, weakened their coalition and the Orange Revolution failed shortly.

Six years after the Orange Revolution, Viktor Yanukovych, thug from Russian eastern Ukraine, was barely elected president and it was business as usual for his Kremlin-influenced policies. Yanukovych had Yulia Tymoshenko, his primary political adversary, arrested and jailed in 2011. She presently is serving a seven-year prison sentence as Yanukovych eliminates political adversaries in time-honored Russian tradition. The miracle of actual freedom in Ukraine turns out sad and grim, as politics in Ukraine historically do. I fixed an orange flag to our gate until all that was left were shards.

Remy Departs

Tina and Remy vacation in Hawaii for a couple weeks. I don't see the big deal with Hawaii. It's hot. I don't like it hot. It's humid. I don't like it humid. All the tourists in the world are already there. I don't like crowds.

I fly to Phoenix, buy a '96 Dodge ¾ ton 4X 5-speed Cummins diesel pickup, sell the Mercedes Turbodiesel and Mariyka's Airstream. I buy a '67 Avion truck camper for the back of the Dodge for road trips.

The '85 BMW K100 RS motorcycle I add to the collection is a beautiful piece of ergonomic sculpture, that tries to get me killed every time I ride it. I rode BMW motorcycles all my life, and never encountered an evil piece of shit like this one. I trade for a trailer just to haul it for repairs or numerous times it quits on the highway. I haul it to Steve Prokop, legendary BMW mechanic in Dundee, Oregon. Prokop's initial bill is $2,338.50. I trailer the beast home. First ride, I pass a Mustang 5.0. The driver won't let me by. I take my opportunity and pass him at about 110 mph. The motor dies grinding, a mile later. $2,858.10 to Prokop and a used motor with 30,000 miles, the beast dies in a hairpin turn. I go down, right lung collapses. Three days in the hospital costs $15,000. The ambulance ride is $1,200. A loose fuel tank connector is at fault. Prokop admits no responsibility. The son of a bitch claims he's blameless. Before I sell the bike for $1,200 for parts, the rear end seizes at 75 mph. I load it on the trailer one last time and advertise it on Craigslist, gone later that day for $1,200 as a parts bike.

O.Z. Lysiak

John Amos parks an old Boston Whaler full of pine needles under a tree at his house years ago, sells it to me for $1,500. The fiberglass hull is sound, but all the wood as well as the trailer is rotted. I sling it with straps in my shop, clean out the pine needles, refurbish and rebuild. Exiting the Whaler, I lose my balance and slam my left shin against the rigid interior gunwale. A few days later, my left foot too swollen to fit in my shoe, I'm in emergency at our local hospital and the surgeon keeps me overnight, surgery in the morning, blood clot removal. I sand and paint the interior, sand and paint the bottom, build and install a hardwood bench, the console, custom Plexiglas windshield, a forward seat/storage, forward hatch, all lovingly finished and varnished.

Sasadi and Ade contribute $2,000 toward a brand-new 50 horsepower Nissan outboard motor, a 60th birthday present. I rent a slip and fish salmon out of the Whaler for a couple years—until an ad for a Harley shovelhead gets my attention. I trade the Whaler for the Harley. My mistake. The Whaler is a great boat. The shovelhead is a piece of shit.

The Harley Davidson 1976 AMF Electra Glide, an incredibly slow 1200cc's, falls apart at every opportunity. Before I sell the Harley to a guy in San Francisco for $6,000, I lose 40 pounds so I can make it up the hill to the county dump without downshifting to third gear. The Harley is heavy, but as cool as can be as far as classic motorcycle esthetics. I buy a 2000 Moto Guzzi 1100cc Jackal in Sacramento, on the way home, for $3,900. I give my wife the $2,100 difference to keep the peace.

The Moto Guzzi is my best motorcycle ever, with the exception of the BMW R50 I rode across the country in 1965. I ride the Moto Guzzi for a couple years and sell it, time to dismount for good. Older, heavier and slower, my reactions are dulled by decades of overuse. The Moto Guzzi doesn't care about my shortcomings, lets me fall

Art, Crime & Lithium

over in a parking lot because I can't get my leg off the floorboard in time: embarrassing, and reason enough.

On my 60th birthday I decide to quit drinking for good. I adore good tequila. Beer goes down too easy. The reason I quit is I'm not nearly as funny drunk as I think I am. Alcohol wipes out any beneficial properties of lithium, which I take to counteract the ups and downs of bipolarity. I don't want to die a drunk like my father. I have plenty of reasons to quit, and none to fool myself. I don't ease out of drinking, don't follow a program and don't require advice. I do it because it makes sense, like quitting cocaine, pot and an extensive list of potent mind-altering drugs. I've been there and done that, to excess, with enthusiasm. Migraines subside to where I hardly notice. The day after is when the pain kicks in. I can't find words I need to complete thoughts or sentences. 60 years old, and I'm on the right track, finally. I had more fun and caused more trouble than any ten people I know, and survived. Now I'm trying to mind my own business and keep my mouth shut: not easy. Or I maybe trying to bore myself to death for a change of pace. The middle ground isn't something I'm equipped to deal with.

Serena telephones an invitation to her Grand Canyon show at the Kolb Gallery. The show is a big deal in Serena's career. I try to politely ease my way out because the show is being held in January, 2006. Driving from the Northwest to Arizona in nasty, dangerous midwinter weather in isn't something I'm enthusiastic about. Serena insists. I relent and rig the Dodge with new tires to make the winter journey. I fill the camper with water, propane and supplies. Tina makes it comfortable. We take the dogs to our local kennel, cross over the coastal range to Interstate 5. At Ashland the mandatory-chains sign is flashing, cars and trucks pulled over chaining up. I slip the transfer case into four-wheel drive, and we drive up and over the pass and down the other side, past Mount Shasta into the Siskiyous in California, toasty and secure.

Past Sacramento on Hwy 99, in steady rain through Stockton, Manteca, Modesto, we find a Nicaraguan restaurant in Fresno, overnight at a truck stop to the hum of diesels, breakfast at Bakersfield and Interstate 40 past Tehachapi in Barstow. At Williams we link up with Hwy 64 north to Grand Canyon National Park.

The temperature is four degrees above zero at the Grand Canyon the day before Serena's show. I have no clue how long the propane will last, and turn the heater off when we go to bed, toasty enough with layers of covers and each other. A long icicle hangs from the spigot in the morning. My heart sinks. I imagine all copper pipes cracked and about to leak as soon as the camper thaws. One by one I light the burners on the stove. Warmed by the bright blue circular flames, a few minutes later the icicle thaws and a stream of water flows out of the spigot: no leaks

Serena's family dinner at the El Tovar Hotel starts as an intimate group, but expands to more than eighty people wanting to share in her big moment. Being invited to show at the Grand Canyon means inclusion into an exclusive group of artists. Serena is a star.

Earlier in the day, Serena and I walk through the show as we have many times before, picking out favorites, figuring last-second changes. No changes to be made, the show is hung and set. Serena wants to know which painting is best in show. The collection is spectacular: watercolors and large, brilliant, colorful oils. I pick an oil painting, in muted gold and dark tones, of a rapids ripping through the basalt at the base of the Colorado River. Serena paints the Grand Canyon from the bottom up, from the inside out, unusual and original. If the painting doesn't sell at the show, she'll give me a shot at trading her out of it. Now it hangs in our living-room.

Every river-rat in the west must have been at the show, paying homage to the woman who expresses what she knows about rivers, rapids, and those who risk everything for the thrill and joy of rowing. The show is a success, packed shoulder to shoulder. It's nearly impossible to make it across the room. Serena appears on the walkway above the gallery, and makes a short speech thanking everybody.

We say goodbye in the morning in a motel room full of groupies, and drive south through Prescott, Quartzite and Blythe, to secondary roads to Julian and a state park to camp in, before hooking up with Remy in San Diego the next day.

Hot to show us the sailboat he bought—a 28-foot, sloop–rigged, fiberglass–hulled, American Marine cruiser with a Yanmar diesel—moored in Mission Bay, Remy rows us out to the mooring and shows off his project, which he renames the *Wet Dream*. Remy knows nothing about sailing, but that doesn't stop him from taking the *Dream* out into San Diego Bay.

Coming in under power one evening from a day–sail, Remy hooks a commercial crab-pot with a trailing line on his propeller. The crab-pot doesn't give, and the propeller shaft rips out of the boat. He is towed to a shipyard, where his boat is put in dry-dock. Damage repaired, Remy gives the *Dream* a navy-blue paint job, with eight coats of hand-rubbed epoxy marine paint.

Remy earned a bad knee from working construction, finds a job tending bar at BASIC, a downtown bar and pizzeria where beautiful young women come to ply their shapely voodoo. Remy's girlfriend Heather is a ten-plus in a crowd of almost-tens in four-inch pumps. She is also a slut, fucking his friends. The pressure on good-looking women to spread the joy around is immense, and Heather apparently spreads it wide. Remy maintains that the only constant female in his life is his cat, Whiskey, who is always there when he comes home. Tall, dark, handsome, with an engaging smile and charming innocence, he has his pick of loose lookers at the bar.

Remy entertains dreams of opening a bar and restaurant of his own. The owners of BASIC recognize his abilities and his easy connection with people. They consider helping him make his dream come true.

Home on the coast, I work reclaimed-wood deals through spring and summer. Business is good. I work primarily with Patrick Wilkins, who has a reclaimed yard in Eugene, and works word of mouth: no advertising or web pages. Patrick is honest, reasonable, punctual and occasionally funny. I prefer to work with Patrick because with him there's never any scam. Patrick tells it like it is. That's how it shows up, trucks roll, checks arrive.

Tina and I take ours dogs, Lily and Cooper, to the beach at every opportunity. Lily is a Yellow Labrador Tina acquired in Norwood, a hard-headed lab but charming, engaging and entertaining. In Basalt her barking brings an exasperated deputy sheriff to explain one more complaint, and the fines begin at $100. Lily regularly tears into the garbage cans of the guy next door, who is in a wheelchair with a leprosy-like malady that claimed his fingers.

With plans for the five-pound meatloaf I had baked, some for dinner and the rest for sandwiches at work, I place the pan with the meatloaf on top of the oven to cool and watch the evening news. Almost immediately I hear a crash in the kitchen and come running. Lily gulps the last of the hot meatloaf and makes for the bathroom to hide behind the commode. I dive and trap her. Lilly is a strong girl. I hold on and pummel her hard as I can. Hand sore, I reach for the wooden-handled spatula and beat her. Lily slinks off. In the morning we're business as usual, like nothing happened.

In Oregon, Lily has room to move. We acquire Cooper, a Chesapeake Retriever from a couple in Eugene who can't handle him in an apartment. They try to give Cooper away to a couple with a koi pond. Cooper eats the pond and the koi. They're desperate and happy to drop him off with us. I open the back door of their yuppie SUV. Cooper shivers, uncertain. I tell him to get out, and walk him down to the pond. Cooper shivers, looks at the water, then me, then the water again. I tell him he's a good dog, get in the water. With a leap he jumps in, swims concentric circles, slaps the water with his forepaws and barks, pleased. Cooper likes to dive, to bring up sweet root-balls to munch. We now have two psychotic dogs.

Lily hooks up with Buddy and Nikki, John Amos' white and black dogs from next door. Four dogs now terrorize the neighborhood raccoon population. Lily comes home covered in mud and blood, with the remnants of a raccoon tail in her mouth.

I have a show of mobiles, *Balanced Obsession*, at the Triangle Square Gallery in Port Orford. The owners of the Triangle Square Gallery, Joyce and Doug Kinney, are both artists. They're the most reasonable gallery owners I have encountered in decades in the business. Every once in a while they'll call with news one of my pieces sold, and send a check. We're friends. I ride whatever motorcycle I'm on at the time to the gallery, where Doug and I discuss politics. The right wing takes a beating in our discussions.

Sasadi's first son Ethan is born January 27, 2006. The Odunsi clan, Sasadi, Ade and Ethan arrive from Brooklyn to the Oregon coast for Thanksgiving. Bobby, Tina's oldest son and his then girlfriend, wife-to-be Amy, arrive from Spanish Harlem. Remy arrives from San Diego.

Wednesday before Thanksgiving, we have a Dungeness crab feed. Thanksgiving Day, Tina insists on tradition with turkey and trimmings.

"Here's to those of us who are here, and here's to those who aren't," I say before Thanksgiving dinner. At my mother's Christmas table there was always a setting at one end of the table, left obvious, with food and drink for those who weren't with us.

Bobby, our barbeque master, shows off his meat spicing and grilling skills over open hardwood coals in the fire pit. The day after, we broil salmon.

I look for Remy, to talk about his life in San Diego, his job, how the restoration of his sailboat coming along. He's off by himself, on the bench by the pond, engrossed in *You Can Have It All*, a self-help book. His grandfather, Al Peterson, sat on the same bench the summer before, whittling. They both enjoy the solitude and magic of the spot between two ponds alive with wildlife, soft with wind rippling the water's surface silently.

Thanksgiving gathering over, the kids fly home to their own lives, their own problems and solutions. Tina and I plan to drive south with our Avion camper on the ¾-ton Dodge diesel 4x4 through California, stopping to visit Remy in San Diego before crossing the border at Tecate to points south in Baja. The truck gets new shock absorbers, new tires, and expedition equipment for any eventuality, with spares. Heat, cooking, refrigeration, water and toilet systems work. We'll leave after the first of the year to miss holiday traffic.

Tina answers the phone. From the tone in her voice, I assume it's her sleazy scumbag pedophile ex. He's not to call here.

It is. He tells her Remy is dead, killed by a car as he walked along Interstate 5 in San Diego on New Year's Day.

Sixteen hours later, driving straight through on Interstate 5, we're in San Diego at Remy's apartment. The drive is like being skinned alive breathing carbon monoxide. We both know the reality, but don't believe it.

The medical examiner's office won't let us see Remy's body until the mortuary picks it up. Tina fills out the forms and gets Remy's personal effects. Remy's

Art, Crime & Lithium

toxicology report won't be available for at least a couple weeks. Sasadi, Remy's big sister, the recognized organizer in the family, makes mortuary arrangements from Brooklyn for the following morning in South San Diego.

We stay at Remy's apartment, sleep in his bed. Tina's adamant about finding out about what happened to Remy and why, what party he went to. She insists somebody slipped him some LSD or some sort of a mickey, that had him walking the interstate intoxicated, out of control. She wants reasons that'll exonerate her baby boy from having done anything stupid.

First thing the following morning, Tina and I drive to the mortuary in an African-American neighborhood. The guy who opens the door is African-American. Photographs decorating the walls are of Coretta Scott King and Martin Luther King, easily recognizable African-Americans. Employees walking the halls are African-American. The head mortician, an African-American, tells us Mr. Joseph, an African-American, will be with us soon. Our queen of organization has outdone herself.

First, it is inconceivable Remy is dead. Now we're in an African-American mortuary, with a mortician who speaks through stainless steel braces in solicitous whispers but cops to having been a coke-snorting, limo-riding, whore-hosing music group manager in Portland, Oregon, before he imploded and lost his wife and family. He is a custodian in a San Diego church when the head mortician offers him a job. We are making arrangements for Remy's viewing and cremation with him this morning. Mr. Joseph is an interesting guy. Once we get around to simply talking, he loses the solicitous whisper and speaks in a normal manner. We share a coke-snorting, whore-hosing rock'n'roll background.

Tina signs the papers, pays with a credit card. Thirteen hundred bucks, and they'll run Remy through the municipal crematorium and deliver his ashes in a plastic box. I have a creepy '30s film-noir vision of the kind of people who work in a municipal crematorium, continually placing cadavers onto a belt moving toward the flames, no way to be certain the ashes are Remy's. At this point it doesn't matter. All we really have are memories. I'm amazed Tina keeps it together as well as she does. We view Remy's remains at 4 p.m.

Our little group—Tina, Sasadi, Bobby, Remy's father and I—gather outside the viewing room, desperate for strength from each other, or from wherever the strength for what we're about to deal with comes from. We enter the viewing room. What's left of Remy is on a gurney, with a sheet covering him from the shoulders down. Tina gave permission to harvest Remy's vital organs. The makeup artist who worked on Remy does a creditable job of smoothing over the split in Remy's skull, and makes the kid look as presentable as possible, considering he'd been run over from behind at 60 mph.

The cadaver on the gurney vaguely resembles Remy, in an other-worldly, pasty–gray, cosmetically dead sort of way. On the positive side, Remy never knew what hit him, didn't suffer stepping from the plane of the living to oneness beyond corpulence. The air in that small room is so thick, so full of pain, a guy with a chainsaw with a diamond-tipped chain couldn't cut it. A sound comes out of Bobby that I never heard come out of a human before. I leave before my lungs collapse and wait outside, basking in a setting, municipal-carbon-monoxide-tinged sun.

Tina is adamantly determined to find something or someone other than Remy responsible for what happened. She speaks with the police, to no avail. We go to the house where Remy partied New Years Day before the accident. Remy's cell-phone is in the trash. Nobody knows anything helpful. Apparently Remy works all night and takes a cab to the party when BASIC shut down their New Years celebration. Nobody sees Remy leave the party. He walks down the on-ramp to Interstate 5 at Sea Bird Drive, and on and off the shoulder and first lane. One driver sees and avoids him. The next, a woman, doesn't see him. She hits and kills him. The toxicology report says there is nothing in Remy's system except for an inordinate amount of alcohol. Remy was hammered out of control.

Bobby talks Thomas Perry, rigger and assistant director of the University of Minnesota rowing program at Mission Bay, into giving him a ride out to Remy's sailboat so he can shinny up the mast and hang Tibetan prayer flags. They're for the memorial ceremony, to be held on the beach in direct and full view of Remy's *Wet Dream* moored to an engine block.

Under typically warm, blue, clear, Southern California skies, with flowers propped up in the sand, anyone and everyone who wants to say something about Remy has an opportunity. His grandmother Geneva has her say, so do his mother, brother and uncle, as well as cousins and friends he grew up with. Heather, his tearful slut of a girlfriend, shows up in heels. I can't say for certain Remy would have liked his ceremony, but I liked it well enough for both of us, and read a poem I wrote for him.

BASIC hosts Remy's wake. The pool table is converted into a flower table. More beautiful classy young women, dressed to the nines in heels and black stockings, than I'd ever seen in one place shed hot tears openly. Remy visibly touched a lot of lives. The owners love him.

I haven't had a drink for more than two years. When I order Don Julio anjeo, the bartender fills a whiskey glass to the brim. I pull out my wallet. He puts his hand on mine.

"That's not necessary," he says. "I know who you are."

An unusual night for tequila: no matter how much anjeo I drink, I'm sober. Once again I'm the designated driver, and chauffeur walking and stumbling wounded to safe havens all over the San Diego.

Since arriving in San Diego I walk the neighborhood daily, get up early and take to the streets, following my nose like I have on streets in cities all over the world. One morning I discover a French crepe-breakfast joint. Tina invites herself along the next day. The place is barely open when we walk in. The owner, a good-looking petite brunette with a French accent, invites us to sit wherever we please.

Tina gets to the heart of the conversation with this: "If I hadn't chosen you, he'd be alive now," referring to the morning she sent Remy off to live with his father.

Concrete slurry fills my lungs. I can't breathe. I must have made an extravagant answer because the proprietress bolts from the kitchen to see what's wrong. I explain our predicament and apologize. No way can I eat crepes after the guilt-and-shit sandwich I'd just been fed. I pay the bill.

I regain composure and tell Tina to either take me to the airport or clean her stuff of the van. Fourteen hours later I pull up to our front door on the Oregon coast. Cisco, who is taking care of the place, locked the front door. I sleep in the van.

I build an urn out of the finest figured walnut for Remy's ashes. She brings them home. Tina always wanted to have her youngest son close to her. Now she has what's left of him in a walnut urn, on a redwood shelf in the foyer. I make a frame for a photograph of Remy, shirtless on the deck of the *Wet Dream*, sailing. I hang the photograph over the disk sander in my shop, along with photographs of others friends no longer among the living.

Gilah, in one of our occasional telephone conversations, mentions that couples who suffer the death of a child often separate because guilt is so overwhelming. Tina and I are still together.

I don't know that Remy would still be alive if she didn't choose me. I determined to be last in her long line of losers. Remy's dead because he got out-of-control hammered at the wrong place at the wrong time, is all.

Early on in our relationship she told me I wasn't the best fuck of her life, intending to wound me in a drunken moment. She wasn't the best fuck of my life, either. I figured we were even, and didn't tell her because it didn't matter.

Nobody said it would be a picnic. This is combat for identity 'til death do us part. And more than anything else, Tina says she loves me.

Meanders

I wrote *Barely Inside the Lines*, a novel; *Filet & Release*, a non-fiction collection of columns; *The Chromium Kid in the American Zoo*, a poetry collection; *Scars in Progress* and *Geezer Rumba*, poetry chapbooks. *Boston Literary Magazine*, a high quality quarterly ezine, has published my poetry regularly for years. I write daily.

A backlog of mobiles sits under cover in the shop, dwarfed by the wood collection both reclaimed and figured, and woodworking tools. Mobiles are wire and mostly air. Wood is substantial. Patrons tend to buy substantial art, whether two- or three-dimensional. Mobile patrons are sophisticated and live in urban environments. Apparently, living in non-urban environments is more important to me than grooming sophisticated patrons. The backlog continues to sit under cover in the shop.

My art business philosophy has been to do whatever it takes to cover basics, in order to make what I want the way I want to make it. I'm a lousy salesman of my own work. My work sells best when somebody else sells it.

A worm-drive saw, electric hand drill, sheet-rock screws and a hand sander were the tools of choice for my first attempts at making primitive furniture: coffee tables, wood boxes, and pickup truck sides. Twenty years later, I build figured hardwood dining tables, coffee tables, chairs, lamps, children's toys, cradles, boat-benches fitted with wooden dowels and glue. Collecting tools, and learning through experience what can be accomplished, is responsible for the upgrade in quality, but I still depend on my ability to solve problems. I'm a self-styled

Art, Crime & Lithium

wood-butcher with a penchant for good finishes. With every project I get better. The level of my skill has allowed me to build our house and most of the furniture in it. I almost lost a couple of fingers on my left hand, working with the table–saw, building a spalted-alder pantry for my wife. Once I understood what had happened, I wrapped my profusely bleeding left hand—with two dangling fingers—and drove to the emergency room at the local hospital. They took care of me immediately, and the doctor sewed my fingers back on nicely. The fingers function fine today. I went to the shop to face the 10,000 rpm table saw with the understanding the saw wasn't at fault, my lapse in attention was. I finished the pantry.

Neither drugs nor alcohol have been a problem since I quit, although in the interest of fairness I had a good time getting loaded until it got in the way. The problem resides in the nature of drugs. If a line of cocaine makes you feel better, then another will make you feel twice as good, and so on. Pretty soon, what felt good is an expensive habit you can't shake, that makes you paranoid and suicidal. Alcohol makes you sloppy and stupid. And you puke. What makes you feel good virginally makes you a cesspool of snakes once you become a slut—via weakness, craving, and lack of control.

I was lucky because I was able to quit tobacco, alcohol, pot, acid, mescaline, hashish, cocaine and others I can't remember, because I fried synapses seeking enlightenment through drugs, better living through chemistry. What the drugs didn't frazzle, my inherent bi-polarity and migraines did. I'm amazed to be able to function and create.

Exasperated with the craziness, including mildly suicidal episodes, I have endured for decades, I'm dedicated to mitigating emotional imbalances caused by blood chemistry problems, caused by lack of a simple salt. Ingestion of 1,800 milligrams of carbonate lithium daily, for more than 20 years, has done little to mitigate the cycle of emotional distress, which comes on without warning, eroding what normally passes for enthusiasm into a chasm of near despair.

Drugs, especially alcohol, negate what positive effect lithium carbonate might provide. Dr. Paula Trautner, a psychiatrist I saw once a month in Colorado, pleaded with me to cut down or quit the alcohol consumption, which I was unwilling to do. At the time, I'd drink several shots of tequila and chase them with a 12-pack of beer almost every evening, when I was benevolently disposed. Dr. Trautner was unquestionably the best shrink I ever saw. Unfortunately I was too arrogant to take her advice at the time. It was much later when I finally saw the wisdom and the clarity of her advice, and acted on it.

In nearly–Spanish, based on vernacular without benefit of grammar, learned thirty years ago from Quintana Roo to Guayaquil, I explain I need a reasonable room to my accommodating cabbie. He drops me off at the Hosteria de Convento, a former nunnery with common courtyard, quasi-religious artwork, comfy couch and chairs, trellised bougainvillea, blue-tiled outdoor cooking and washing facilities, a metal table with chairs, and an ancient color TV—hooked to an antenna perched on a rooftop-high wooden pole, delicately spun to enhance two channels playing non-stop Hispanic soaps, game shows, movies and occasional football matches. Exposed logs support tall ceilings in my corner room: raised concrete bed with mattress and fresh sheets, tiled floors and wainscoting, sun-warmed shower with commode, hasps and padlocks on a peeling door, with louvers that highlight an intriguing shade of aqua over repetitive surfaces and angles from dawn to glorious, warm, Baja California Sur day. Across the street the Hermanos Gonzales taco stand spills into a boisterous intersection, under a tree whose roots muscled out paving since before Francisco Villa. I

Art, Crime & Lithium

dine on *pescado empanizado, almejas, ostra, pulpo*. Three bucks buys dinner and a drink. Latinas flaunt curvy, homemade rhythms, ay yay yay.

On the midnight flight from Portland to Guadalajara last night, I'm going to see a Dra. Lorena Estrada Talamantes, Mexican woman dentist, who agreed to pull all my teeth and fit me with dentures. I'm beyond dealing with the pain. The latest in a painful line of dentists quotes me $10,000 for dentures. I get advice from a commercial fisherman pal, make a few calls, research the net, call the dentist in La Paz, make an appointment and book a flight. The entire process takes a day.

In the heart of a psychic, spiritual, emotional and mental breakdown, I flew out of La Paz more than 20 years ago. If a silver turboprop, with a knockout brunette stewardess welcoming passengers, sits on the tarmac at La Paz airport, I'm not getting off the connecting flight from Mexico City. Lucky for me, turboprops have been phased out long ago and I don't need to fuel questionable meanderings. The cabbie doesn't speak English, but understands creative Spanish. The ride from the airport is $20. The room at the hostel is $15 a day. I leave my bag in my room, formerly a nun's quarters, and take to the streets to locate the dental office at 222 Altamirano. First thing tomorrow morning, I have an appointment with—hopefully—the last dentist I ever have to see.

The office is done in cool grays and blues, with an aquarium in the wall, separating waiting room from dental-business leather recliners and stainless steel implements, all air-conditioned. A squat young Latina in white, with a white mask, leads me to a recliner. I wait.

The doctor speaks flawless English, attended dental school in the US. I'm stunned, not by her English but by her beauty. Early forties, graceful womanly curves, anthracite hair pulled back tight, dark eyed with tattooed brows, Dra. Lorena Estrada Talamantes is easily the best-looking dentist I have ever seen.

In a pale blue frock she dons a white mask and, armed with dozens of Novocain vials, loads the stainless hypodermic. Numb, I laugh—entertaining visions and positions featuring my lovely dentist. She wants to know what's so funny. I can't say. She insists. I relent. This is a very exotic situation, I tell her. I can't say for certain, but I believe there's an indication of a smile under her white mask. She's a nice woman, and doesn't hurt me nearly as much as she could have.

Two and a half hours later, her frock is bloodied and twenty-two of my teeth are on a stainless tray by the recliner, along with a pile of Novocain vials. She gives me a prescription for painkillers and antibiotics, and an appointment to take impressions for dentures. Hilda, the receptionist, gives me a ride to my hostel where I collapse. I wake up at sunset. The pillow is bloody. I'm hungry. A couple blocks away on the Malecon, on La Paz Bay, is a fruit smoothies place. I order two with the works.

Meandering daily on the Malecon, I encounter local fishermen trolling the sidewalk to take gringos with money fishing. They display fishing rods, lures, a 25-foot fiberglass *panga* with a 75 hp Honda outboard anchored off their cast iron bench, and a loose-leaf binder with photographs of successful expeditions. I'm interested, but balk at $250 a day. The next day I agree on $150 with suntanned, bald, Hector—elder statesman, all-around hustler, and obviously the guy in charge of the Malecon sidewalk fishing–crew, playing cards and drinking beer under the sunshade in the boat.

I buy a cheap plastic digital alarm clock, so I'll be ready for my 5 a.m. pickup. The night guard in his sleeping bag makes room for me to pass. I open the creaky iron gate enough to step into the street and close it behind me., Minutes later, a white Toyota pickup pulls up. Hector gets out, introduces me to Enrique, the driver. We stop for tamales on the way out of town, south and east to daybreak on our way to Bahia del los Muertos, the Bay of the Dead.

The skipper of our fishing *panga* nets and stores baitfish in the forward hatch, has six fishing rods with Penn bait-reels rigged ready to go. He shoves off, fires up the big Yamaha and makes for open water. The combination of daybreak splayed over the clear depths of Bahia de los Muertos is mesmerizing for the half hour trip to the fishing grounds, where layered rock formations gradually darken downward, contrasting with flowering saguaros, ocotillos and desert layers climbing to pastel villas dotting the ridge above. Dark schools of snapper swirl up out the depths below the rock shelves as Efren, our skipper, throws out handfuls of small silver baitfish for chum. We bait up, cast out and hook into 20 to 30 pound snapper—strong, healthy fish.

Hector gets our attention. He spots a whale thrashing its tail in the bay. A half hour later, the whale intermittently goes through its thrashing routine in the same spot. Hector thinks the whale is in trouble. We pull in our rigs and make for the whale.

The whale is caught in a net. Close up, we see the whale rise, skin chafed raw by the futility of being caught, unable to work itself free. The whale's awesome tail slaps the water in frustration. It can demolish our boat if it wants, but I believe the whale understands we mean it no harm. We pull up close enough to the whale to clearly see its eye looking at us, blowhole opening and closing. I pull in the net, with disgusting, rotted sea-life caught in its plastic mesh. Enrique quickly cuts the net, freeing the whale on one side. Efren pilots the boat to the other side. I pull in more net slimed with disgusting goo. Enrique cuts the whale loose from the net. The whale sinks out of sight. We pull the remainder of the net into the boat. Efren is concerned because the net belongs to a local fisherman, the basis of his living. We wait. The whale breaches, blows, several hundred yards south.

Hector comments the whale is on its way to Peru, had enough of Baja. The whale breaches, blows, and sounds again—motivated, free.

Two large snapper, my share of the day's catch, I prepare as a seafood stew and fish fry at the hostel, for staff and guests. Salsa for my culinary effort comes from my favorite fish taco joint, under the big tree across the street from the hostel.

While I'm waiting to be fitted with my new Mexican dentures, Enrique drives me to Todos Santos to explore what remains of my adventures there 20 years ago. The buildings are vaguely familiar. Manuel, who drove me to the airport, tends his own bar at the Tequila's Sunrise across the street from the Hotel California. We chat. He's busy.

Dra. Talamantes fits my dentures. I pay Hilda the receptionist $1,200, and book a flight home via Mexico City and Guadalajara. The battery in my truck at the Portland Airport parking lot is dead when I arrive.

Not having children of my own may be a blessing. I won't impart chemical deficiency, mental illness and bipolarity. Tina provides me with all the family pain and joy I can stand. She says her grandchildren are mine. They're not, although they need grandfatherly love all the same. I didn't know my own grandparents, so I base my knowledge of how grandparents act on what I read, movies I saw, and grandparents other than mine. Sasadi has three sons – Ethan, Zack and Alexander.

When Ethan was four I took him down to the pond to teach him to fish, rigged him up with a hook, worm and bobber, and carefully explained how to cast. We were at a standoff for a while. He desperately wanted to , but just as desperately didn't want to listen. At one point I turned my back and started to leave, but caught myself and gave it one more try. Ethan eventually caught a nice bass. I asked if he wanted me to release the bass. Ethan told me he wanted to cook and eat his bass. Good boy.

Art, Crime & Lithium

As I struggle with chemical imbalance, I struggle with weight. When my attitude sinks, so does my will to do anything remotely physical. Since my weight problem is cyclical, I stash my fat-boy pants for expansive times. I've tried the cocaine, salad, fruit, daily workout and no carbohydrates diets. They work to a certain extent, but I always wind up back where I started. In the last ten years I figure I lost more than 100 pounds, only to gain it back and be faced with the same situation again. Or I can accept myself for who I am: old, bald, fat, curmudgeonly, partially deaf, ambulatory with the aid of joint prostheses, fitted with Mexican dentures I seldom wear, bi-polar with dwindling reserves of enthusiasm.

A clan gathering of Tina's family, down to the cousins and kids, was scheduled for a spring meet on Whidbey Island. We packed the Avion, drove north to the Port Townsend ferry and commenced with backslapping and hugging on arrival. Tina's family is enthusiastic, capable and good cooks.

Nancy Welles lives down the road in Langley, where she managed a bookstore for 20 years. We're in touch in the last few years, but haven't seen each other in other in over forty. Tina, cousin Kevin, and I spend an hour on Nancy's deck, overlooking Langley and Puget Sound, in a pleasant, civilized and minimally emotional visit. Nancy looks like Nancy, forty years, two kids and a husband later. The sound of her voice transcends decades.

Later that spring she stops by our house on the Oregon coast, on her way home from burying her older sister Pat. Nancy had already buried her father and her mother. She held her mother in her arms as she died. Nancy buried her ex-husband. We sit on the bench by the pond. The wind blows across the surface of the pond, rippling the water in gusts. She has a brother and two sons to take care of.

Gilah Hirsch flies from LA for a visit on our stretch of Oregon coast. A visit from Gilah is special indeed. I often wonder what makes Gilah run. She teaches full time, and mitigates politics of the art department of a major university. Gilah constantly entertains guests from around the world at her home in Venice, California. She travels all over the world on educational, spiritual or research projects. Gilah makes films, but first and foremost Gilah is a painter. She recently had shows in several Eastern European countries. Gilah is an excellent writer. I try to convince her to write her adventures, but she's too busy running. Gilah does more in a day than I do in a week. A visit from Gilah is no small thing, like having a real-life Indiana Jones stop by to share a few days and stories.

Claudia Muir was Hoffman when I knew her in Colorado, married to David Hoffman at the time. We met while I worked on their home on Wilson Mesa. Claudia and I shared conversations on Alexander Calder. She visited my studio, and became one of the foremost patrons of my kinetic work. Claudia sponsored a show of my work at her home in 1994. I made $7,000 that day, but more important, I understood people respect my work. Claudia and I always danced around sexual involvement, but never did the dirty deed. We came close, but regard for her husband made us toe the line. Claudia is extremely proud of what passed for self-control and integrity between us. She said it made what we share better.

She may be right. Experience proved that exceptional women I was involved with sexually evolved into even more exceptional friendships once our involvement moved on.

Serena Supplee saved my life. We went through the cycles to get to true, loving friendship, when friends love you in spite of who you are instead for who you are.

My wife Tina and I have been together 17 years, involved in friendly daily combat for identity.

One More Ride

Medically, Latin explicatory doubletalk comes first. Then, Lily's vet blurts "MALIGNANT," flat out, citing biopsy results from the tumors he recently removed from her right hind leg. Make her as comfortable as possible, he adds. Not easy to tell a guy the dog love of his life is going to die soon. Lily's a good dog, and life being what it is, the time arrives. I don't tell her, in case she fools the vet and beats the odds.

Today it's extra important to go for our daybreak walk the around the pond. At the far end of our walk I give her an enthusiastic ear scratch, to which she responds with throaty moans. Lily's got more soul and sensitivity than most females I was intimate with over 50 years. I should have scratched their ears instead, and saved us all a lot of trouble.

I kiss my wife, give Lily a goodbye pat and head north along the Oregon coast on US Highway 101 in my '96 Dodge with a '67 Avion camper.

Ray L'Hommedieu and I meet for lunch in Tillamook, at the same Mexican restaurant where we always meet. Ray is honey-do painting the guest bedroom in the cute-beyond-belief cottage he and his wife Therese share on the beach when I call. He welcomes an opportunity for a break. We drink diet Pepsi instead of slamming beers with lunch these days.

He hands me a sketch of a shelter we constructed out of reclaimed and requisitioned materials in 1970, on Nancy Welles' gold-mine claim in Calaveras County, in the Sierra Nevada foothills. Ray's a thoughtful guy. I couldn't remember the details his sketch provides. Ray didn't do nearly as many drugs. I'm fortunate to have him as a friend.

After crossing the Columbia River I call Nancy Welles on Whidbey Island, Washington. She had called and asked if I'd read poetry at Brave New Words, a fledgling poetry festival on Whidbey Island. Nancy volunteers me. I agree.

On Highway 101 to Raymond, Washington, I take a right on Route 6 through dairy farm country—rural, rolling, green, gray, drizzly—and camp at Rainbow Falls State Park in tall moss-barked firs that night. In the morning, after coffee and fried eggs in the Avion, I ease onto the entrance for Interstate 5 at Chehalis, figuring the worst of the rush-hour traffic in Tacoma and Seattle will have subsided. Seattle traffic continues to be a monumental pain in the ass, no matter what the time.

Brilliant fields of screaming yellow daffodils outside Mt. Vernon line the Highway 526 short cut to Highway 20 and Deception Pass, gateway to Whidbey Island, home to Whidbey Island Naval Air Station. Pilots practice touch-and-go landings. Tankers, fighters, and sub-chasers thunder overhead continually, in contrast to the cuter-than-poodle–curls, superficial, politically-correct pitch of the island.

Nancy and I stroll around Main Street, lunch at a local Langley pizza joint. The obvious lack of economy in the country takes seconds to discuss. When we had money, we spent it. When we didn't, we got by on no matter how little, with the good sense to live within our means.

Our sexagenarian conversation over pizza on this sunny day is spiked with death. Loss, grief, and pain intrude on our normally rosy, quasi-realistic outlooks on life. Guilt is brutal, debilitating, all-consuming, unless you realize the gambit is about life, and put emotional

Art, Crime & Lithium

pain in perspective behind you. Takes time. Nancy has grim stories of her own, but comes to the rescue with a hard-to-top tale.

While they were married, her ex-husband issued an ultimatum: that things had to change to what he wanted or they'd be divorced. Okay, she said, and initiated proceedings. He died shortly after. Had she known he was going to die, she said, she wouldn't have divorced him. Her ex loved smoking pot. Nancy rolled a fat one, went to his funeral, played the grieving widow over his corpse while she slipped the joint into the breast pocket of his suit coat. She wanted him to make the transition to the next life good and stoned. He was cremated.

Life isn't fair. Fairness is a concept conjured by humans. In time you get over emotion, histrionics, accept the inevitable and get on with the quality of your own goddamned struggle. I don't drink now, but found excellent, high-dollar tequila to be effective in mitigating the jagged rawness of loss.

Despite work, death, and raising two sons, Nancy finds time and resources to travel to Kenya, France, Sicily, Spain, Portugal, Italy, and plans to visit Turkey next. She's annoyed with being treated like shit by the TSA when she arrives home, and fails to understand why American authorities deal with terrorism by treating American citizens as terrorists.

She maintains an enduring sense of humor, and is the best-read person I know. Nancy loves to read, does it for a living, is my literary angel and comes up with new, engaging authors each time I run out of patience with what passes for contemporary literature.

Twenty-one poets, young and old, female and male, famous and not, Phd'd, MFA'd, street-hip to maximum nerdy, representing every persuasion, take to the stage with varying levels of enthusiasm at the inaugural Brave New Words poetry festival at Greenbank Farm, April 18.

I'm honored and pleased to be one of the poets reading, give it my best, including an emotional rendition of a poem about shooting my dog Cooper. I spot liberal doggie types by their expressions once they comprehend what the poem's about.

Scheduled 15 minutes on stage, I allow minimal time between poems to get the maximum out of my time allotted. The audience either appreciates my performance with applause, or is glad to see me get off the stage.

Luckily, there's no wait Sunday morning at the Mukilteo ferry, although Seattle's traffic-crush spills over onto Highway 2 on the uphill side of Stevens Pass with weekender recreation-hungry city dwellers flooding Cascades playgrounds with pent-up frustration. The east side of the pass sports eight-foot-high snowdrifts on either side of the highway. Skiers enjoy Stevens Pass last runs before spring melts the snow-pack away.

The snow is gone by Leavenworth, Washington, a town totally devoted to anything and everything Bavarian. South of Wenatchee, Washington, the Columbia River Gorge unfolds with fractal formations in varieties of muted desert hues. Expansive apple orchards bloom along either side of the Highway 28. A short drive through eastern Washington farm country, and I set the cruise control for Idaho on Interstate 80 east.

Sundown finds me at the exit for Cataldo, Idaho, thrilled to find an RV campground open with a spot on the Coeur d'Alene River, the only client this early in the year. Surrounding snowcaps reflect orange-pink as I hand the campground proprietor $20. We discuss the yellow and flat-black '67 bored and stroked 440 hemi Charger, his baby. He won't sell.

Fried steaks and salad in the Avion. Bars fluctuate on my Motorola cell-phone, flicker if I stand outside and tilt my head just so. I call and tell my wife I'm okay. Bars dissipate. To the bright light of the Avion's small wall–lamp, in the upper berth, I read *The Last Good Kiss* by James Crumley, a present from Nancy. Crumley can write. I hang on for a while but succumb, exhausted.

Nancy warns me not to drive Interstate 90 in the dark because the stretch between Spokane and Missoula is winding, treacherous, and dangerous. I cannot imagine driving this road in winter.

Mid-morning I'm south of Missoula, Montana, on Highway 93, looking for the dirt road turnoff for Ronn and Charlie Alexander's place. Ronn and Charlie always live on dirt roads, the way they like it: the further away, the better. I make instinctive decisions, and pull into their driveway high up on the west side of the Bitterroot Valley, on the edge of national forest.

About 30 years ago I gave Ronn a Hupmobile rocket hood ornament I liberated from a Colorado junkyard. Ronn requests a 4" by 6" solid block of wood for a base. I have a solid piece of reclaimed oak in my shop. I mill and plane it to specs and give it to him when I arrive. If Ronn were a tree, he'd be an oak.

Amid the wealth of American automotive classics stashed behind Ronn's shop sits a pale green '52 Chevrolet coupe with gargantuan bullet holes in the windshield, a portrait of Montana soul in steel and glass, sculpted with firepower. Keeping the Chevy company in a line are two '38 Plymouth pickups and a '49 Ford coupe in various stages of repair. Ronn shows me the '54 Chevy station wagon in his shop, a project he's been getting ready for more than 20 years. When I lived in southwest Colorado, we hunted '54 Chevy parts at local junkyards.

Ronn is my favorite living philosopher, a no-bullshit, real-deal, Arkansas-rooted, California-raised and, after 25 years, naturalized Montanan. He's deliberate, specific, and refuses to be rushed.

A rusted, gray, lichen-encrusted 1926 Studebaker Phaeton with rotted wooden spoke wheels occupies a place of honor in the yard. Ronn perceives the Studebaker as American automotive art. His wife Charlie sees it as junk, and wants Ronn to haul it to the dump. They've been married 40 years. The Phaeton remains, testament to standoff and a standard of married life.

Ronn makes the same walk in the neighboring Bitterroot National Forest for decades. Today he shares his walk with me. We cross the barbed-wire fence from his property and start uphill through spruce and pine, slowly and softly on fallen needles. The delicate, sweet aroma of the trees permeates the forest. It's warm, no breeze.

Ronn's 70-year-old knees are shot, but he refuses to get replacements. I've had a knee and hip replaced, so going slow is fine with me. We talk cars, parts, work, wives, kids, grandkids, geezers enjoying each other's company. When there's nothing to say, we shut up and walk.

Truck-driving instructor and driver for a company that feeds firefighters, Ronn doubles as on-site troubleshooter and homespun guru in fire camp, during the working season from June through October. It's still early for the forests of the West to engage in their annual trials by fire.

Charlie's call to dinner brings us into the house. She is a consummate professional of the homemaker's art, with a stocked freezer, pantry, and excellent homemade things to eat. Charlie also always has a job. She was recently laid off by the Washington Corporation, which she envisioned as the last job she'd ever have, and immediately found a job with a Jeep dealership in Missoula. Of course that didn't last long. Now Charlie has her unemployment compensation and medical insurance ducks in a row, eyeing retirement with confidence and relish. Ronn is concerned about what to do if they're both home full time.

A faded Old Glory, most likely one that never comes down, waves softly atop an extra tall flagpole in the distance. Gary Marbut's house is around the next bend of the dirt road I've been climbing for the last few miles on

Art, Crime & Lithium

the Clark's Fork, across the valley from the Alexanders. His self-sufficient dome comes into view. No doubt about it. This is it.

Gary appears, ear to phone, discussing Second Amendment business. He makes his living fabricating gravity-operated target systems in a concrete bunker set into the hillside, and markets them for law enforcement and other government entities. Besides the target business, Gary is president of the Montana Sport Shooting Association, teaches concealed-weapons classes, self-defense classes for women, shoots competition combat hand–gunning, and hunts elk with a pistol.

The elk we have for dinner is one Gary personally invited and prepared. Our conversation remains pretty much in the parameters of Gary's singular preoccupation with arms and the right of the populace, particularly Montanans, to bear them.

Gary is of the opinion good citizens should have guns, and need them if liberty as we know it is to continue. He doesn't trust government, especially the federal kind, which has a nasty habit of eroding rights for our own good. I have no argument with this.

What about machine-guns and assault weapons, I ask.

"It says 'the right to bear arms' in the constitution," he replies. "There's nothing in there about machine-guns or assault weapons. If you want a machine-gun, you should be able to have one."

We cover the gamut from Diane Feinstein to Charlton Heston. Gary has issues with Feinstein, Barack Obama, anything and anyone liberal. He employs right-wing scare-tactic catch-words,like "socialism", spiced with an abundance of conservative talk-show rhetoric. I hope he's smarter than this. We've known each other for 40 years. When we get after it, anything goes. Gary's entitled to his opinion. I suggest he get elected to the United

States Senate if he has issues with Senator Feinstein.

The theme from *The Magnificent Seven* plays full-bore in my head on Interstate 15 for Deer Lodge, Anaconda, and the Idaho border, spectacular with excruciating vistas floating over flea-sized cattle herds against mountain backdrops engulfed by skies bigger than oceans, where shifting cloud continents display whimsy through fantasy on serious winds. The *Magnificent Seven* theme stays with me through Idaho until just before Wyoming, where I luck into a disc jockey who plays real-deal music on an obscure country-and-western radio station. This must be where my America is hiding out. I'm sorry when the station turns to static on I80 east for Green River and Rock Springs, park my rig at the RV lot at Little America, and order a trucker's steak and salad at their restaurant.

Up at 4 a.m.; the *Magnificent Seven* theme is gone and, in a few minutes, so am I. Dawn flickers in the distance off the interstate in the east, the star-flecked sky hasn't shrunk a bit, trucks heading west have their orange running lights and low beams on. I sing the *St. James Infirmary Blues*, my absolutely favorite road song, to my Cummins diesel rhythm section.

At Wamsutter I turn south on a dirt road shortcut through Wyoming oilfields to Highway 13, to Colorado. Once oilfield-pickup rigs, mostly Dodges and an occasional Ford, packing welding rigs on flatbeds, disperse to their assignments for today, I'm alone on the well-maintained dirt road. Occasionally I'm faced with a semi tanker heading straight for me, at what I approximate to be 80 miles an hour on this barely two-lane dirt and gravel road. I ease my rig off to the side and let them pass.

The liveliest aspect of the parched high desert, punctuated with rigs, is the herds of antelope who don't seem to mind industrial intrusion. I pull off the main two-lane onto a service road leading to a series of industrial structures, large diameter piping, and gauges, roll down the window and aim my Nikon at a herd of antelope who allow me to photograph them to my heart's content, apparently oblivious.

I admit to a sense of relief when 50 miles of dirt road finally intersects with Highway 13. There is an immediately marked improvement in the quality of roadway. Breakfast has been on my mind for quite a while. I pull over, fry eggs and corned beef, make a fresh pot of dark Sumatran coffee, and feel a lot better about everything. Later that day I check into the KOA campground in Steamboat Springs, lock onto their wireless signal, check email messages, and go to town to seek out the large steel mobile I hung lifetimes ago at Colorado Mountain College while teaching a kinetic art class there. It still hangs in the entry of CMC's administrative building. Like seeing an old friend, the meeting triggers a flood of memories and emotions.

I wake to two inches of snow in the campground on the Crystal River, in the shadow of Mt. Sopris, south of Carbondale. Snow in late April in the Rockies is no big deal, usually melts off by noon. The camp host is Omar, a pleasant, Brit-accented Pakistani. The campground is a trailer enclave of exclusively Hispanic workers and their families. I find a spot by the river mind my own business, content to listen to the water's lilt.

McClure Pass is a portal to what used to be home turf, with familiar, extravagant, expansive vistas. A left at Delta, and the Uncompaghre's are in sight in the distance. A right at Ridgway takes me over spectacular Dallas Divide to the turnoff at Placerville for Telluride. I drive by the house I built up the street from the fire station. Someone else lives in it now. The ex sold it and moved on. The house looks good and solid, bleached bones of one dream and hot meat of another.

Ben Kerr, manager of KOTO and a pal from the "old days" in Telluride, when I did the Saturday night radio show from nine 'til midnight, before money tweaked any semblance of sense in that town, agrees to air an announcement that I'm reading at Back of Beyond Books on Saturday Night. In return, I agree to record my show's "call" for posterity: "This is the Uncle O Saturday night dinosaur show, spinning them dinosaurs out for all you dinosaurs out there. No shuck, no jive, we're staying alive. This is KOTO Telluride."

A visit to the grave of Peter Spencer, friend and former editor of *The Norwood Post*, finds me at the east edge of Telluride's box canyon below Ajax, Bridal Veil Falls, and Bear Creek at the cemetery. I tell Peter he was the only editor I got along with in more than 40 years of professional writing, thank him for the opportunity to work with him at *The Norwood Post*, the most productive and creative writing run in my life. I miss Peter Spencer. He was a hell of a guy, smart, capable, a long-shot player who understood why the West was wild.

L'CHAIM, "to life" in Hebrew, is inscribed on his gravestone. I take it to heart, and drive out of that twisted circus of a town where more money than sense persists as a way of life, down along the San Miguel River, where I fished in respectful and joyful solitude for more than 20 years.

Cresting Norwood Hill, after the tight serpentine two-lane drive up-canyon with the drop immediately to the right, the confines of the red-rock canyon walls expand into vistas punctuated by the Lone Cone to the south and Tukhanikavits to the west, and a lot of southwest Colorado and southeast Utah in between. I drive through Norwood, don't stop at the house I lived in on Cedar Street; it's been an emotional day already.

West of town, a left on the dirt road takes me past Darryl Elder's junkyard and hog farm. Darryl stacked a four-car high fence along the road, which he mashed out and restacked. The Saab I drove to Telluride many lifetimes ago still occupies a place high in Darryl's fence.

Art, Crime & Lithium

Maurice Richard lives off the grid, on 90 acres up the west side of Norwood canyon, past Darryl's American-classics art fence. He has a collection of what some might call junk and others stash. Old cars, buses, motorcycles, road equipment and piles of assorted parts are scattered amid the junipers.

Maurice and I met in Norwood in the '90s, became friends and teamed up as Meshugene Brothers Construction, to build log stairs on a condo project in Telluride. Maurice is one of those guys who intrinsically understand how things work: a mechanic, builder, electrician with major league photovoltaic expertise, jeweler, a good guy and a better friend. He helped me wire the barn my wife and I live in. I was glad for his help, attitude, expertise and company.

We discuss old and new times, current and future projects. I commission Maurice to design and build a small gold-and-emerald bauble to replace one my wife lost.

On back roads via Redvale, Naturita, Bedrock, Paradox and LaSal, through spectacular, massive, red-rock Paradox Valley, I'm on my way to Moab. This is the land of Butch Cassidy, the Sundance Kid, and the Hole-in-the-Wall Gang, who often stopped for supplies at the Bedrock Store between jobs and posses. My friend Rose Morse now owns and operates the store, but unfortunately for me this is her day off and she's in Grand Junction shopping. I climb the winding road out of the valley, through the labyrinthine white and red rounded rock canyons before the Utah border, and climb again to the deep green of the Manti-Lasal National Forest dominated by 12,721-foot Tukhanikavits, patriarch of the La Sal range. I pause at the ever-gushing spring water faucet at the crest, fill a water jug and wash my face like I have for 30 years, less than an hour to Serena's house from here.

When I told Serena I'm reading at the poetry festival on Whidbey Island, she got in touch with Jim Webster at Back of Beyond Books in Moab, and instigated an evening of my poetry and prose.

With a day's grace before my reading, Serena takes me down the daily from Hittle Bottom to the mid-point takeout on the River Road from Cisco to Moab. We ran this stretch numerous times. I bring my Nikon at Serena's insistence. Rounding a bend across from White's Ranch, where John Ford, John Wayne and Maureen O'Hara made westerns, I spot a great blue heron. The boat rocks, the river undulates, closer to the heron every second. Finally, the heron stretches its great wings and rises. I depress the shutter and take one of the finest photographs I've ever taken, perfectly sharp, clear, and every detail visible.

Jim Webster and Serena introduce me to approximately 50 people in the audience at Back of Beyond Books. I tell a story out of my childhood in Philly to break the ice and settle down. Saturday nights, my father and his cronies would gather at our house for dinner and poker. Once my mother cleared the dishes, my father would go to the refrigerator and pull a bottle of vodka out of the freezer, didn't bother with ice. He'd pour everyone around the table a shot. Then they apologized to each other for whatever they were going to say in the course of the game.

I apologize to the audience up front for whatever I'm about to say that will offend them, and get on with it. An hour and a half later they applaud. My books sell after the reading.

That hour and a half is one of the most important of my life. It represents sales, to the bookstore. To me, it represents respect. My books are on shelves with books by authors I admire.

The Bonneville Salt Flats was going to be my next stop, but the pull of the Pacific has me pedal to the metal. I take photographs of the salt flats at the Bonneville rest stop. At Winnemucca I turn north on 95, then west on 140, a desolate-as-can-be ride I'd been intending to make for years.

Art, Crime & Lithium

Lily guards the place at her usual spot above the driveway. She barks and wags as I emerge from our underpass. We take Lily to her final visit to the vet the day before Thanksgiving. I bury her down by our pond, next to Cooper.

I keep taking my daily lithium, and for nearly a year walk the beach alone, with occasional thoughts of dogs on scent slipping over driftwood, bolting circles berserk, riling gulls into rising, blasting heedless through surf, moist muzzles brushing by, hauling ass up the beach: joyful, sweet, saving grace of days spent tinkering with enthusiasm's used-to-be.

Seven weeks after April Fools Day, two years ago, we take in two puppies and walk the beach daily at dawn, rain or shine.

Better now than never.

About the Author

A self-proclaimed curmudgeon, Lysiak drives and maintains a 30-year old El Camino. He drowned his cell phone in a pond. He is a beach addict and lives in a barn with his wife, two local young brown mutts and an affectionate, battle-scarred 13-year old orange tomcat. Lysiak has been devoted to good clear writing, poetry and the art of mobile making all his adult life.

Made in the USA
Charleston, SC
09 May 2013